The Rule of Crime and Me:

An Intimate View of
ANN RULE

SHARED BY HER FRIEND OF
THIRTY YEARS

by Anne Jaeger

Praise for *The Rule of Crime and Me*

"Ann Rule was my friend and mentor for decades, and I so enjoyed Anne Jaeger's very personal account of her friendship with 'The Queen of True Crime.' An exceptional author and one of the best people I have ever known, Ann Rule deserved this loving portrayal."

- Kathryn Casey, bestselling True Crime author

"Not only is Anne Jaeger one of the Pacific Northwest's legendary local tv news journalists, she's also a top-notch crime writer. *The Rule of Crime and Me* is a fascinating, brisk memoir about Ann Rule, one of America's favorite criminal writers and Jaeger, who covered the Diane Downs murder case alongside Rule herself. Part breezy television news memoir, part epic investigation, part biography, *The Rule of Crime and Me* belongs alongside Rule on the bookshelf of any crime buff."

- Jack Ohman, Pulitzer Prize-winning editorial cartoonist and columnist for the San Francisco Chronicle

"In *The Rule of Crime and Me,* investigative reporter Anne Jaeger shares a unique perspective of Ann Rule, 'The Queen of True Crime.' A lasting friendship between the two writers formed over three decades ago when both covered one of Oregon's most shocking crime cases. Jaeger, renowned for her stunning interview with the notorious killer, not only shares insights about the Diane Downs case, she reveals details about the fascinating life of one of America's most beloved authors."

- Leslie Rule, bestselling author and daughter of Ann Rule

Book design by Jeff Patterson.

ISBN: 979-8-218-60837-8 (hardcover)
ISBN: 979-8-218-60838-5 (paperback)

Contact for media interviews or speaking engagements:
4TrueCrime@gmail.com

Table of Contents

This book is an accounting of true crime, events which are true, that happened to real people. It is based on events as I saw them and report them to you. No names have been changed.

To Ann, my dear friend.

You never had the chance to write your own life story before you left us. May this book give your millions of readers a glimpse of the true Ann, the person behind the fame, and our adventures along the way.

Part I

Chapter 1
The Rule of Crime

The first day I met Ann Rule wasn't a meeting to be proud of. I was late for opening arguments, slated to start at 10 o'clock the first full day of the Diane Downs murder trial. Downs, a twenty-seven-year-old mother, had been accused of shooting her three children in Oregon, killing one of them while trapped in her car on a "sightseeing trip" after dark. In 1984, I was a television news reporter in my mid-twenties and the Diane Downs case had consumed me since the shootings the year before.

If you want to make friends and get along with other reporters covering the same news, don't cause a kerfuffle in court. Especially on opening day. Unless you think it's some mind game, a power trip to let them know who's boss. In which case, you'll probably torque them off enough that your insensitivity will put them into overdrive to best you.

All morning, I checked my sources at the courthouse, got engrossed in some other news, then rushed in just before the opening bell. Much like in Jazzercise, spin cycling, and yoga, most reporters have favorite spots to sit during jury selection and trial. These seats are "saved" for the media to guarantee access to a seat when the trial is so popular the line snakes the courthouse lobby on the third floor, as it had been during Downs' trial. But it's first come, first serve.

By the time I reached the first or second row on the left side, which was reserved for local media and court artists, there was no room in the house. I'd been waiting for this trial for a year and there was *nowhere* to sit to report on it. My mind launched into computer mode, my eyes like grocery store laser beams, tick, tick, tick, scouring the media benches; I knew everyone except a young woman sitting next to Ann Rule, who I knew to be a famous writer.

But Rule and the young woman beside her hadn't been there during jury selection, so I had no idea what I was stepping into.

"Hi Ann," I said. "My name is Anne Bradley and I'm a reporter here. I recognize you, and I know all the reporters in these two rows, but not *her* – " I gestured toward the young woman around my age sitting next to Ann. " – And I'm so sorry, but the judge saves these rows for the media so *you'll* need to move."

Ears pricked up, heads swiveled toward me straining to hear: *What did Anne Bradley just say??* I was already a little jittery about *how* to ask this in a nice way in the intensity of the moment, but this came tumbling out!

Unbeknownst to me, I was asking Ann Rule's *daughter* to give up her seat. My neck started burning from the chest up at the prospect of a mother fending for her young in a courtroom of spectators who watched me on the news.

Can you imagine how that might have gone over, if Ann was a different person?

But what did Ann Rule, star author, do?

Yes, there was a very uncomfortable pause. Then Ann's eyes twinkled, the corners of her mouth lifted and she said in her sweet lilting voice, "How about if we all just scoot closer together and make room?" Ann could have left me hanging there, sweating it out in the aisleway, but she quickly found a much better solution.

I didn't know until later that Leslie, Ann's second daughter, often took notes of witness testimony and captured great photographs for her mother's books at trial. I mistakenly thought she was a Lookie-Lou sitting in the designated media spaces. When Ann introduced Leslie I was scarlet-faced.

I scooted closer, sat down and shut up.

Despite a twenty-seven-year age difference between us, Ann always described our relationship as girlfriends. During our friendship, she wasn't a mother figure to me, nor I a daughter to her. Somehow our relationship transcended age. We talked about intimate aspects of our lives, men, sex, the whole gamut. She said I was one of her funniest friends, and her humor kept me in stitches.

In 2015, Rule was interviewed for the Lake Oswego newspaper and said this about our friendship: *Leslie and Anne became friends, but it was Anne and I who really bonded. We had the same sense of humor, and we loved to go on adventures…Over the years, both Anne and I have had successes and tragedies and we've always been there to support each other…The thing I admire most about Anne is her ability to do so many things. I didn't know she was a Master Gardener, but her yard is amazing. She was a superior TV reporter. Anne's interview with Diane Downs was the best one of all, and it's the one that all the other shows used.*

Somehow this courtroom scene was the start of our thirty-one-year friendship. Not quite as auspicious as a reporter or any "nice girl" would like, but we laughed about this first meeting our whole friendship.

Over the years when I came to visit Ann for the weekend, as soon as I wrapped my hand around the doorknob, and stepped one foot inside, I'd hear her snickering to her assistant and best friend Donna Anders.

"Oh, here's that pushy reporter who tried to kick Leslie out of court," Ann would tease me.

Leslie and Ann Rule, both authors. Courtesy of Leslie Rule.

Our eyes would meet and I'd be embarrassed all over again. We laughed at the audaciousness of the unlikely first foundation of our friendship. It never got old.

Maybe you can understand the way the tide turned from foment to friendship after that in a letter of recommendation Ann wrote for me nine months after Diane Downs' conviction. Ann and I had known each other for almost a year when she wrote it. The letter is cherished, and much more detailed than most recommendations I have:

> *February 20, 1985*
> *To Whom It May Concern:*
>
> *This letter will convey, I hope, my regard for Anne Bradley, and my enthusiasm for her talents as a television newsperson.*
>
> *Because part of being an author is going on the road to publicize books after they are published, I have been interviewed on talk and news shows from Boston to San Diego, and from Miami to Seattle – with so many stops in between that it makes me dizzy to think about it. A thousand or so interviews in the last five-years may not have made me an expert of who's good in news, but it certainly has given me the opportunity to see many, many T.V. personalities up close and under fire.*
>
> *I have seldom found a young woman in T.V. news with the exceptional qualities Anne Bradley possesses.*
>
> *Anne and I spent two months together last summer (along with three dozen other reporters) covering the Diane Downs Trial in Eugene, Oregon. I was there to gather material for a book; Anne was continuing to cover this bizarre story for the Eugene T.V. station where she works. I <u>know</u> how accurate she is – because I was there in the trial each day myself. Anne never missed a trial session, and afterward, you could find her at an old typewriter she'd carted into the courthouse lobby – and chained it there – so she could get her story in shape for stand-up news.*
>
> *Anne Bradley seems to me to be cut of very special*

material. She is no "cookie cutter" product as a newsperson. She strikes me as exceptionally intelligent and compassionate. She doesn't just report the news; she shows the viewer every facet of the story she's working on. She is honest and she is fair, and it was interesting to see how well respected she was in the eyes of the district attorney's office and the sheriff's detectives. We all know that if a reporter "burns" an official once, there are no more stories. And those of us who have lasted in this business know too that, in the end, it is the ethical reporter who gets the story.

In November of 1983 – five months before Diane Downs went to trial – Anne Bradley obtained an interview with Downs that captured the woman absolutely. Bradley showed the Eugene public a brilliantly psychopathic woman in a special that is so compelling that I refer to my tape of it several times a week as I write this book. (Anne's taped material was the basis for a special done at a larger television station in the Northwest and which won second prize in the New York International Film Festival in the television documentary category.)

I doubt that there is a better way to get to know someone than in the boiler-room atmosphere of a press corp bonded together, for a murder trial that lasts for weeks. And, more than that, as we spent three-and-a-half days together on the roof of the courthouse waiting for a verdict. Ann was adept even at coming up with something for the 5 o'clock news when there was nothing to report.

Anne is gutsy – without being pushy – empathetic without being a patsy. She is an individual; viewers will not forget her or mix her up with the gal on Brand X channel. She works hard, and she is a self-starter. She is young enough to be full of enthusiasm for her career and has the energy to go for it. But she is old enough to have beyond the cheer-leader type of reporter. She is very attractive, she dresses in a way I always hoped to – but never got the knack for – and she has a compellingly warm voice.

Anne Bradley also happens to be a sincerely nice human being. I met a lot of nice people in the press corps in Eugene last summer, but Anne stands out among my two or three favorites. Even though we are a generation apart, I consider her a friend. She has been very kind to me, sharing information and insights into Diane Downs, things that she had a chance to see after months of being first with stories about Downs. She didn't have to do that; there was nothing "in it" for her. She is well-respected by her fellow media reporters.

I have no doubt at all that I am going to turn on my television set five – or seven- years from now and see Anne Bradley doing nationwide news on one network or another. I guess the best thing I can say about her is that, if I were running a television station, I'd hire her in a minute.

Thanks for listening!
Ann Rule

Thankfully, as you can surmise, our first ("you'll have to move") Downs' courtroom detente' became an inside joke for decades. A comment that could have put us toe-to-toe in a power struggle and left me sputtering, evaporated into thin air because of Ann's charm.

"That case changed my life," Ann always said.

It changed mine too, in very personal and professional ways.

Me and Ann Rule on the Small Sacrifices movie set.

There has always been so much to admire about Ann Rule: her

selfless nature, her love of animals, her loyalty to true friends, her relentless research, her writing skill, dedication to her craft, and the true crime genre she re-created. The list is long, and the pages here are full.

So this is my love letter to Ann Stackhouse Rule.

If you're an Ann Rule fan like I am, we'll break some new ground together and fill in some gaps. We'll trace her childhood in detail, explain her public and private self, and her motivations in life. We'll explore hard work, tenacity and how bloodlines nurtured a little girl from an itty-bitty Midwest town into a writing and research powerhouse.

I'll share new behind-the-scenes intrigue about Diane Downs, and a few true crime stories you've likely never heard, while also touching on Ann's greatest achievements and disappointments. You won't find a rehash of her books here because, heck, who could do it better than Ann Rule?

No one.

Chapter 2
Home Rule

Ann was born in tiny Lowell, Michigan in 1931, the same year as the town's big centennial celebration. Lowell's first hundred years were much more prosperous than those that followed Ann's birth, when an economic boom brought by the railroad withered due to time and circumstance.

Standing on Main Street in Lowell today puts you smack in the confluence of then and now. I'm telling you, this place still remains the town where Ann was born on October 22, 1931. But the city remains as nicely suited for a new family today as it was back then.

In early 1931, Ann's parents Chester Ray Stackhouse "Stack" (1905-1978) and Sophie Marie Hansen (1906-1995) were both educators, living in Cadillac, Michigan. Stack, an athletic director, and Sophie, a teacher, married December 20th, 1930, and within two months were pregnant. Anticipating the birth, they settled on having their firstborn in Lowell, at the home of Sophie's aunt Magdelena "Lena" Cook Luz, who was a midwife. A doctor made a house call just as Ann arrived. Unfortunately, Stack had to keep working back in Cadillac while Sophie sat out the rest of her pregnancy in Lowell.

Ann's mother Sophie and Father Chester "Stack" Stackhouse in 1920's. Courtesy of Leslie Rule.

Despite the country roiling from the Wall Street Crash of 1929 and the vise clamp of the Depression, Stack was always able to get jobs easily. He was a self-made man, with a great education, and a strong motivational personality.

In late summer of 1931, Sophie was well into her last trimester of pregnancy with their first child, Ann. Aunt Lena's house would have been awake "at sunrise with the firing of bombs"[1] outside, which were strong enough to shake the beds, windows, and all of Lowell. She likely tried instinctively to shield her unborn child from the bomb's concussion. What in heaven's sake was going on? The town was a-twitter about it.

Turns out, Lowell's bomb blasts were a calling card of sorts to mark— not Ann Stackhouse's impending entry into the world, but another birthday—Lowell's 100-year anniversary. Yes, the wake-up bombs were birthday icebreakers! The disruption was enough to trigger Sophie's labor pains, but Ann's parents were hardy stock. Sophie waddled out to Main Street with her aunt's hand bracing her elbow.

The weather edged toward 100 degrees, and the little town was about to witness a spectacle. Over three days,

---

[1] Lowell Ledger, Lowell, Michigan, "Centennial A Blaze of Glory From Start to Finish!" August 13, 1931

Lowell's population of 2,000 ballooned to 60,000, with townspeople and newcomers lining a three-mile parade route down Main Street. Lowell's newspaper called it the "Centennial:A Blaze of Glory From Start to Finish!"

The paper said, "We doubt if any town or city in Michigan ever offered its visitors a more interesting or magnificent sight."

Unremarkably, no citizen was quoted snarking openly that the daybreak bombs *may* have been overkill.

That centennial was quite the to-do. When I visit Lowell to research Ann's life for this book, the Lowell Area History Museum Director Lisa Plank told me, "They did a carnival, they had a hot air balloon ascent. They did all sorts of things to mark the occasion."

According to the town newspaper, the real side splitter came during a Civil War reenactment when a local man, Elmer White, was trying to make a live "patriotic" eagle scream to honor the War Between The States but lost his fake mustache instead. That's what you get for trying to make a live eagle scream, I guess. Lowell was obviously a little town thinking big. Plank said there were many events citywide.

Two months after the earth-shaking celebration, Ann came into the world with Aunt Lena's help. At the time, only women with difficult births went to hospitals. Sophie's brother, who grew up to be a local doctor, couldn't yet help with delivery because he was only seventeen years old at the time. Ann was the very first grandchild. Upon arrival, Ann was named after her maternal and paternal grandmothers, both named Anna.

By all accounts, the first-born Stackhouse thrived in the loving domain of educated parents. Lots of reading, playing and walking. I asked Ann years later if her father was nice to her and Ann said, "My daddy always told me I was the prettiest little girl he'd ever seen."

The sweetest smile on her face then intimated touching thoughts of her daddy's voice whispering his praise to her.

Ann's middle name was also her daddy's middle name. In fact, this newborn, Ann Rae Stackhouse, could not be bested.

In a story that became family lore, the aunts were walking through town with baby Ann in her stroller. Ann was babbling along as a man bent down to greet her. Somehow Ann's babble was heard as a complete sentence. Instantly, the man straightened up, shoulders back, astonished, and shouted "This baby can talk!"

The aunties snapped up, looking indignant that anyone would suggest otherwise, "Of course she can!" Proud aunties sniffed the air, turned on their heels and got walking again with their talking progeny.

Besides being an "early talker" Ann was an early reader. She cherished hours at the library, coming home with piles of books, studying pictures and listening to stories read by her parents. She was a quick study and well-spoken. Even still, nobody knew who Ann Stackhouse would grow up to be someday. How could they?

There would be one more child welcomed into the Stackhouse family in Lowell: Ann's brother Don born in 1933. The family complete, the Stackhouse brood would live in Western Michigan until 1935, but there were plenty more fireworks to come.

Ann and her much beloved younger brother Don as children. Courtesy of Leslie Rule.

I wanted to see Lowell for myself, so, in 2023, I traveled two thousand miles from my home in Portland, Oregon to Michigan along with Doug Welch, the lead detective from the Diane

Downs case.

Selfie of former Diane Downs Detective Doug Welch and me flying to Michigan on our research trip. Used with permission: Doug Welch.

Doug and I have been buddies since the trial, and he was also Ann's friend, in addition to being featured in Ann's *Small Sacrifices*. As lead investigator in the Downs case, Welch's role in the trial, book and movie were more important and extensive than my own, but we lived the same facts.

Doug, Ann and me, having a good time together in 1984 at my Eugene apartment. Courtesy of Doug Welch.

We were anxious to see where Ann came from, to trace her ascent from small town Michigan girl to world-renowned author. Inside? I'm as giddy as a child at my first amusement park. But outwardly, I try not to let on that my tummy's on a rollercoaster.

Touching down in Grand Rapids, Doug drove us north to Lowell. I served as navigator.

As Doug tells it, he went on the trip because he "enjoys

the challenge…A job to do, some research and investigation; that's something I enjoy."

"My goodness, you've done it for years, Doug," I say. "How long were you an investigator at the Lane County Sheriff's Office?"

"I was there for just short of twenty-eight years and investigations were twelve years," he says.

Doug's first murder case as lead investigator was Diane Downs. Back in his early days as a patrolman, if Dispatch didn't want reporters to hear breaking news over the police radio, Doug had to find street corner pay phones to call the cop shop for crime locations and details.

Navigating us to Lowell, my smartphone called out directions and made the trip easy. Doug as driver was working far below his pay grade.

We decided to get off the beaten path on our trek to Ann's hometown. We ended up rumbling across the Fallasburg Covered Bridge, built in 1871, which covered the Flat River leading into Lowell. Doug and I really appreciated these stately covered bridges; where we live in Oregon, there are around fifty-four of those charming wooden relics.

The Fallasburg Bridge (1871) outside Ann's birthplace is one of the nation's last covered bridges back East. Author's photo.

The Fallasburg bridge was a real sentinel over the river. There are so few left. The old weathered gray wooden span to Lowell bridges the dim past and the present. Standing in the sunshine, the Fallasburg bridge silhouetted in front of a robin's egg blue sky ahead of me, I wondered how old Ann was when she first saw this – likely no more than two years old. As one of the last surviving "kissing bridges", this treasured relic displayed long-gone names painted or engraved into the white pine timbers inside, like *Clyde Alotich 1900* and *BF 1920*. There was no visible evidence of any kissing shenanigans echoing from the past under the gabled roof, but a 150 year old replica sign warned "$5 fine for riding or driving faster than a walk." Historically, that was likely just fine for a romantic walk beneath the peak.

We passed over slowly hearing heavy *clack-clack-clacks* of timber under our tires. I'm all nostalgic about seeing names from Ann's time. As for my buddy Doug, the ride or die investigator? Not so much.

"No, not at all. Not at all," he said.

From his point of view, we were in this thing for facts and I had a seasoned professional at my side on the journey. But there were stark differences in our interests.

Sometimes Doug says we're like "peanut butter and jelly." I guess I'm the jelly.

Doug remarked after our trip, "I took these sights at face value, and you...always wanted to look deeper...Your interpretation was, I guess, much more extensive. You put feelings to your observations. And I was just there to help you." Doug's steady demeanor kept us on track while I waxed nostalgic.

I'm walking in Ann's footsteps, I thought to myself.

We did both wonder why the bridge, back in the day, was called a "Kissing Bridge." To us it looked utilitarian but beautiful–a way to get from one side of the river to the other. But if you consider the times, the old morals and the stereotypes, kissing was considered risque for single girls both during and before Ann's day, even for engaged couples. Historically, there were few places young couples could kiss without being seen and tattled on. So, walking pace was perfect. A stroll facilitated an easy smooch here and there for couples shielded by the tall tunnel surrounding them. And perhaps that's why very few female names were carved in the wooden beams from that time. If a young man etched your two names in a heart, there was sure to be trouble at home when mother found out where you'd been. They *knew* what you and your beau had been up to in that kissing bridge.

Old graffiti inside the Fallasburg Bridge near Ann's birthplace. Lowell, Michigan. Author's photo.

Considering all this got me in the right frame of mind for what was coming up ahead in Lowell. A quintessential middle American town. Doug said the town evoked comparisons to his childhood home in Pierre, South Dakota.

"I remember the houses [in Lowell] are similar to what I remember, and the narrow streets, sidewalks. It brings back memories," he said.

The streets boasted vibrantly painted old businesses with simple but eye-catching embellishments, decorative cornices over classic dentil or corbel brickwork and curlicue flourishes on window hoods–long forgotten architectural embellishments wiped out by Bauhaus and mid century modern design.

It was fancy back in the day, now renovated to conjure up its former glory of the Great Depression when Ann grew up.

Brightly refurbished downtown Lowell. Author's photo.

In the Victorian moment, a lot of wealthy people resided in Lowell, especially since the railroad came to town in 1858. The homes of the rich, mostly merchants that we saw were testaments to the town's wealth: ornate houses with fancy front porches, circular turrets, and steep roof lines, were painted vivid colors of energetic blues, greens, purples, and yellows, still standing like icy confections of a bygone era.

The Director of the Lowell Area Historical Museum told us that in the early 1900's, when Ann was born, "The city of Lowell was the social hub that brought people together" from all over Kent County.

Residents of Lowell, back in Ann's day, sit a spell. Courtesy of Lowell Area Historical Museum.

Wheat milling, fruit orchards, poultry farms, and a button

business thrived in 1920's Lowell. Workers at Lowell's button factory were earning five cents per bucket filled with forty cups of hand punched buttons. The buttons were drilled and polished from freshwater mussel shells from the local rivers. In the first half of the century, before plastic became the standard, "cultured pearl" shell buttons were highly sought for women's clothing–and the very best shells were found in the two rivers, the Flat and Grand rivers running through Lowell. The shell harvest was enormous—four to five tons of shells a month. A ton of shells made 210,000 buttons–a stunning number given the rudimentary manufacturing techniques of the time. The museum had a fascinating display showing how shells became buttons back then, an era of American manufacturing when handmade pride in workmanship and quality mattered.

How shell buttons were punched out from freshwater clams in Lowell button factory before the advent of plastic buttons. Author's photo.

The shells went to good use, but most of the mussel meat either fed pigs or rotted. Plank said after talking to a woman who grew up on a pig farm nearby, she learned a steady diet of mussels made pork meat taste "fishy." The woman swore she never knew what real pork tasted like until she moved off the farm.

On that trip to Lowell, I was surprised to learn, almost incredibly, that no one seemed to recognize Ann's name, her miraculous accomplishments, bestselling books, nor that Lowell is the birthplace of this internationally acclaimed crime writer. I asked Plank, "Are you surprised about this bestselling author being born in Lowell?"

Plank cheerfully responded, "Actually, no. We have a lot of authors that have come from Lowell."

Plank named Colonial American historian Howard Henry Peckham's twenty-one books on American history, and Chris Van Allsburg, the author and illustrator best known for his children's books *Jumanji* and *Polar Express.*

Plank didn't read true crime and hadn't heard of Ann Rule.

The museum had a special bookshelf dedicated to hometown authors, but no Ann Rule books among them. Plank explained, "Lowell always seems to nurture a love for arts and writing, so I think it makes sense we've had a renowned author with a claim to Lowell in her life."

Why no Rule books? Stands to reason that no one there knew Rule's connection to the town. And in my estimation, the true crime genre gets snooty short shrift in the oh-so-sophisticated literary world. Despite true crime's popularity, people still discount its merits. Perhaps with the discovery of Ann Rule's litany of bestsellers and oft-replayed TV movies, her works might someday join other Lowell authors on that lofty bookshelf.

After all, Lowell is less than forty miles from where Ann got an up-close look at her first criminals.

Chapter 3
Rule's First Killer

Ann met her first killer in the upstairs of her grandparents' home. This key experience in 1940, when Ann was about nine years old, would drive her future obsession with decoding murderous minds.

Between 1931 and 1941, Ann's mother, Sophie, took Ann back to Stanton, Michigan, where her grandma and grandpa ran a mom-and-pop home detention facility, the Montcalm County Jail. The sheriff's residence and the jail were housed together under one roof. The sheriff was the policeman and the jailer. Ann's grandfather cuffed the criminals and guarded inmates. Ann's grandmother booked suspects into jail and cooked three meals a day— not only for the suspects, but for her own family—in the first-floor kitchen. It's nearly impossible to fathom children growing up in jail without nightmares today, let alone condoned by parents, but it was perfectly normal for any family in the homey one-stop criminal justice operation of the times.

Ann's first killer had a tremendous influence on Ann's future. Ann remembered her name as Viola. No last name, just Viola. But Ann never forgot key details about the woman who shaped her future without knowing it at the time. Killer and child were strangers in the jail when the encounter took place. Based on Ann's recollections the meeting began very innocently.

Ann remembered that Viola wore her hair in pin curls, fashionable for the day, and black lace-up shoes with white ankle socks. On the day they met, Viola's body was completely still, except for an anxiety made conspicuous by her hands, which were obsessively crocheting. One loop at a time into one square at a time, hundreds of individual loops would eventually be woven together into a comfy lap throw. This rhythmic meditation served two purposes; staving off boredom and keeping "what if" at bay. Viola would exhaust her yarn by day's end, and inadvertently hook-in a very curious nine-year-old child.

In contrast to most childhood chores of making our beds or setting the table, Ann's job in the jail was on an entirely different spectrum. Grandma served up the meal, and Ann delighted in sliding dinner trays to the male prisoners through a slot in the pantry wall. With only the men's nose and mouth visible through a slot a bit bigger than a front door letter box, the inmates cocked their heads to the side as they spoke kindly to the kid serving meals.

"How are you today, little Missy?" they'd ask her.

Ann would tell me later that those brief conversations were bewildering, because the prisoners were smiling and polite – not very different from her dad or lawmen uncles.

But Ann had her run of most of the jail in her little Mary Jane shoes. Her small footprints skipping, hopscotching, jump-roping, and nimble fingers throwing jacks in the corridors. Ann spent happy summers and holidays in a bedroom down the hall from the female inmates. Only a single hallway door divided the family from felons. There were two cells upstairs for women and "insane" female patients, as they were called back then. The men were sequestered downstairs on the first floor in a larger wing adjacent to the jail office.

Ann took pride in delivering meals directly to the women. The food came up from the kitchen in a dumbwaiter. Sliding the trays out from the food elevator rising from the floor below, Ann gingerly balanced the trays to her waist and counted her steps to these two "cells" spirited upstairs, feeling like a big girl in this alternate universe. Meals became a conduit for Ann's personal connection with a few women inmates, including Viola.

I remember recoiling one of the times I interviewed Ann for this book, when she was about eighty, and Ann told me that she had loved *sleeping* alone inside those two upstairs jail cells. It was surprising to me that her grandparents allowed this when the female cells were empty. Ann laughed at my gobsmacked reaction to this detail. I was flailing at the mere thought of a child spending the night in jail "but, but, but, Ann, you were a *child*!"

Ann countered quickly with an irreverent grin, "Well, the cell door wasn't locked!" As if this tidbit blunted the vision of a child sleeping in an inmate's cell alone. Here's what went through my mind: a child leaning very close to the metal bars watching a new chain stitch gets snagged by a murder suspect with a crochet hook, a dangerous weapon. The child was now easy prey, a hostage, for a felon. Fortunately, that never happened during Ann's experience, but laws about children in jails with inmates were lax or nonexistent then. Her freedom makes me wince today.

This formative time for Ann was critical to desensitizing her to any possibility of danger we may harbor. Like her grandfather, Ann saw suspects as men and women who made mistakes. Ann was programmed differently by her past. While other authors' resumes chronicled published titles, Ann Rule is the only true crime author I've found who could list "grew up in jail next to killers" as life experience. Ann's childhood is jaw-dropping to the rest of us and would not be repeated.

Ann was one of only three children I've heard of growing up in jail. The other two were her cousins, Karen, who now lives in California, and Jim Sampson, who is still in Michigan.

Last year, when I sat down with Jim, Ann's first cousin and twenty-one years her junior, he told me that "I was born in jail. Yeah, that's where I grew up, the Montcalm County Jail."

Jim did not pass GO, he went straight to jail from the hospital! Jim's mother, Freda Hansen Sampson, and Ann's mother, Sophie Hansen Stackhouse were sisters. Sophie and Freda's father Christian Hansen was sheriff and operated the jail with his family while Ann was a child there. Later on, Freda's husband Elton Sampson, Jim's dad, won the top job for eighteen years after war service as one of General George Patton's drivers.

Ann Rule at nine years old as a flower girl in Elton and Freda Sampsons wedding. This is about the time Ann met her first killer. Courtesy of Jim and Mary Sampson.

Elton Sampson's jail was very different from Sheriff Hansen's, but so were the times, nine years apart. Jim and his sister were shielded from knowing *too much* about the prisoners, likely to protect them from being frightened of tight living quarters with hardcore characters. Unlike their cousin Ann, Jim and Karen were forbidden to open that hallway door separating their rooms from female inmates. They often heard the women screaming, crying all night, or talking loudly with foul language,

"We'd hear many of them," said Jim. "They came in intoxicated, and they were not pleased to be where they were. I learned a lot of new words as a young child…and many nights would be rather restless because of the yelling and conversations they had."

Jim lived "in jail" for sixteen years. Being a sheriff's kid might have been a detriment, especially during the 1960's anti-government days. But his friends saw the jail as a novelty, an amusing if eccentric curiosity. Jim told me they'd say, "Mom, I'm going to jail…" or "I'm at the jail and I'm staying overnight at the jail."

Jim noted matter-of-factly, "But to me it was just, this is my house. Come over to play at my house.'"

As I listened to Jim, I was thinking of the baggage this

could cause to fragile children from less-nurturing jail families.

Both Jim and Ann grew in strong, loving families. As adults they wanted to help people. But they came at it from different angles: Jim's time in jail led him into social work, mostly focused on helping children, for thirty-four years, and Ann's internal compass set her on a quest to figure out the motivations for crime, the intricacies of the criminal mind, and to warn women of the pitfalls.

In an article for a Seattle newspaper, Ann talked more Viola, the crocheting felon who chain stitched into Ann's psyche "Viola…was awaiting trial for fatally shooting her husband when she caught him with her best friend in a [Chevy] truck she'd bought him with her waitress's tip money. She explained it was 'justifiable homicide' and warned me to never trust women [like Viola's *former* best friend] who pluck their eyebrows into 'those itty-bitty lines'."[2] Aside from the aberrant life lesson, Viola taught Ann crocheting with a helpful beauty tip too. To which, Ann said, laughingly, "Where else could you learn such valuable information?"

I was so intrigued with Ann's encounter with Viola that Doug and I made it a priority during our trip back East to find out more. We wanted to find out if Viola's case really was justifiable homicide, or if she was convicted of murder instead.

On a chilly spring day in 2023, Doug and I sat in a back room of the new Montcalm County jail on a March afternoon, scouring every name in dusty old jailhouse logbooks, looking for Viola. The Undersheriff, Andy Doezema, told me nobody had looked at those ancient books since they were last closed decades before I was born.

---

[2] Ann Rule, *What's a nice girl like Ann Rule doing in a genre like true crime?* (Seattle: Post-Intelligencer Writer in Residence, December 2007)

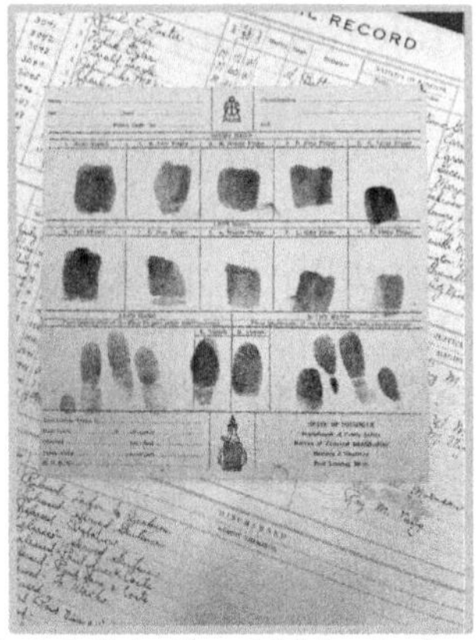

Jail records and fingerprints left in the old Montcalm County ledgers. Author's photo.

There weren't many women's names in the jail books from 1930-1941, and, frustratingly, there was no trace of Viola. We also searched books before and after those dates, but I knew Ann had an outstanding memory for detail.

One complicating factor in finding a prisoner was an old practice of recording inmates held for crimes outside Montcalm County jail only as "lodgers" and not by name. Why? We never got a good reason, except "lodgers" were merely held in the jail, but sent elsewhere for adjudication– their gender, age (and sometimes their crime) were included. For example, if a woman in Detroit murdered a man, went on the run and she was caught in Montcalm County, the woman was listed as a "lodger"--until lawmen from Detroit picked her up and drove her back where the killing took place to stand trial. Such was the antiquated system of small-town jailers during the Depression years and before.

Viola definitely struck a deep chord in Ann Stackhouse, propelling her to become Ann Rule, The Famous Crime Writer later. Ann the author didn't take things at face value, meticulous research unearthed facts for publication, but the whole jail experience confused Ann early on. She told the Seattle Post-Intelligencer that "At seven or eight, I believed children chose what they wanted to be, and I couldn't understand why anyone would want to go to jail… decades later, I'm still searching for answers, but I know the correct terminology now: I'm tracing the psychopathology of criminal behavior."[3]

Ann vividly recalls hearing Viola profess her innocence, but she knew something was questionable about her story. Viola's penalty wouldn't have been for murder if she'd been defending herself from death or serious injury when she shot her husband. Justifiable killings are seen as "no-fault" homicides. Then, again, maybe the killing wasn't quite "justifiable homicide" – big, new words for Ann that captured her imagination as a child. She never knew how Viola's case turned out, but there was something about Viola's demeanor that certainly made Ann feel safe enough to trust the killer then, or at least safe enough to feel the woman's breath on her shoulder while learning to crochet through metal bars.

Yet, there was also something about her crochet teacher that was also deeply disturbing to her.

While Viola *seemed* like a nice enough lady, Ann was shocked to see utterly no remorse in her new "friend." It was obvious to Ann, even as a child, that it was very wrong for this woman to shoot her husband in cold blood. She began thinking, *How could someone do that?*

The whole saga made me want to find out more about the killer who piqued Ann's interest in the criminal mind. In my quest to find details about Viola's story on the Michigan trip, I came across a Joyce Earl in Stanton's jail in the 1940 Census. Joyce Earl is the only woman I could find whose story might match Viola's. Ann likely met both women if they were not one and the same.

The story was so similar to Viola's that it occurred to me that perhaps Viola could have been Joyce's nickname. Earl was a secretary in a car body shop and a waitress at the time of her crime; Ann said Viola was a waitress who saved her tip money to buy a Chevy. Ann remembered she was nine when she met Viola; Ann was that age in 1940. Her parents were living in Ann Arbor, Michigan then, and since Ann visited her grandparents'

---

[3] Ann Rule, What's a nice girl like Ann Rule doing in a genre like true crime? (Seattle: Post-Intelligencer Writer in Residence, December 2007)

jail on holidays, this *might* make perfect timing: Easter vacation fell at the same time Joyce Earl was incarcerated. Whether my hypothesis is correct or not, it's likely these two would have also met each other as Ann skipped her way to the second-floor women's cells. In twenty years of dusty records, Earl was the closest match that Doug and I found for Viola. It's likely that this will remain a mystery—if she was still here, I'd ask her—but it's certainly a solid conjecture based on the facts available.

After an extensive search, I didn't find any record of a trial, but by 1941, Joyce Earl was out of jail. Maybe the evidence did indeed prove justifiable homicide in her case. She was working as a waitress again, then remarried and divorced, on grounds of extreme and repeated cruelty. Her husband had definitely abused her. Earl married and divorced for a third time by 1955. Both husbands were machinists. Earl's final marriage ended by 1956. Alone, Earl moved to the Pacific Northwest, living 180 miles from Ann Rule for the rest of her life. Earl died on Christmas, 1969.

Earl's case was investigated for several months, while she was locked in jail, but it's highly likely the woman never went to prison.

There are similarities between the two women: same jail, same time frame, but no smoking gun.

Naturally, Viola left a big impression on Ann; she talked about it in interviews for the rest of her life as her first brush with a killer. Although Ann might not have dreamed of becoming a true-crime aficionado nor a writer until midlife, Viola unquestionably initiated Ann's lifelong passion for crime writing. Viola's story, tucked way back there in Ann's memory bank, became a driving force in finding out *why* people committed crimes.

Ann and I had this in common, and we'd often talk about it together. In one chat we had in the late 90's, when I was around forty, I was describing a young man in Eugene, Oregon who got so angry about his neighbor's tree that he called the guy into the street, knocked him down and sliced the neighbor's head off with his shovel. Clean cut, guillotine style.

My question was rhetorical: "Ann, what makes a man cut off somebody's head over a tree instead of just walking away or calling the police? I just don't get it. Is a tree really worth a murder conviction?"

What psychological triggers drove murders? That was our obsession. I followed up with, "That's what's always fascinated me about crime- why would we never see killing as an option, especially over a *tree,* and these people just have at it? *Why* do people do it?"

Ann answered emphatically, "Me too!"

Thinking back on the whole conversation, and having reread the books she wrote up until the time the conversation took place, now I think "Bless Ann's heart for playing along." But this was more than that. We had killers and cases in common to hash over. What latent psychological timebomb makes someone kill a partner over a lover or money, when divorce wouldn't bring prison time? We agreed that the belief they wouldn't be caught (which is the overwhelming theme in most cases) just didn't make sense. Odds were not in their favor. The bottom line? Killer's minds worked far differently than ours. Ann and I shared a drive to figure out why.

It was always fascinating to have these in depth talks with the Queen of True Crime. The "why" of it kept Ann Rule writing books for sixteen more years after that conversation. Her curious nature was instilled by her parents, but as far as crime and punishment was concerned, it came from her grandparents' jail.

The Stanton Michigan Sheriff's Residence and Jail, her grandparents operated, still stands today. It's now the University of Michigan Extension Office. Ann spent a lot of time here as a child. Author's photo.

Chapter 4
Rule's Roots

Not long after Ann met Viola, her cherished grandfather passed away and the entire county mourned with her. Ann's grandfather, Sheriff Chris Hansen, was known as the "Father of Montcalm County," a sheriff who never fired his gun in the line of duty, but was a good shot, treated inmates as people who make mistakes, got criminal confessions easily and won all his consecutive elections handily. Sheriff Hansen was by all standards, then and now, quite a man.

While most kids have little interest in what adults do for a living, Ann was fascinated by her grandfather's job. She heard people call him Sheriff from the time she was born. She knew it was a mighty title. As she grew up, she'd find out how hard-won his success had been.

"Christen" Hansen was born about 45 miles southwest of Copenhagen in a small farming town of Aarlose, Denmark on March 31st, 1874. Christen was the fourth of six children born to Hans Hansen and Karen Marie Neilson. Two siblings died in infancy.

Aarlose & Terslev about an hour southwest of Copenhagen, Denmark. Author's photo.

Aarlose wasn't a fancy buggy town. Few people could afford more than a wooden wagon and a horse. It wasn't a town so much as a place where owners carved out pastures for livestock. Lumbering along in the family wagon, you'd see their thatched cottages. The poorest neighbors lived with livestock under their roofs, and the lucky few had barns for their horses, dairy cattle, pigs and chickens. Wide divots in the dirt roads, forged along pioneer trails, directed "traffic" when farmers delivered their milk to the co-op.

Denmark had no real natural resources, since wheat failed. Instead, farmers and the whole country eked out a different kind of gold from the land. From dawn to dusk, families churned premium butter, and raised pigs for bacon. These exports to England and Germany were enormous. Christen Hansen's family made a hard-earned living this way: butter was their "bread."

The town made big news in 1911, when two boys playing in a potato field dug up fourteen pounds of silver, buried by Vikings in the tenth century! Close-knit neighbors, their hands raw from milking, nearly fainted. They'd been starving next door to a vast hoard of silver. Even more jewelry and coins were found again there recently. This cache, now in a Denmark museum, was discovered near Arlosevej road, traveled daily from the Hansen farm.

All the Hansen babies were baptized at the historic Lutheran church in nearby Terslev. The church absolutely glowed in the sunlight. The stunning 800 year old building with a shining red tower was the oldest brick church standing in Denmark built with a bright yellow limestone finish quarried from an ancient pit.

Christen Hansen was anointed in the big church font, in continuous use since the 12th century. Poor Christen and other newborns were plunged head-to-toe three times in this imposing granite vessel.

Christen Hansen was christened in this baptismal font dating back to the 12th century. Courtesy of Terslev Kirke.

Hansen's life revolved around the Lutheran stalwarts, "grace alone, faith alone, scripture alone," and hard work. At fourteen, Chris had to drop out of school (held every other day) when the Lutheran confirmation of adulthood made him a full-time worker at the dairy. A farm that would never be his. The teen wouldn't be able to inherit his father's share of the co-op farm they owned with another family. That would go to his eldest brother.

Chris Hansen had a dream, and he'd be forced to go elsewhere to achieve it. As Chris grew up the population skyrocketed 169%. There were no jobs. He had few choices. Encouraging news pricked his ears. Friends talked about moving to the "land of opportunity" in America. Hundreds of thousands of Danes got on board after 1867. But, a steamship ticket cost a year's wages and turned inside out, Chris' pockets held nothing but dirt. So, Chris mounted up in the King's Royal Horse Guard, hoping to save money for two years[4] in the Army.

The young man finished his service as the turn of the century closed in, but his pockets still didn't jangle. Hansen needed fast money. He found it two thousand miles away in Ivittuut, Greenland. For three years he mined the world's largest deposit of a very precious, rare mineral called Cryolite. "White gold" was odorless and colorless, but dangerous. Cryolite was a

---

[4] (Obituary file, White Pine Library; Ancestry.com, census; Stanton Clipper-Herald, 2-6-1938, 1-7-1941, 9-5-1941.)

magic trick. It disappeared completely under water. If you couldn't feel it with your fingers, the "rock" was invisible. Native Inuit called it "ice that never melts." Mined almost to extinction, the mineral made lightweight, affordable aluminum. Working on a 175-man crew, Chris got worried when men had trouble eating, breathing and turned into skin and bones. Seeing older men sputter for air, Chris finally left Greenland with cash in his pocket.

He headed home to Aarlose to say goodbye to family. He wouldn't see home again. The steamship Hekla sailed for his biggest adventure yet. And his next chapter would be even more remarkable than the first.

Chris Hansen shipped off to America about 1898 on the Hekla Scandinavian Line.

In 1898, at the age of twenty-four, Christen Hansen arrived at Ellis Island with $12 dollars in his pocket–more than enough for a train ticket to Montcalm County, Michigan where he'd know some other Danes. Chris got a job as a mason and began building stone foundations for houses.

When Chris met Anna Maria Cook, the daughter of a farmer who fled Germany, he knew he wanted to start a family. They found contentment living in Edmore, Michigan. The couple's firstborn was Sophie, Ann Rule's mother.

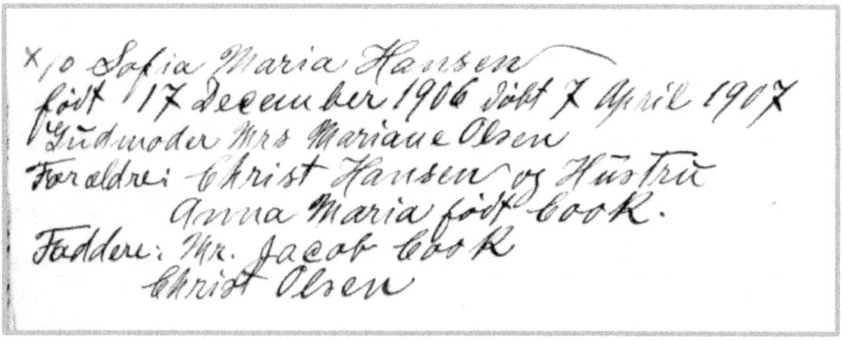

x/o Sofia Maria Hansen
født 17 December 1906 døbt 7 April 1907
Gudmoder Mrs Mariane Olsen
Forældre: Christ Hansen og Hustru
Anna Maria født Cook.
Faddere: Mr. Jacob Cook
Christ Olsen

The Baptismal Record of Ann's mother, Sofia Maria Hansen, December 14th, 1907. The family's Lutheran church in America recorded events in Danish, listing names of father, mother, and grandparents. Courtesy of First Congregational church of Stanton, Michigan.

Their house was a constant beehive of happy activity, with five more children following between 1906 and 1924. And in those years, Anna watched her husband come alive as a man with an eighth-grade education, drive and determination. In his home township, Chris became treasurer, supervisor, deputy sheriff and justice of the peace in succession. This man's innate skill allowed him to learn quickly on the job and move up the ladder.

In 1924, life hit an emotional snag with the family's sixth baby, Richard, born September 16th. Their second boy would be their last, as Anna and Chris were getting older, forty-four and fifty respectively. Richard Marion Hansen was a treasure to the family, the four Hansen sisters arguing over who got to hold him, feed him, change him. But it was Sophie, Ann's mother, then seventeen, who cuddled, cooed and cared for Richard as if the boy was her own. The oldest and the youngest shared a special bond.

Richard was almost a year old when Sophie and her mother Anna notice he wouldn't eat and was crying inconsolably. Dr. Becker, Edmore's hometown M.D. and family friend, made a house-call. Richard was crimson-faced crying, and drawing his tiny hands and feet up to his chest in pain. The sight was hard to bear. The Doctor was not hopeful about the outcome.

Silence came on September 15 at 4:50 p.m. Baby Richard Marion Hansen died – the day *before* his first birthday. Sophie took the passing especially hard. "*Her baby*" had died. Dr. Becker signed the death certificate proclaiming *follicular colitis* as the cause–a rare disease in infants when the colon became inflamed perhaps due to a virus or infection.

Richard Marion was laid to rest at the Hansen family plot in Vinewood Cemetery a few days later.

Life didn't *go on,* back then, as much as it *moved on.* Sophie had a hard time losing Richard. Even as an elderly woman, her eyes went to a film strip of inner memories when she talked of it. Ann's daughter Leslie saw this happen, "Grandmother Sophie was devastated when Richard died. I don't think she ever got over it."

Chris Hansen dug deep for gratitude, as they all did. Sophie and sister Emma headed to teachers' college. Sister Freda married a lawman she met through her father. Millie worked at the courthouse and brother Carl went to medical school. And Chris Hansen grabbed the brass ring.

In 1928, the family picked up stakes and moved to Stanton.

Chapter 5
Ruling Stanton

Doug and I circled back to Stanton from Edmore on our trip into Ann's past. Edmore had shriveled in the intervening years and picturesque views of Lowell faded in the rearview mirror. Stanton might not have been as pretty as Lowell, but there was one monolithic structure reminding us of its prominence in Montcalm County: the sandstone and brick courthouse right smack in the middle of town on Main Street. The jail residence Ann's extended family grew up in sat behind that old courthouse.

Over the course of our friendship, Ann told me stories about these places, but I wanted to see them for myself and fill in details about her upbringing.

What was amazing about Stanton, Michigan after 1934 was the small dynasty Ann's family built in Montcalm County:

- Her grandfather Chris Hansen became sheriff
- Her grandmother worked at the jail
- Her Aunt Freda married Undersheriff Elton Sampson who later became sheriff
- Her Uncle Carl was the Medical Examiner
- Her Aunt Millie (Amelia) worked in juvenile court
- Her cousin Bruce was a prosecuting attorney

The Hansen children circa 1918. Ann's mother Sophie, the eldest, is pictured in the center of the photograph. Courtesy of Leslie Rule.

As a child, Ann couldn't wait to follow in their footsteps. Hansen was, without a doubt, one of the greatest influences in her life. She idolized both him and her father. There were no female coaches back then, and no female sheriffs either, but Ann was most attracted to the flashy lights and sirens of police work. Even at about four years old, Ann would beg her parents to follow the sirens. At the jail, Ann must have been at her grandfather's hip, soaking up the job like his junior detective. The badge. The holster. The gun. Ann Stackhouse's dream job.

As Rule told reporter John Sparling in a 1997 interview, she kept a copy of her grandfather's 1940's forensic science book as a lifelong treasure. It was outdated, sure, but the principles held true. As she said, "Every killer leaves something of himself at the scene and takes something away no matter how minute'." This was fascinating to Ann! Even without the benefit of DNA, her grandfather could pick up a cigarette butt, bullet or torn piece of cloth and trace it back to a killer. Rule used the same minutiae to weave stories in her books. It was often the little things that tripped up a suspect.

Ann's grandfather, the sheriff, used brain over brawn to get confessions and arrests. Ann also thought of herself as a psychological detective trying to crawl inside a killer's mind to see what makes them tick and explain crimes. Her grandfather paved the way. Chris Hansen, as he was now known, was the person who instilled this driving curiosity in her about the *why* of crime.

At a time when "thug" cops beat suspects into submission faster than drinking a steaming cup of coffee, Hansen dispensed with the pervasive "good cop/bad cop" police interview routine. Chris Hansen knew by experience that good cops get the confessions, not the nasty ones.

Ann Rule also let people talk and listened carefully to what they said. There were clues in their conversations. Hansen solved cases by treating people with respect, not ruthlessness; Rule did the same.

Musical talent runs in some families. Perhaps solving crimes does too?

Opening the old jail logs describing the crimes happening during Ann's grandfather's time illustrated that small towns didn't just mean petty crime. Bank robbery, pedophilia, rapes, carjacking—the crime mirrored any other place. All the wickedness, secrets, and peccadilloes of crime in Montcalm County between 1930 and 1941 were hidden in those huge jail logs I read. Combined, the books, which looked like canvas tomes, contained more than 3,600 names of all the people who earned "accommodations" at Hansen's jail. Other names in the old dusty arrest records proved sweeping societal changes. Perusing the logs, I read names of women reported to be "insane." This hit a sympathetic nerve, as I knew that a man back then could silence or get rid of his wife simply by claiming she was crazy, and she'd be locked up based on his word alone. I saw a few of those women's names in and out of jail, but they weren't committed. They had to go back home. Wives without money of their own didn't have the means to leave abusive husbands and a man's word superseded that of a woman. A man raping his wife was not a crime. The current undersheriff, Andy Doezema, said he "can't remember anyone ever asking to see these old registers," while explaining what information to find where. Inside was the nitty gritty, the hits, runs, errors of each inmate, stripped of sentiment, in short, "just the facts, m'am." In all, suspects of mail fraud to murder were listed.

Montcalm County inmate records kept at the Stanton, Michigan, jail run by Ann's grandparents, Sheriff Hansen and his wife Anna, between 1930 and 1941. Author's photo.

There were no war stories written in the logs about the sheriff's hand reflexively jerking his service revolver from the holster, because he never shot at a suspect in or out of jail.

Newspaper cartoon of Ann's grandfather: "In 24 years as sheriff Chris Hansen never

fired a gun in the performance of his duty! Stanton, Mich."

Nor details of his ability to get confessions easily, a skill for which he was renowned statewide. But there was a chilling case that illustrated how Hansen earned his reputation.

A crime that changed a boy's life.

It all started a quarter mile from the banks of Clear Lake, a lake outside Stanton, Michigan, which was a tad murkier than the name implies. Clear Lake was a tranquil country fishing hole full of bass and crappie, mostly wild except where two private farms bookended the water. The land was said to be sandy loam, dry and warm in spring for early crops. Summer corn liked it too.

Benjamin Perrien and his wife Sylvia had a homestead farm there at the turn of the 20th century. It was a good prospect to settle down, have some kids, and work the farm. Between 1914 and 1920, the Perriens' pocketbook was stable, but sadly, the household was not growing. The couple was barren, year after year. The yearning made it easy for the Children's Aid Society to convince the middle-aged couple to foster eleven-year-old Celestine Colester, because her mother couldn't support her. Celestine moved in, but the relationship fractured and Celestine was taken away by welfare workers.

The farm and the couple aged alone, for another twenty years. Benjamin, seventy-one, and Sylvia, sixty-one, wondered if a boy was a better match this time? Much like Celestine's history, eleven-year-old Robert Eberhardt's mother abandoned him after his father died. Robert picked up chores along with school at the farm.

Like clockwork before nightfall, Benjamin lumbered into the kitchen, bending over the sink to wash his face after a long day's work. Surreptitiously, three men quietly entered the Perrien home unseen. One of them shot Benjamin execution-style in the back of the head. A get-away car waited outside.

Robert found the body bloody and lifeless. Woozy, he called for help. "Mrs. Perrien…Mrs. Perrien!"

Not fully understanding what had transpired, Mrs. Perrien shouted to call the sheriff. Eberhardt's body, hands and voice shook, but Sheriff Hansen was on the way. In the kitchen, the farmer's wife took one look and dropped to her knees sobbing. Her husband was gone. Sixty-seven-years of marriage ended on the kitchen floor.

Arriving at the scene, Sheriff Hansen was immediately struck by the boy's small stature, thinking he looked much younger than thirteen. He was a thin and small sixth grader, with brown hair and eyes and a ruddy complexion.

Sheriff Hansen sat the witness down to ask him to explain every detail. The sheriff used a calm, fatherly tone with a tinge of a rhythmic Danish accent. From news reports about the crime, it's easy to fill in the conversation based on facts.

"Son, I'm sorry to have to ask you about this, after what you've been through today," Sheriff Hansen said. "But you are the only witness who can help us catch the men who did that." He pointed to Mr. Perrien in the kitchen.

The boy nodded nervously in agreement.

"You are sure you saw three men, right?" Sheriff Hansen said. "What kind of gun did the shooter have? A revolver, a rifle?"

"Oh it was a shotgun for sure," said Robert.

Hansen's son-in-law, Deputy Sampson, was in the kitchen assessing the damage. The old man's body was slumped down in front of the sink. Bits of brain matter stuck to the wall.

There was stippling at the entry wound at the back of the head, proving the shot came at fairly close range. There was a gaping hole in Perrien's face.

Sampson surmised the weapon was fired less than 12" from the old man's head. He searched the room for a fired casing, but found nothing.

Then, the deputy took a second to catch his boss's eye in the other room and motioned for the sheriff to follow.

"Robert, you rest here a minute while I take a look around, alright?" Hansen told him.

"Well, looks like a close range shot with a long gun, but there's no shell casing anywhere in here," Sampson said to his boss.

The sheriff and deputy decided to look outside, canvassing the yard for the evidence and the killer's tire tracks.

Outside, the lack of evidence became evidence. They saw one set of footprints heading from the kitchen door, following short of a snowbank. Pawprints from the family dog continued, cresting the bank, then headed back to the house. No foreign tire tracks were found. The lawmen gave a knowing glance at each other, and Hansen went back in.

"Robert, thank you for being so patient," Sheriff Hansen said. "I want you to take a deep breath and let's go over this again."

And this was where the youngster's story started to get hinky.

"I told you already, the two men came into the kitchen and shot Mr. Perrien!" Robert insisted.

But Hansen caught the lie. "You said there were three men, Robert."

Clearly agitated, the kid said, "One man was waiting in the CAR!!"

Looking up from his notes, never losing the child's gaze, Sheriff Hansen slowly inched a little closer to the witness. "How can this be? First there are three and now *two men*?"

There was no answer.

"So…can you help me understand what happened to the shell casing?" Sheriff Hansen asked. "We can't find it near Mr. Perrien's body. Did you see it in the kitchen after the rifle was shot? And there are no tire tracks leaving this property, Robert."

Fidgeting was followed by sputtering.

"I don't know," Robert said. "I don't *know*."

There was a long *heavy* pause between them, as a dog darted past. From his seat, Sheriff Hansen saw the dog crawl out from under a bed in the next room.

"Excuse me, Robert," he said.

At this moment, Hansen *knew* or *thought he knew* exactly what happened. He got up and walked straight to the bedroom. The evidence was under the bed right where the dog left it. *There it was*, a 16 gauge shotgun shell and the murder weapon.

Hansen showed it to the witness. Robert's eyes widened, nose flared, his story changed.

"The man made me do it," Robert said. "He forced the shotgun into my hands! Said he'd kill me if I didn't do it, errr, shoot!"

Sheriff Hansen's calm approach eventually persuaded Robert Eberhardt to confess. The crime and confession was big, splashy news across several states, reading "FARM BOY, 13, KILLS AGED BENEFACTOR" and worse.

BOY CONFESSES TO GUN SLAYING OF AGED BENEFACTOR

STANTON, Mich., Jan. 3.—Sheriff Chris Hansen of Montcalm county said this morning that 13-year-old Robert Eberhart had admitted the shotgun killing of his 73-year-old benefactor, Benjamin Perrien, of Clear Lake.

Hansen explained that Robert's dog assisted in solving the case when it retrieved an empty shotgun shell from a snowbank and carried it into a bedroom.

When deputies found the shell they succeeded in breaking down several conflicting stories the boy had told, about the shooting which occurred yesterday afternoon as Perrien leaned over a washbasin in the kitchen of his house.

Robert had lived with the Perriens two years because his mother had been unable to provide for him.

He told the sheriff Perrien had been "mean" to him and refused to let him go on a vacation.

Newsmen, always misspelling Eberhardt's name, called the sheriff a hero for cracking the murder so quickly, attributing it to Hansen's record of confessions. Hansen solved the crime with just one shell casing. In news reports, Hansen explained that Eberhardt threw the shotgun shell out on the snowbank after the shooting. The dog played fetch, brought the casing inside in its mouth, and hid under the bed. The sheriff humbly said, "The dog solved the crime."

No hometown jury would read these news reports and find the kid not guilty of murder.

Man brutally killed. Youngster confesses. A long life

sentence would be justified.

After the bloody rampage on the banks of Clear Lake, Robert Eberhardt would likely face execution if the crime had been committed in another state with capital punishment on the books. Juvenile executions were rampant in the 1940's. Nationwide, fifty-three young men (in their twenties) were put to death for crimes committed *before* their eighteenth birthdays, according to the Washington Post[5]. Would thirteen-year-old Robert Eberhardt's twitch and gyrate in the electric chair if he murdered elsewhere? Could be a slam dunk case. Criminologists of the day argued death was a "just retribution for unspeakable crimes, deters crime, protects society, and preserves the moral order."[6] But Michigan didn't believe in executing killers of any age.

However, investigating the crime didn't satisfy the sheriff. Sheriff Hansen wanted to know the *why* of it, just as his granddaughter Ann Rule would have. Eberhardt told him the old man hit him with a bucket and wouldn't let him have time off. The grievances fell short compared to what the sheriff saw in the kitchen.

Still, the sheriff didn't believe in the death penalty for thirteen-year-olds and neither did Ann Rule. Michigan has long been a no-death penalty state. Rule was against capital punishment until later in her career. Ann's position on this was very clear as she aged. She supported the death penalty—for adults only— because in many cases killers murdered more victims after being paroled. Robert Eberhardt was no serial killer, but *everyone* knew the Perrien killing.

---

[5] "History of the Juvenile Death Penalty" (Washington Post Archives, July 9, 1988.)

[6] Jennifer Brookland, "They Thought They'd Die In Prison. Now They're Justice Advocates On a Mission," (Detroit Free Press, May 23, 2023.)

Confessed Killer---

Robert Eberhart, 13, said to have confessed killing his employer Ben Perrien, Clear Lake, Mich., farmer, with gun used in shooting.

Newspaper account of killing. The caption reads:"Robert Eberhart, 13, said to have confessed killing his employer Ben Perrien, Clear Lake, Mich, farmer, with gun used in shooting."

At sentencing, the prosecutor recommended Eberhardt be sent to the Michigan's Boys' Reformatory in Lansing. The probate court agreed. News reports didn't follow up on the case of the guilty boy with a dirty gun.

After reform school, the eighteen year-old enlisted in the Army in 1947.[7] Staff Sgt. Robert Eberhardt was buried at a military cemetery, with full honors. Having served his entire adult life in the Air Force.

The Father of Montcalm County

Benjamin Perrien's death was Hansen's last big case. The sheriff won re-election by the largest margin ever recorded in

[7] "Robert Eberhardt Enlists In Army"(Ludington Daily News, July 18, 1947.)

Montcalm county. But within months of the victory, Hansen released personal news that shocked everyone:

September 2, 1941

Because of ill health I find it impossible to carry on my duties as sheriff of Montcalm County and, while I am reluctant to lay aside the trust the voters of Montcalm County have placed in me, I believe it is for the best interests of the people of the county that I vacate the office so that a successor may be appointed. Please accept my resignation as sheriff of Montcalm County, effective September 30, 1941.

Sheriff Hansen had not been feeling well for more than a year. He put health issues aside thinking, as many of us do, that he'd bounce back. But the symptoms worried him enough to call his son,

Doctor Carl Hansen, Ann's uncle. If ever there was a doctor to bring bad news to a patient, who better than your own son? The medical examiner diagnosed prostate cancer.

Hansen's last entry, which I found written in his own hand in those ancient jail inmate records we found, *is indeed* September 30th, 1941.

Hansen was sicker than people knew and passed away six months later, March 30th, 1942. He was so revered that police radios privately broadcast the time of death statewide.

On the day of the funeral, the cities of Stanton and Edmore shut down, and all court workers were released at noon. Stanton judges, bailiffs, prosecutors, jail staff, friends, townsfolk and family followed the hearse to Edmore, where Sheriff Hansen's career began.

The memorial service in Edmore's coliseum was big enough to accommodate 400 mourners. The place was packed. Every person in line wanted to say a personal goodbye to their beloved former sheriff, lying in state up front. There would be no rushing that day.

In full dress, sheriffs, deputies, police officers and FBI men statewide stood sentinel.

Ann, ten years old, and her extended family filled up several rows.

So many flower arrangements were sent, it was hard to see the speaker's dais when mourners finally sat down. After the Lutheran service, the crowd stood without speaking, heads down, as the casket was carried down the aisle and loaded into the hearse again to drive to Hansen's final resting place.

The procession grew even larger then, winding its way to Vinewood Cemetery on the outskirts of Edmore. A newspaper reporter for the Stanton Clipper-Herald commented on the "largest attendance that had ever been present at a funeral in Edmore" for the "father of Montcalm County," as Chris Hansen was known.

Hansen was buried near baby Richard. Father and son both died the day before their respective birthdays.

On my trip to Michigan with Doug, I asked him to drive me to Vinewood Cemetery. The sun was shining, bees clustered on flowers, buzzing loudly on shade trees overhead.

After learning so much about Ann's grandfather, I wanted to pay my respects to him as well. Putting flowers on his headstone, I felt like I was honoring the love Ann had for him, the respected positions he held, the long miles he traveled from Aarlose to Greenland to Stanton.

I placed another bouquet on the headstone of his wife Anna, who lived another nineteen years after her husband's death, passing away in 1961 at the age of eighty-one. Both lived exemplary lives, and unwittingly nurtured one of the most successful true crime authors of her generation.

Chapter 6
Rule Roams

In the last decade of Grandfather Hansen's life, Ann's family was on the move. Her father Chester "Stack" Stackhouse got new coaching jobs hither and yon. Ann used to say about life as a coach's daughter, "If you win, you move. If you lose, you move." Stack's job took them from Cadillac, Saginaw, to Ann Arbor, and later to Lincoln University, PA (where in 1947 Stack was the first and only white coach at a historically black college and university). Those achievements were followed by moves to Willamette University in Oregon, Stanford in California, and finally back to Western Pennsylvania in Slippery Rock.

Together, Ann's family moved six times in fifteen years. The rigors of moving were old hat to Ann. She'd make more transitions before finally settling in Seattle for the rest of her life. I'll touch on a few, but not all, of her family travels that might provide insight.

Ann was a baby the first time the family pulled up roots for Stacks coaching career, in 1932. The Stackhouse family trekked east to the huge industrial metropolis of 80,000 in Saginaw, Michigan. Sophie and Stack rented an apartment in a large boarding house on the corner of Sheridan and Emerson Streets. The building looked more like an old barn or school than a house. It was a large, unique, white apartment house with two separate doors bookending one short side, each door covered overhead by semi-circular turrets. Inside, the Stackhouses' apartment was on the small side, but Sophie did her best to make it homey. On the wall over Ann's bed, her mother hung the bust of two angels, the cherubs placed as protection from Heaven above. Angels were important to Ann.

Sophie Stackhouse proudly shows off newborn baby, Ann. Courtesy of Leslie Rule

Many people may be surprised to learn that Ann had a powerful spiritual side, and that she believed in angels. In fact, she wrote the foreword for Leslie's book, *Where Angels Tread – Real Stories of Miracles and Angelic Intervention,* and shared an amazing account of a narrow brush with death when she was a child. I won't offer any spoilers here, but I will say that Ann believed with all her heart that she would not have survived childhood if not for help from beyond.

In the book foreword, Ann also talks about starting first grade in Saginaw. She was pleased as punch being allowed to walk home from school alone. Coming home one afternoon, walking by Mrs. Willis' house, a squirrel made a beeline for Ann, scrambled up her chest and onto her shoulder. Quite a sight!

Ann showed a love of all animals early on in her life, but this cowgirl walked home from school on her own without the benefit of a traveling photographer's show pony and chaps. Courtesy of Leslie Rule.

Mrs. Willis, who raised the orphan baby, then gave the pet to Ann. But the squirrel's surprise antics didn't win everyone over. "He once ran up my Grandmother Hansen's leg," Ann wrote.

Apparently, Grandmother Hansen didn't know about this unusual pet, "and she did a dance that no one could forget!" Poor Gramma Hansen.

While the Stackhouses lived in Saginaw, city neighborhoods were segregated, with black families relegated to the east side. Many of Coach Stackhouse's students came from neighborhoods deemed "hazardous" for white investment because they housed residents of color or were even *near* residents of color.

Mortgage lenders' institutionalized practice of discrimination, called "redlining," dictated who could live where and who got loans. Stack and Sophie abhorred segregation, treated all his students with respect, and welcomed the boys on his team into their home for dinner, regardless of their race. Stack believed in the kids he was coaching at East Sag High and inspired them to reach their potential.

Growing up, Stack was a star player and leader on the football, basketball and track teams. He coached all three. He was a tall, handsome, imposing man with a kind face. He taught his students and his own children to assess character, not color.

CHESTER R. STACKHOUSE
ASHLAND, OHIO, HIGH SCHOOL
Chippewa Athletic Editor '28
Chippewa Editor-in-Chief '29
Life Athletic Editor '28-'29
Varsity Basketball '28-'29
Varsity Football '27-'28
Varsity Track '28-'29
Y. M. C. A. '29

Ann's dad, Chester Stackhouse, in 1929 flanked by his long list of accomplishments in the Central State Teachers' College yearbook.

The first year at East Saginaw High in '32, Stack discovered a staggering talent. One of those teenagers in particular blew Stack away during gym class drills. The exercise: Coach set a bar three feet off the ground and told 50 kids to jump it from a standstill, straight up, feet together, and land on the other side. Mind you, that was like jumping the height of a kitchen countertop, feet together.

"C'mon give it another try. Put some power in your thighs!" Coach said as the boys stumbled through, fell, tried again.

Stack remembered when Bill Watson stepped up.

"When Watson's turn came, he bounced over it easily," Stack later said. "When I went home at noon I told my wife I had just seen an Olympic champion."

Coach knew the average male athlete could only gain six to ten inch jump height in a year if lucky, and this kid was only sixteen years old and clearing three feet with room to spare.

Stack recruited the young man to the football and basketball rosters and for the Trojans' track team. Stack was an anomaly for his time, as one of the first high school coaches nationwide to honor black and white athletes alike.

But according to Stack, Bill was so thin at 115 pounds that "he could easily have slept with in the shadow of a clothesline."

Mighty Bill Watson at Saginaw High School – 1933-35. Football, basketball, track and field star and Stack's protégé. Record setter in shot put, broad jump and high jump. First Black student athlete in history elected captain University of Michigan, two-time U.S. decathlete.

Stack mentored Watson, offered advice about what to eat, and showed him how to visualize each competition in his mind before the event. He was training a champion. Under Stack's tutelage, Watson beefed up to 190, with wicked scores in shot put, hurdles, discus, broad and high jump. With Watson on the team, they won state championships. Watson set personal records. Stack then helped the University of Michigan recruit the high school track star.

Almost in tandem, the two joined the track team at Michigan, where Stack became assistant coach. Under legendary UM coach Charles Hoyt, Watson was the first Black American to win the U.S. decathlon championship, the first ever Black American captain of any college athletic team, and won twelve individual Big Ten Conference championships, including three consecutive championships (1937–1939.)

This kid proved he had the brains, attention to detail, and the endurance to be an Olympic star, and Stack was still in the wings providing stability and encouragement to get there. Newspapers started hailing "Big Bill" as the "one-man track team."

But the racism of the times was limiting; Watson might have been team captain, but the athletic prodigy was always associated with the color of his skin. The Associated Press called him "a finely proportioned negro." Time magazine compared Watson to Jesse Owens, "last week it appeared the 1940 Olympic hero would be another midwestern negro, 190lb. William DeLouis Watson…" The word "negro" was historically thought to be "politically correct" compared to "colored" at the time. Change would come slowly.

Just as experts were doling out compliments with caveats, the bomb dropped. The 1940 and 1944 Olympics games were canceled when Bill was in his prime. World War II erased all chances of Watson manifesting his dreams in any Olympic arena.

When he aged out of future Olympic games, Watson pivoted. He was hired on as personal secretary to famed heavyweight boxer Joe Louis, amid the fighter's stint as the longest single-reign champion in boxing history.

Watson stayed near the ring for a few years when another job prospect popped up: Detroit police officer. He signed on as one of its first Black patrolmen. Watson was on the force two years before the disastrous Detroit 1943 Race Riots. Black citizens protesting unconscionable police brutally and deeply rooted racism were attacked by white citizens fighting to keep them out of their neighborhoods. Nine white people were killed in the melee and twenty-five Black people—seventeen of the twenty-five were shot or beaten to death by police. President Roosevelt deployed 6,000 army troops to quell the uprising.

Bill soldiered on through this at work, earning eight meritorious service commendations for outstanding service. He was the bodyguard to both the Detroit Police Commissioner and a judge in the 1950's.

Before civil rights leader Martin Luther King gave his famous 1963 speech during the March On Washington, he delivered the same "I Have A Dream" address in Detroit. Watson probably worked the rally, but his beliefs were flagging.

There was so little change. He watched the gut-wrenching slide of Detroit: America's richest city to one of its worst. After twenty-five years on the force, his second dream waned just like the Olympics and Watson retired at forty-nine years old.

There is a tragic end to this man's story. One incomprehensible, inexplicable, puzzling, heartbreaking ending which would no doubt take Chester Stackhouse to his knees. Stack, the egalitarian who mentored Watson, and took him to great heights. And in 1947 was the first coach across the nation to hold thirty-five games between white and black students when he coached at Lincoln University, a historically Black university.

About seven years after Watson's police retirement in 1966, serious internal cracks seemed to fracture at the surface. On Wednesday, February 28th, 1973, he was hauled into a precinct after reportedly confronting two police officers on the street. No doubt the humiliating experience for a former cop went from bad to worse when officials concerned about Watson's safety and theirs, took away the permitted gun in his pocket. He was allowed to leave the station.

Three days later, Watson screeched his car to a halt seeing two cops ticketing a driver for smoke coming out his tailpipe. This routine traffic stop ended with a handcuffed arrest. The record doesn't say if the driver is Black or white, but a witness said that Watson yelled for the two policemen to "turn the boy loose."

Watson spat out a few choice expletives at the Black cop on the scene, words that ended in, "I'm going to kill you."

Next this decorated former cop flew out of his car, ducked behind his door aiming through the window at the patrolmen. He used the door as a shield and started firing.

There was a wild gunfight. Officer Virgil Hollins, the Black patrolman, fired eight shots from two magnums, the white officer squeezed off three rounds from his .38 pistol. Neither officer was injured, but one of eleven shots hit Watson in the chest.

Big Bill was dead in the street.

William "Bill" Watson, the famous athlete who ran head-first through color lines with the emotional muscle to withstand the chiding in high school and college with Stack's encouragement, who was once Michigan's winner, robbed of Olympic glory, died at fifty-six years old after seeing his second dream go down the tubes in hatred and numbing segregation-driven poverty amid screams of police brutality. And perhaps, mental illness.

I wonder if the same thought crossed Stack's mind as it does mine: did the fatal shot pierce Watson's heart where his badge used to be?

Chapter 7
Rule: Ann Arbor to Oregon

The river of life broke open some new paths, then retraced its steps and switched back on itself over time for the Stackhouse family. This was the case back in Ann Arbor of 1939, long before Big Bill Watson's dreams sunk in despair. The year held great promise for the Stackhouses.

Moving to Ann Arbor, they built a lovely three-bedroom brick bungalow for $7,000. Conveniently, the house on Pauline Blvd was a twelve minute walk to Michigan Stadium, where Stack worked as a coach. Ann was eight, joyous that she might get her own room again. Here, Ann learned one of the most important facts of life: you can't acknowledge what you don't see.

After going to the movies, Ann asked her mother why movies only showed shadows instead of people. "For me, it was like listening to the radio," Ann wrote in her daughter's book *Where Angels Tread: Real Stories of Miracles and Angelic Intervention.*

Right away, Sophie took Ann to the optometrist.

The eye chart's big "E" was a haze. Her vision was bad, 20/200, with profound nearsightedness.[8] Ann got her first pair of glasses in elementary school, but few people knew she was legally blind throughout her life.

Ten years and another city later, Ann graduated from high school in Coatesville, PA (wearing glasses). Ann and I didn't talk much about her high school days, but I do know that by the time Ann hit senior high, she'd been on a whirlwind cycle of packing and unpacking with her family. I moved a lot

---

[8] Rule, Leslie October 11, 1991, *Where Angels Tread,* McNeil Publishing.

in my childhood too, but my father was a journalist, not a coach. Both professions required moving to new cities for greater opportunity.

Ann reading as a four-year-old. Her parents, both teachers, instilled a love of reading from a young age. Courtesy of Leslie Rule.

So Ann and I would talk about what the moves required from children: you needed to make fast friends, learn subtraction when your last school only taught addition, and behave like you'd never met a stranger.

Honestly, it was a pretty lonely existence for a child. Just when we'd put down a few roots, then we were off again, sometimes in the middle of a school year. The constant moves meant we lost touch with old friends. We had to fit into new groups, attitudes, styles, surroundings and with new teachers. I remember moving from Toronto, Ontario, Estevan, Saskatchewan to Yakima, Washington, then sister city, Selah in quick succession. A boy in my third grade class had LSD written on his eraser. I thought those were his initials!

Girlfriends invited me to their churches. Different churches than the ones I knew. I asked Mom, "Why do they always talk about BEVERLY at church? Who's Beverly?" My mother puzzled at this, finally figuring out the pastor was saying "VERILY, verily, I say unto you." Sure was easy to get things twisted as a kid. That same year I was forced to give up the Beatles for the Monkees. The Beatles were de rigueur in Selah!

Ann said she often felt like an outsider. So did I. But we

learned how to make friends quickly, acclimatize to our surroundings, study people intently and listen to *their* stories. I was far more chatty growing up, having been an only child most of my life, but we both agreed having a ready sense of humor also helped us make hard transitions.

In 1949, Sophie pulled out the old cardboard boxes again. Ann was eighteen years old and the movers were going cross country this time, to the other side of the Continental Divide, where no Hansen or Stackhouse ventured before. Chester brought his family to Oregon, where he got a great job at Willamette University in Salem. He was a triple threat there – football coach, track Coach, and Athletic Director. Stack's track team won State Championships in 1951 and 1952. He innovated quickly, starting the enormously popular Willamette Relays, the precursor to the Steve Prefontaine Classic held today in Eugene. The whole family had moved out west together, but Ann was now college bound and got a dorm room in Willamette U's residence hall.

The girls' dormitory, called Lausanne Hall, gave Ann autonomy while also allowing her to sit at the family dinner table any old time she liked. Her parents lived nearby. However, lest you think eighteen-year-old college girls had real freedom then, you'd be sadly mistaken. In '49, far less than two percent of teenage girls went to college. Societal expectations funneled most of them into M.R.S. degrees (slang for becoming a wife) instead of into serious careers. Their mothers had it no better. Women weren't allowed to have bank accounts, make contracts or wills, buy and sell property, or serve on jury duty.

At Willamette University, "gals" had to wear skirts, dresses, saddle shoes, loafers, maybe with a penny slid into the decorative slot on top of the shoes. Handbooks of the day give disturbing dating advice such as: "When asked on a Coke date don't order a banana split. The gold-digger is soon shunned. Telephone a man only if necessary. He sees through a flimsy excuse, so you have cheapened yourself for nothing. Don't talk about the men in your life, real or imagined. Talk about him or, better still, let him talk about him." Thank goodness 1949 is in the history books.

Ann was a friendly frosh, meeting people easily. Her quick wit added to her charm. One of Ann Stackhouse's first friends at Willamette University was Betty Mae Settecase.

Betty Mae Settecase talked about her long friendship with Ann when we met in 2019. Author's photo.

I interviewed Settecase at her home in Oregon's wine country in 2019, after Ann passed. Betty Mae, then a woman in her eighties who looked years younger, remembered their first meeting like this: "I thought she was from a foreign country because she really was different than the rest of the kids going to school there."

Ann was wearing this "Teddy Bear" coat at Willamette University in Salem when she met Betty Mae Settecase in 1949. Courtesy of Betty Mae Settecase.

Betty Mae was, shall we say, a little put off by Ann's appearance; a big oversized 1920's Teddy Bear coat, cat eyeglasses setting off her auburn red hair. Nobody at school looked "like *that*," according to Betty Mae.

Well, Ann's joie de vivre quickly overshadowed her appearance and the two ended up in the same sorority. They were lifelong friends. Betty Mae never gave a second thought again about Ann—God forbid—"wearing polka dots and stripes together" because she was hilarious.

"I don't think there's much that ever came out of Ann Rule's mouth that wasn't funny," Betty Mae told me.

One of the most amusing things Ann did came at breakfast every day. She read the newspaper out loud to her close cadre of friends, but she changed the names of people accused in crime stories. Instead, Ann inserted the names of her roommates and Betty Mae as the suspects. For example, "Yesterday, Betty Mae was arrested for smoking outside the boys dormitory. Another roommate, Alice tried bailing her out but couldn't raise the money to spring her."

Oh they had a ball! Betty Mae said they'd all be in stitches trying to swallow breakfast.

The two didn't date much, if at all, at Willamette, but Ann made up fictitious boyfriends for her posse. According to Ann, Betty Mae's pretend boyfriend was "Kyle Rote," a good-looking football player from Texas. He later became a noted NBC football commentator. For the rest of their lives, Ann would call Betty Mae asking, "Mrs. Rote, what are you doing?"

The two were supposed to attend weekly sorority dinner meetings on Tuesday nights, but they'd skip out to Ann's family home instead. After inviting her friend to dinner the following Tuesday, Ann asked Betty Mae, "Mom wants to know if there's any food you don't like?"

"No, I eat almost anything," said Betty Mae. "Except parsnips."

"Oh, that's good to know," said Ann.

Low and behold, what was on the Stackhouse family table that Tuesday? Parsnips. Betty Mae didn't remember if they ate the vegetable, but they all had a good laugh about it while passing the 'snips.

Ann, with college dorm-mates, is on the left wearing polka dots, at Willamette University in Salem where her dad was Athletic Director. Courtesy of Betty Mae Settecase.

"We'd laugh all the way to Ann's parents' house *and* all the way back," said Betty Mae, with a wide grin.

Dinners at the Stackhouse's were always fun, and delicious. Their home, built on a hill, sat prominently on the highest peak overlooking south Salem. The house was unusual for 1949, with a waterfall coming down the wall near the front door. Betty Mae said she couldn't get over a light switch turning water on and off with the flick of the finger. Such modern conveniences.

A few years later, in 1963, when Sophie and Chester moved to a farm outside of Salem named "Seclusia," Betty Mae said the waterfall made a repeat performance in their next home in Turner, Oregon.

Betty Mae, Ann, and their other Willamette friends got together all through the years, eventually calling themselves the Jolly Matrons. Ann's book acknowledgements frequently mentioned the group or individuals who had been her friends the longest in life. The Matrons met in Seattle drinking wine and laughing at Ann's stories for decades. Eventually, attrition took its toll, and each woman either became too frail to continue in the group or passed on. I'm sorry to say, Betty Mae is gone now too. I loved hearing her stories; it made me feel like we were both with Ann again. But it is not hard to imagine "Mrs. Kyle Rote," Ann Rule and the rest of the Jolly Matrons discussing books, sipping wine and laughing until they snort in the hereafter.

A Jolly Matrons reunion in 2000. Ann sits on the far left with many of her friends from Willamette University. Courtesy of Betty Mae Settecase.

Part II

Chapter 8
Rules of Engagement

In the fall of 1950, Ann decided to make another change. She wanted to switch schools and move to Seattle. She entered the University of Washington as a sophomore. Ann loved Willamette University, but wanted to test her own wings on a campus where she wasn't always "the coach's daughter." When Ann left Willamette, even her closest friends like Betty Mae had no idea what Ann's major would be.

At UW, Ann majored in creative writing, an easy "A" and started leaning hard into a career in criminal justice. She minored in criminology, psychology and penology. She would later earn an Associate of Arts degree at Highline Community College in Des Moines. Some experts see penology as the science of punishment, prison management and rehabilitation, others view it as the study of science and philosophy. The rehabilitation principle is used today as prisons fill, because most criminals are eventually paroled. There are many facets of penology, which Sheriff Hansen seemed to understand decades before schools taught it and prisons employed it.

Ann loved criminology classes, studying the causes of crime: prevention, statistics and behavior. Stackhouse would need to know all these facets of criminal justice if she wanted to be a police officer. Finally, this woman, who would spend half a century investigating why heinous crimes were committed, loved her psychology and abnormal psychology classes. Insert any of the names of the monsters Ann wrote about (and meticulously researched) and you'd move to the head of the class in abnormal psychology.

Ann said she never thought of being an author back then. Yet, it was in those creative writing classes she found something she never expected either: William John Rule. Bill, as he was known, was a graduate of Highline High School in Burien, Washington, and was now studying at "U-Dub." Bill was good looking, with blonde-hair and blue eyes, and was a student in one of Ann's writing courses.

Bill Rule about the time Ann met him in a writing class at University of Washington. Courtesy of Leslie Rule.

Betty Mae Settecase expressed confusion to me about the pairing, "When she married Bill, I was surprised. He was handsome, but very slight. Not the football types [her father Stack had around]". Seems Ann had no interest in muscled types anyway. Bill had a different stature: sinewy and athletic in his own way.

Ann's first take on him was not complimentary. She thought the cute blonde guy was dumb because he slept through class. What alternate explanation could there be? Well, Ann found out later—Bill Rule was up all night working at a gas station to pay his tuition. Ann had an unfailingly soft touch to the unfortunate and Bill was cute as heck. Let's just say one thing led to another and the relationship took off.

While they were dating, Bill lived on a boat. Not a houseboat, mind you, but a small boat tied up at Lake Washington. One afternoon, the two students were having a romp in the tiny cabin in the only fold-down bed, slightly narrower than a twin. The cabin was so tight, you could barely turn around. So cramped that the single bed folded up into the wall to save space. Unexpectedly, Bill's father John Rule showed up out of the blue and rapped on the bough of the boat,

"Billy. Hey! *Bill?* You in there?" he said.

Fearing discovery, Bill and Ann started making hand gestures to communicate. The gist of this pantomime from Bill was "Ann, I'm going to have to fold up this bed and lock YOU into the wall with it, okay?"

Keep in mind, there were no closets, no bathroom to run into. What was a girl to do but nod?

"...Um, okay, I guess so," Ann said, gesturing with her palms up.

Superimpose all the sight gags, thus hilarity you might find in a modern rom-com (or in Ann's time, Pillow Talk with Doris Day and Rock Hudson (1950)) and you'd still underestimate these two amateurs caught canoodling in the afternoon.

Eventually, Dad found his own way in, bent down to clear the cabin headroom when Bill straightened himself up.

"Hey, Dad...uh...um...hi...I..."

Dad sat blithely on the only seat available because Doris Day was stuck in the single bed tucked into the wall. Bill, always nervous around his father, felt his heart beating out of his chest.

Dad took no notice and began a *lengthy* conversation. Bill gave staccato answers, as his father nattered on and his girlfriend nearly suffocated in that folded bunk. Bill prayed his dad would exhaust himself and shove off. Dad blathered on for what seemed an eternity, and finally left. Ann and Bill would laugh about this escapade for years.

Back on campus, Bill was studying to be a writer or perhaps a teacher. His career path would also take a circuitous route to graduation. Meanwhile, Ann picked up her degrees and finally landed her dream job: police officer. She'd work out of downtown Seattle at a time when fewer women were on the force.

Ann's first day did not go well. She was put in charge of taking an incarcerated young girl at the Reformatory to the hospital. The teen said she was sick and needed to lie down. Ann left the room to find a bed. When she returned, the teenager had vanished.

Lesson learned. The girl was found hiding at her parents' house.

Looking back, Ann said she was surprised she wasn't fired. Not a stellar start for a new officer, but Ann kept on trying.

Ann's next assignment topped that. In my mind's eye, the following is how my overactive imagination saw the day progressing when I heard the story from her.

She needed success. *Badly.* This was the first day, her first time being thrown out on the streets alone. Unseen eyes tracked her.

The park was slow that night and the weather was cold. Despite the temperature Ann needed to kick into a higher gear. Her 3" heels click, click, clicked as she headed toward a nearby park bench. The ricocheting sound intensified her emotions, echoing off nearby old brick buildings and vibrating through her. Nervous, she was unsteady on her feet.

A few more steps, she thought, to calm herself. Now a bench was within striking distance of her outstretched hand, ready to brace her. Her resolve was flagging and her tummy growled, but there was no going back.

Resting at the bench back, Ann leaned a minute, gathering her composure, then shoved off as if nothing happened. Her impervious look said, "I did *not* almost fall, must be your mind playing tricks."

This job was more difficult than she imagined. She was working hard to not get psyched out, to let the jitters win.

The week before, Ann was told that "Today would be the day."

Hearing the words "Get ready…" made time move too quickly from the calendar to the clock. She knew within hours, minutes, then seconds they'd be pushing her into the park. Alone.

She'd tried to prepare, but for *what* she wasn't quite sure.

She better keep on moving. Her current strategy was garnering no results.

I need to find a new spot, she thought, wincing.

Then, in one more pounding heartbeat, it was over. Immediately "they" sprung out of their cars and ran toward her.

It was a bust.

Ann Rule's first day on VICE duty as a sex decoy for the Seattle Police Department didn't snare any predators that day. But Ann was enormously relieved the mission was over.

Yes, this is how *I envisioned* Ann Rule's first day as an undercover cop in Pioneer Square trying to snare a man flashing unsuspecting women in the park. Police women wore skirts and heels on duty in the 50's, her partners hoped this made the perfect ruse. It's easy to see why they chose Ann for the job. With fewer women than men on the force, your badge number comes up pretty quickly. When telling me about her real early adventure, she snickered "I was a virgin and they sent me!?"

Most of all, Ann was grateful the sex predator wasn't out that day.

Indeed, the thought that Ann was actually sent out trying to lure a flasher is enough to scare the daylights out of me! Ann *was* naive about sex but knew enough to be anxious about walking alone in a park like that. Her parents had always been very open about how nature worked and Stack later taught college sex education classes on closed circuit television. This did not mean Ann had ANY experience!

Ann pretends to be a vixen with her college dorm friends in 1949. Courtesy of Betty Mae Settecase.

Ann had the most ingratiating way of telling her story. My rendition is more embellished than hers, but she was walking in three inch high heels, a skirt and heavy coat. Her superiors directed Ann to walk a specific path where the exhibitionist previously appeared. She followed directions closely but the perp wasn't caught that night. This was her one and only experience as a sex decoy.

When I heard Ann's story more than ten years ago, it made me bend over with laughter. She was hilarious. Ann snickering, lips pursed, her shoulders bobbing up and down as she stifled a full laugh, enjoying the folly.

Sixty years later, Ann admitted to having been scared to death that day, saying she had *no idea* what she was doing, was supposed to be doing, nor what she'd do if she actually *saw* the suspect. She was the lure, with no way to communicate with the undercover cops in cars.

Her colleagues held police radios, guns and handcuffs.

Ann had her purse.

Ann had joined the Seattle Police Department as a provisional officer, waiting to pass all the tests required. Ann never forgot those days, always laughing under her breath that they chose her, still a virgin, for VICE duty. She worked the next year and a half on patrol until the police exam rolled around. Naturally, the written test was a cinch.

But. That. Eye. Exam.

At the time, department brass wouldn't hire an officer without 20/40 vision. Ann said back then, contact lenses were not allowed. Officers had to be able to protect themselves, or a partner, if their glasses were knocked off. And as we know, Ann was almost legally blind. She failed the eye test. She turned in her badge. Her poor eyesight short circuited her lifelong dream of being a policewoman. The experience broke her heart.

Suffering the disappointment through her glasses, the fog from her tears made it darn near impossible to see her way home. Ann, so grief stricken, avoided the precinct at all costs. Ann told me, she went *way* out of her way for years steering clear of the memories at the Seattle Public Safety Building. But Ann's time on the police force paid off later, when many of the officers and detectives she knew became sources in her stories.

Chapter 9
Rule: Happiness to Heartache

After that, Ann turned the page reluctantly and focused on her relationship with Bill. And she became a social worker.

Ann and Bill soon decided to get married and announced their engagement. Joy abounded. You can bet those "Hansen girls" (mother Sophie and her three sisters) burned up the long-distance telephone lines in twitterpation!

The happy couple decided not to get married in the Northwest, but instead in a church holding far more meaning to her mother's family — the First Congregational church of Stanton, Michigan. A legacy church, her grandparents Chris and Anna Hansen had been going there for decades. A wedding in Stanton made more sense since Ann had spent so much time there as a child, and her extended family was closer to the East Coast than the West.

While Doug and I were back East researching Ann's life, I went to see the church where Ann and Bill got married. Wandering around the church one Sunday, I saw the altar where Ann and Bill gave their vows. The altar was silhouetted in front of a large stained-glass window of Jesus in a blue robe, a red shawl wrapping around his hip and over his right shoulder. Very vibrant. The church seemed almost new, with modern technology — a big computer screen upfront and a sound system running in the back.

Remembering pictures of Ann in her wedding dress, it was almost as if I could see her walking down the aisle, with Stack "giving her away."

Most of all, I envisioned what Ann and Bill Rule might have seen as they turned to walk down the aisle as husband and wife. I picture Ann's father, mother, aunts, uncles and their families standing in the pews and beaming at this first-born Hansen grandchild, now a new bride. I'm feeling, well, sentimental about an event I never attended, one held four years before I was born. Judging by the photographs, it's an event I would love to have witnessed.

Hilarious picture of Ann on her wedding day in 1954 with her father Stuck. The reason for their surprised faces is lost to history! Courtesy of Leslie Rule.

Almost seventy years later, standing in the church on that trip with Doug, I was hoping nobody would misinterpret why a strange woman was gawking in the sanctuary long after Sunday service. I got busy trying to find out Ann's ties to this place, while Doug waited in the pews. I ran into the pastor, Randy Bennett, who was leading a youth group in the basement.

The pastor explained that the First Congregational Church of Stanton did have quite a history. Founded Lutheran in 1874, it burned to the ground in the early 1950's, with an enduring congregational spirit to rebuild. Ann's relatives had probably seen the conflagration from the courthouse jail where they lived a few blocks away. The whole town watched the flames licking the sky as the old church billowed up in smoke.

First Congregational Church of Stanton, founded 1874, engulfed in fire. The baptismal church for many of Ann's relatives. Courtesy of First Congregational Church of Stanton, Michigan.

Much as Lutherans believe in the resurrection of Christ, a new church would rise from the ashes. The lovely new brick church was completed two years before Ann's nuptials on September 1st, 1954.

Ann and Bill Rule were married a month before her twenty-third birthday. The family circle and faith was not broken, even by fire.

The Rules only had a few months of wedded bliss before the real gut punch hit. A wound so deep and wide it left a lifelong scar. Ann's only brother Don Rex, a twenty-one-year-old pre-med student, ended his life by carbon monoxide poisoning.

Ann already knew something was wrong when they dropped Don off at the Seattle airport after the wedding. Don and Stack were headed back to Palo Alto. Stack was finishing his degree, and Don would complete his senior year at Stanford before heading to Harvard. Ann couldn't help but notice Don was extremely depressed. Ann waved goodbye as the plane taxied from the gate. Her gesture got slower and slower as her dread sank deeper. Ann *knew* she would never see Don again. She started crying, and walked away with an intense sense of dread.

Unless you've lost a sibling—having been swallowed whole by memories or what if's— the repercussions are hard to fathom. Stifling the pain can be a lifelong endeavor. The angst over the death of Ann's brother led her to volunteer at Seattle's Crisis Clinic hotline years later. She was determined to give her heartache a purpose by working to prevent suicides. That crisis line job changed Ann in ways she could not have fathomed.

Chester (Stack), Ann, Don, and Sophie Stackhouse. Photo take around 1934.

Ann and brother Don with their parents. Courtesy of Leslie Rule.

I understood the depth of her pain over her brother's death. We both lost siblings way too early. In my friendship with Ann, we talked about my sister's death from congenital heart failure. Jill was nine years old when she died, a month shy of our birthdays, both in July. The deaths in our respective families came relatively early: I was almost six when my sibling died and Ann was twenty-three. But age made no difference when recalling loss, and while we talked, she empathized instinctively with my pain. She never filled in any blanks about Don's passing during our talk. And I never asked. I saw silent tears beneath her glasses, but she remained so still you might not see unless sitting right next to her.

There was a gnawing anguish in her eyes protecting an incalculable loss locked inside.

Chapter 10
Family Rules

New life changes made the Rules' heads swivel. Bill was drafted and they moved from Seattle to New York State, where Bill worked on an anti-aircraft battery after the Korean War. They lived on the Tuscarora Indian Reservation until Bill was transferred to Texas two years later. Then, children. The first daughter born to Sgt. William and Ann Rule came in 1956 in Niagara Falls, then Leslie in 1958 in Washington State, along with their brothers in 1961 and 1964.

All the children were delivered naturally. Ann was so into natural childbirth that she joined the Natural Childbirth Society and quickly got elected president of the Northwest chapter. The Society taught women how to have babies without using drugs during delivery. Ann was an all-star. During one delivery, a nurse saw Ann's arm go limp and shouted, "She's OUT!" Nope. Madame President had just trained her body to relax and let nature take the wheel.

After Bill's stint in the Army, the family lived in Bellevue, a town between Lakes Washington and Sammamish. It was a good place for Bill; he loved to swim. Bill was a very strong swimmer, routinely putting in three or four miles a day. As a twenty-year-old he swam the 22 mile length Lake Washington in ten hours. He swam so often that he was able to save many drowning swimmers. Bill taught the whole family to swim and they'd spend summer afternoons together lolling on beaches.

The best entertainment came in the summer of '62. The World's Fair took over Seattle that year, and Ann and Bill's three kids were excited for a chance to go. The extravaganza dovetailed with an important visit from Aunt Freda's family back East.

Freda, Freda's husband, Elton Sampson, and their two children drove the two thousand miles in a travel trailer. Elton was sheriff in Stanton, living with his family in that same mom-and-pop jail, twenty years after Sheriff Hansen passed. Elton and Freda's children were Karen, about fifteen, and Jim, nine. You've already met Jim. There was a large age gap between the children and Ann, so you'd be forgiven for thinking Ann was an aunt to Karen and Jim, not a cousin. In 1962, they were kids, and she was in her thirties with three kids.

Single tickets to the fair were less than two bucks, kids a dollar. And oh, that Space Needle! The uber modern marvel with slender alien arms of steel stretching skyward, fingertips balancing a UFO restaurant up sixty stories high. Ann and Aunt Freda marveled that people could keep lunch down at the flying saucer restaurant as they circled 360 degrees every forty-seven minutes in the air.

Ann in her Aunt Freda's wedding in 1940. Courtesy of Jim and Mary Sampson.

Everybody clamored to go up the Space Needle. Well, almost everybody. The kids were so excited they begged for the chance. "Please? *Please!?*" You would have thought their very lives depended on it. But Ann hemmed and hawed. The Needle was so tall that their necks strained as they tried to take in its size. Always a worrier, Ann simply couldn't let her children go up, and there was no way she'd get on that space capsule elevator along with them. She was gentle but resolute in her refusal to let them ride. She explained carefully that the contraption "looked too dangerous" and might topple over any minute. The decision was final. No Space Needle for her kids.

The Sampsons were in the other camp, and green-lit the mission. Jim and his sister stepped aboard and watched Ann and her kids disappear below through the elevator's panorama of glass. Leslie, four at the time, saw how worried her mother was. She remembered thinking if it was that unsafe, "Jim's parents must not love him as much, if they'll let him ride to the top!" This makes her chuckle today.

After the Seattle trip, nine-year-old Jim didn't see Ann until he was an adult. Life was hectic for her, raising kids and taking odd jobs to help the family's finances. Bill and Ann scrambled to make ends meet. By 1964, they had *four* little mouths to feed.

Ann began doing door-to-door surveys to stay at home with her children and write. A job most people wouldn't even consider today. She walked from one house to the next asking people to try products and review them, while she marked their responses on her clipboard. Ann would always get a laugh in her book appearances when she'd say, "I was paid to go door-to-door and ask men to drink beer with me."

But it wasn't just beer she was pedaling.

Ann went door-to-door taking surveys in 1967 to test products with homeowners. Courtesy of Leslie Rule.

Before Bugles, a horn-shaped snack, hit store shelves, Ann schlepped the crispy corn cones from one house to another. And, of course, Ann doled out plenty of packages for her kids to try at home.

"At first we liked them," Leslie told me. "Then we got sick of them. They had a weird aftertaste."

This was the way Ann paid a few bills, mothered her children, and tried to get a toe-hold writing. Her persistence was remarkable. After drawers full of rejection slips, and six years of writing, she made $35 dollars for two articles in Seattle Sunday magazine. By year seven, she made $107, then in the eighth-year she made a thousand dollars for small works in the *New York Daily News* and the *Chicago Tribune.* In total, $1,142 for eight years of work.

Ann knew the chances of becoming a book author were slim, that you only had a 1/10th of one percent shot at making it. She told other newbies: "You can't let the naysayers make you think you can't make it, because you can." She took her own advice. And she started overcoming the odds.

Rule wrote true stories for detective magazines. These articles poured out of her. They were written under the moniker Andy Stack—a mash up of her son's name with her father's nickname—and other nom-de-plumes, because male editors told Ann readers would not believe a woman knew anything about police investigation in the 1960's. When they realized Ann knew more about police work than the male writers, the editors relented, saying she could write under her own name. Even so, Ann decided to stick with pseudonymous bylines for safety reasons. She was apprehensive that the suspects might be out of jail by the time the articles appeared and come visiting.

True detective magazines were in their heyday in the 1960's. Ann wrote for five of them, in Oregon, Washington, Idaho and western Montana. The 35-cent magazines, with staged photographs on the cover—usually of women victims pictured in the midst of frightening attacks—had wide circulation and sold nationwide. She'd grown up seeing them in her grandfather's jail office.

Ann detested those covers, and she begged editors to change them. She objected to the headlines, too. The titles, as you'd imagine, were salacious. "The Riddle of Oregon's

Dismembered Brunette" with the subtitle *"A cold-blooded killer hacked up his victim and strewn body parts all over the county."*

Despite the lurid spin editors put on her articles, they were true stories and Ann put careful research into each one. She wrote two to three articles a week, at 10,000 words each (about thirty pages) for the magazines over a thirteen year period. This was a time when her knowledge of killer behaviors grew exponentially, building her vast serial killer profiling skills, honing her expertise about violent offenders and giving her full access to Seattle detectives and their crime files.

Prior to writing for the detective magazines, some of Ann's first published work appeared in confession magazines owned by the same successful New York company. The rules for writing those articles were different. While readers were led to believe each story was true, the writers were required to stipulate that their submitted stories contained a *grain* of truth. Stories in confession magazines had to be realistic enough that the scenario *could happen* to someone, somewhere.

Ann said her inspiration for one of her best stories for the magazine *True Confessions* came from a tiny article in *TIME* magazine. The original article was about a new program for inmates at a Parchmen, Mississippi maximum security prison. Ann's story carried a salacious headline, "I Went to Prison to Sleep With My Sister's Husband," and was based on conjugal visits behind bars. The new prison program in Parchmen did allow inmates to sleep with their wives in prison, but Rule made up the rest using the magazine's well-worn formula of Sin, Suffer, Repent, with a happy ending to wrap things up.

Rule kept writing for *True Confessions* until she said, "I ran out of things to confess!"

All this she did at home with the kids, clickety-clacking on an old typewriter before leveling up to an electric model. Ann must have had tremendous powers of concentration, because as any parent of four children knows all too well: the ruckus can get plenty loud. Ann would say that unless her kids were actually fighting on top of the typewriter, she could write. She was finally earning around $250 bucks an article. In all, 1,400 magazines with Ann's "byline" were eventually stacked knee-high across the lower shelves of an enormous bookcase lining her office wall.

Ann soon left beer and Bugles surveys behind. She was able to become a full time writer in 1969. Starting then, and throughout her entire writing career, there were four topics she wouldn't touch: torture, motorcycle clubs, mob crime families and drug rings. Ann found torture revolting, and the dangerous proclivities of the latter groups kept her at arm's length.

While Ann wrote religiously, Bill had a full time job. But she was uneasy about Bill not being able to live his dream too. The husband she'd met in that creative writing class still longed to pen the Great American Novel. His short story "Leo the Christian Lifeguard" was published in *The Michigan Quarterly Review,* a prestigious literary magazine. He finished a few novels, but never sold them. So, to sidestep any appearance of competition as writers, Ann chose to "write trash" as she called her magazine work.

A few years later, Bill quit his job at Boeing Air, because the monotony was mind-numbing. This was not his passion. In a phone call with Ann's friend Shirley Jackson in 2015, she remembered Bill as a challenging boss. He'd gotten fed up with technical writing and became a teacher at Foster High School in Tukwila. He really did enjoy the students and his classroom.

By now, things have gotten rocky at home. Ann and Bill's relationship hit some turbulence after twenty years and four children.

Ann in her driveway in the early 1970's around the time she realized her marriage was failing. Photo Credit: Leslie Rule.

In the midst of this upheaval, there was more bad news: Bill found a strangely growing spot on his skin. At first, thinking it was nothing more than a mole, he forgot about it. In a time before effective sunscreen, the blonde, fair-skinned swimmer had always been prone to sunburns.

Then, when Ann discovered Bill had been unfaithful, tensions in their marriage escalated. They made the decision to divorce, working cooperatively to make it happen.
Bill was diagnosed with cancer just weeks after discussing final terms of the divorce in 1971.

Surgery to remove malignant melanoma appeared successful, and his skin grafts improved. With the divorce final in 1972, Bill began dating Betty, nineteen years his junior. They married in April of 1974. But Bill couldn't beat another cancer.

Ann stayed in close touch with Bill and his new wife—whom she always lovingly referred to as "her wife-in-law." That was always good for a laugh from me. The three of them got along very well together.

Ann had to make some hard decisions while parenting on her own. She stopped volunteering at the suicide hotline, an extremely stressful job. She wrote more and wanted to help her children deal with the stress of the divorce, compounded by seeing their father become so very ill, after his cancer worsened. Bill Rule died four years after his final cancer diagnosis.

Through it all, Ann kept writing. In the 1970's, with two teenage boys at home, she was the sole breadwinner. And better luck found her. A big wig Hollywood director hired her to do a treatment for an upcoming movie. *The Lords of Flatbush* director Martin Davidson saw one of Ann's articles in *Cosmopolitan Magazine* about a Yakima, Washington love triangle murder and said she was the perfect fit to write the screenplay. They spent months writing a movie script about the case together.

Ann in Hollywood looking very California cool during her screenwriting days. Photo Credit: Leslie Rule.

While working on the film, Ann lived at the Ambassador Hotel in Los Angeles, and her children stayed with friends back home. The Ambassador was nationally famous for being the site of the assassination of Sen. Robert F. Kennedy in 1968, another true crime nightmare.

What was supposed to be a six-week stint turned into seven months. It turned out to be way too long to be away from a growing family in Seattle, so Rule finally left town while Davidson searched for a Hollywood studio to pick it up. Nothing worked out in Southern California, but twenty-six years later Ann covered this great true crime story in *Fever In The Heart, Ann Rule's Crime Files: Volume: 3.*

Headed into the 1980's, Ann Rule began cranking out her hits. She was a full-time author, writing about a bevy of murderers, among them: *Lust Killer (1981)* about Jerry Brudos, *Want Ad Killer (1983)* about Harvey Carignan and *I-5 Killer (1984)* about Randy Woodfield. These paperbacks had a different touch, originally penned under the name Andy Stack, were written more "viscerally" than her later works. All were about men who murdered brutally and repeatedly.

By 1984, while Ann was in Eugene researching her book *Small Sacrifices,* I asked her what kind of crimes she chose to write about.

"I'm looking for stories within stories that lead to other stories," she told me.

Ann had keen intuition about which cases to write out of thousands submitted by readers and detectives. She wanted "sleeper" cases which flew under the mass media radar. She searched for attractive, seemingly successful killers. People who didn't look like murderers. "I'm looking for a protagonist who seemed to have everything--physical attractiveness, intelligence, charisma, education, money, love, and fame. All of those things that most of us think, 'Well, if I had that, I'd be happy.' Yet the people I choose have those things, but they're empty inside. They're sociopaths, so they always want more."

Her eye for crimes turned the 1980's into a prolific decade for Ann.

This was exactly the kind of person Rule wrote about in her first nonfiction hardcover, *The Stranger Beside Me.* This is a book Ann had been working on subconsciously for years, not knowing that her partner at that Seattle Suicide Hotline would turn out to be a diabolical killer. Ann had taken the job to make peace with her brother's suicide and help save other lives. The volunteer work ended up paying off exponentially. Ann got a contract to write about a local unknown serial killer stalking young women. Irony of ironies, Rule had *no idea* the man she worked with, Ted Bundy, was the killer, until suspicions grew after she quit volunteering.

Ann's shift ran from 10 p.m.-2 a.m. while Ted Bundy, a paid work-study student, worked from 9 p.m.-9 a.m..

Every Sunday and Tuesday night, Ann and Bundy were

in a room together answering calls in Seattle's Queen Anne neighborhood inside a decrepit Victorian home whose ceiling tile stains mimicked Rorschach inkblot tests. The musty room was a fishbowl of creaky wood floors, tall windows and few furnishings. Ann and Ted worked in tandem. On the phone, Ann tried to soothe troubled minds while Bundy ferreted out enough information to trace calls and to get police to the scene. Ann said she and Bundy saved lives, individually and together.

Stranger is written from the perspective of the killer's friend—Rule herself—and brought in millions of readers. The literary world took notice of the book's stunning twists and turns as Ann tracked the unknown killer's case, then followed Bundy—from birth to the electric chair—as a brutal and prolific serial killer. He was executed in 1989 for three murders. But his resume was far more sinister, Bundy admitted to thirty additional slayings and investigators believe there were many more.

The book chronicled Ann's internal struggle to come to terms with Ted, the life-saving volunteer, juxtaposed with the bloodthirsty serial killer he turned out to be. No crime book had held the same power since Truman Capote's 1966 seminal work *In Cold Blood*, published fifteen years prior. Ann's first true crime book was truly groundbreaking as well, a one of its kind work, and an incredible read.

Stranger began Rule's juggernaut – while the book wasn't a national bestseller right away, Ann said in several interviews it had "very strong legs." Although *Stranger* did fly off the shelves of Seattle bookstores, it became a blockbuster over time, but not instantly upon publication.

Ann took a break from true crime with her next book, *Possession,* her first novel, published in 1981. The inside cover of *Possession* reeled readers in, "the heart of the story is [Rule's] insight into a woman's reaction to terror and violence and passion after Joanne Lindstrom's police officer husband is killed in a horrible accident, she has to depend on a stranger who becomes her captor and lover in order to survive the Northwest wilderness alive."

The book was a composite of Ann's knowledge of victim behavior blended with fictional settings. Ann said the book was originally banned in Cincinnati for sexual content. *Possession* also seemed to cause a stir back home in Michigan, too. When Ann sent copies of *Possession* to her aunties back East to read, they took issue with a few things despite their staunch support for Ann. On the whole, the true crime genre has been criticized for profane language, ugly subject matter, and gory details. But this was a novel. Ann's cousin Jim (the nine-year-old from the Seattle State Fair trip) was an adult by the time the aunties flipped the pages of *Possession*.

Jim recalled for me their reactions to the book. He explained that the sisters of Ann's mother were a spicy but very conservative bunch, who were raised in more genteel times.

The Hansen sisters bookending their mother, Anna, who's in the middle. Ann's mother Sophie is on the right wearing an apron. Courtesy of Leslie Rule.

After reading *Possession,* the sisters were sitting around a dinner table and started comparing notes. The book sparked a lively discussion among the elderly Hansen sisters.

Sister Freda led off, "Well, I'm not really sure I like a lot of the scenarios."

Aunt Donna said, "Oh yeah, I'm a little put off by that too."

After a brief silence, while Ann's Aunties ruminated, the most outspoken of the sisters finally piped up.

"You mean you don't like the term 'Motherfucking son of a bitch?'" Aunt Millie blurted out.

Sister's Freda and Emma, collectively with Aunt Donna, admonished, "Oh, we don't use those terms."

It was a totally understandable reaction from conservative Christian women of the time. Suffice to say, Aunt Millie getting right to the point was rather shocking to Jim.

But here was plain spoken Aunt Millie in her golden years, "just BAM, there it is!"

Jim, who was in the room listening to this book review, tried his hardest to stifle a laugh.

Ann knew her books weren't every reader's cup of tea – including her family. But her family kept reading them anyway. They held unwavering support for Ann's success. The Hansen sisters' pride vastly outweighed "the touchy subjects," as Jim called them. In time, all of Ann's books would make it onto the *New York Times* Best Seller list. *Every Breath You Take, Don't Look Behind You, In the Still of the Night and Last Dance, Last Chance* all made the list at the same time.

But there would be more "touchy subjects" on her road ahead.

Chapter 11
House Rules

Forty-three years after the Hansen sisters had their enlightening dining room table talk, I was looking for more of Jim Sampson's memories of Ann, on my trip with Doug Welch. Doug drove me to Jim and Mary Sampson's lakeside cottage outside Stanton, Michigan to talk with them.

Jim and Mary Sampson inside their cozy lakeside cabin outside Stanton, Michigan. Author's photo.

Despite the chilly March weather, the cabin was cute and a warm wood stove was already going when Doug and I stepped inside to interview the Sampsons. Doug knew I was excited to meet them and instantly took a liking to them too. Doug can be reserved when meeting new people for the first time, but as he said then, the Sampsons were salt of the earth people and he enjoyed them immensely. I videotaped the interview and Doug helped out by doing auxiliary videos behind us. Unbeknownst to him, he kept accidentally getting in the shot of the Sampsons. No bother, his work as an amateur photographer was welcome and I don't know what I would have done without him there.

My friend was definitely underpaid and overutilized on that trip, especially given his outstanding crime credentials.

As we talked, Jim Sampson put another log on the freestanding wood stove. The surroundings were downright cozy as winter turned to spring in Michigan. And oh boy, the stories started flowing. My heart swelled hearing first-hand about my friend Ann from the family who loved her.

Jim told us about the time he volunteered to pick up Ann at the airport before her appearance at Detroit's CBS station. They hadn't seen each other since Jim was a child and he suspected Rule might not recognize him at the airport.

"I mean we didn't have Facebook, instant messaging and that kind of stuff," Jim told us. "So maybe she wouldn't have a clear recollection of what I looked like [as an adult.]"

Their airport reunion took a hilarious turn when Jim decided to prank Ann BIG as her welcoming committee.

"I developed another persona when I went to pick her up," Jim said. "I went as 'Duke Cook.'"

Duke, you see, owned a pornographic bookstore in Detroit in this scenario. Jim, er, *Duke* Cook asked Ann if she had time to visit his store.

Ann barely looked at the guy as she was scanning the airport crowd, hoping her cousin Jim would rescue her from Duke Cook.

But always polite, Ann said, "I'm not sure that your clientele would be the type that would want to buy my books."

Cook assured her, "Oh, no, I sell everything. I sell *everything*."

Rule's eyes darted downward and swept from side to side. Ann was starting to wonder if this was a joke and questioned, "Jim?" Is that you?" Although, she was still skeptical, thinking that Duke Cook might have been one of her fans who found her before her cousin showed up.

"I don't know who Jim is," Sampson answered. "But we'd like to set up this arrangement for a personal book signing."

At that, Ann was catching on, but she still wasn't sure which direction this strange encounter was going.

That's when Duke Cook, the porno shop owner, finally

revealed himself to be her cousin, Jim Sampson. Their ensuing laughter bonded them together forever.

Ann stayed with Jim on that trip. As two adults, he realized they were family for a reason. Similar traits ran between them.

"I think interest in finding a good deal," Jim said. "The importance of family. Yes, family. *And* having a sense of humor in life." Duke Cook proved THAT at the airport.

I laugh out loud every time I think of this awkward meeting, knowing how respectful Ann was to her readers. I can just see the wheels turning in her head, eyes wide, eyebrows raised, searching for a way out of the meeting. Is this a fan? Is this my cousin? And where is Jim to save me from this porn operator? Jim took quite a chance that day, thinking his cousin could handle it.

We sat together in the lakeside cabin that had been in the Sampson family for two generations, a framed photo of Ann as a flower girl in Jim's parents wedding hung on the wall. Jim and Mary laughed together, lovingly teasing each other about the latest cabin update. A remodel of the bathroom was a must-do for Mary. The first rendition was a big update for them. When Jim and his sister Karen spent summers there as kids, the bathroom was an outhouse. Now, the bathroom was Cape Cod style: bright, white and cute as a button. They ribbed each other about this as Doug and I reset our shots to focus on Mary.

Jim and Mary Sampson in Michigan on the deck of their lakeside home in 2023. Author's photo.

Mary Sampson's an attractive, affable woman who smiled readily and made us feel right at home. I know Mary and I would be fun friends if our universes aligned differently. And I could tell that Mary was just the kind of woman Ann Rule would have connected to instantly. The two became compatriots when driving to Detroit together during Ann's trip and they had to make a pit stop.

As they were stepping out of the ladies' room, a one-eyed cat started curling around Ann's legs, then Mary's. They both wondered if the cat slipped out of its owner's car.

Seemingly alone at the rest stop, the cat wouldn't leave and Ann, the superstar, wouldn't leave either. Mary told me, "We stayed there for quite a long time. Cars come and cars go, and we would think somebody's going to come back for *this cat.* No one did."

Then came Ann's power of persuasion when it came to every living creature.

"Ann convinced us to take the cat home," Mary said. And Ann was very happy the kitty had a new home. They named the one-eyed cat "Freeway" and enjoyed his company. But the Sampsons only had indoor cats and Freeway was not of their ilk. Freeway, the feline, stayed for a while and then disappeared.

A week later, the Sampsons put an ad in the local newspaper looking for Freeway, the one-eyed cat. Immediately, they got a call from the neighborhood vet.

"We have your cat," the vet told them. "We've had your cat for a week, taking care of him. And yes! He has one eye! So, we *know* we have your cat."

Jim went to pick up the rescue kitty at the vet's. Office staff were very relieved to have found the owner so quickly after seeing the ad. What were the chances of finding this stray's owner, they exclaimed. There was just one problem: Jim took one look and *knew* this cat was not Freeway, their cat, and he did not have the heart to tell them about this case of feline mistaken identity.

Jim and Mary adopted this new cat and named it Freeway 2.

On that one Ann Rule trip, she got the Sampson's to adopt not one, but *two* one-eyed cats.

After meeting the Sampsons in Michigan, the three got along so well that Ann invited Jim and Mary to visit her home on Puget Sound. The Sampsons stayed in her "writer's cottage," seldom used for writing as it turned out. They adored it, hidden beneath tall timbers, set back from the Sound. Idyllic, really. The cottage sat adjacent to Ann's home. She called it the "Money Pit." In 1997, some $400,000 worth of damage from mudslides had to be removed by barges. The property on Puget Sound was Ann's first real splurge as a millionaire writer. It might not have been the mansion you might expect a celebrity to live in, but was an expensive beachside property nonetheless. It was beautiful, with lots of flowers growing in pots on her deck and clippings of rose-scented geraniums growing inside on window ledges.

After dinner together, the Sampsons joined Ann in her main house next door, where the real writing was done. The contemporary architectural home had huge two-story windows and a deck out front facing the water. It had a clear clean view of a seawater inlet, which was something of a novelty back in Michigan. The Sampsons were accustomed to vast lakes, not the Pacific Northwest scenery of snow-capped mountains, enormous old growth forests, vast rivers, and coastal waters not far from city limits. Ann enjoyed living on the water and so did the Sampsons.

The bugs also loved sunset on the Sound, attracted by the light inside. And with front doors wide open, Jim and Mary started swatting mosquitoes and other night flyers from their faces.

"Jim," Ann said. "We don't kill things in my house."

I laughed hearing this from Jim, as I too had been admonished for killing a Daddy Long Legs spider at Ann's house. The Sampsons were surprised, but submitted to the house rules, as Ann headed to the bathroom.

Jim remembered that he and Mary were sitting alone when "all of a sudden, Mary jumps up to make sure Ann is indeed in the bathroom. "Ann wouldn't even kill a spider. I'm sure she wouldn't. I mean, she said it, we knew she was serious, 'We don't kill things in this house.' "

But the house was becoming a bug menagerie.

"We had to make sure we worked fast," said Jim. The two of them looked like whirling dervishes, jumping, clapping the air to the front, left and center, before Ann got back from the bathroom. And there was added pressure to the timeline.

"We had to clean up all the bugs that fell over," Jim said. "Yeah, we had to get rid of them."

Destroying the evidence before being discovered! The Sampsons might have understood stray cats wheedling their way into Ann's heart, but there was a disconnect about bugs. Ann never discovered the murdered bugs that summer night, and her star just kept on rising.

Chapter 12
Rule Rising

There have been thirty-five Ann Rule books on *The New York Times* Best Sellers List. Seventeen television movies. And Ann was a proven celebrity in the book world. This powerhouse of hits made Ann either a mentor or target for other authors. She shied away from speaking publicly about controversy. That was not in her DNA.

Privately, there were sideswipes that hurt her feelings but never stopped her. Celebrity brought jealousy, but her notoriety also forged valued friendships predicated on mutual trust, respect and kindness. Fellow author Kathryn Casey understood this from day one.

Seven years before Ann's death, the two became fast friends. Casey is now the bestselling author of nineteen books, her most recent novel is *Bone Cold,* but more than a dozen works are true crime.

In a personal interview with Casey, she told me that Ann read *The Rapist's Wife,* retitled *Evil Beside Her,* long before they met.

"She was happy to see I did the work…that I write like her," Casey said to me. "We just kind of clicked…I really respected her. I respected her before I ever met her because I could tell by the books how hard she was working on them."

The two wrote from the empathetic perspective: bringing victims back to life through the memories of people close to them. They really listened to the victims' devastated families. The women focused on people, not the prisoners. At the same time, both authors understood readers inherently wanted to know how and why a child grew into a deranged killer. They meticulously researched the personality traits, superficial charm, insincerity, exaggerated sense of worth, and the deceit of murderers. I share their curiosity.

They reached deep into early chasms like lack of empathy, narcissism and the antisocial behavior that often shows up by eight years old. All the details uncovered by hard digging. While some authors resorted to headlines and the internet as research tools, Casey said Ann was never like that. "Ann always went to the trials," Casey told me. "She always put in the legwork. She always interviewed people. She spent a lot of time with the families…and I did that, too."

Early on in her career, when Ann started making a living writing crime, her conscience started nagging at her. She wrestled with authoring books about other people's misfortunes, and saw a psychologist. He smiled wryly saying half the world makes a living off the other half: Police, firefighters, doctors, lawyers. In *Publishers Weekly,* Ann said the psychologist told her "What matters is how you feel about people." Even late in her career, Ann admitted she'd never been able to inure herself enough to keep the tragic stories from impacting her emotionally.

Ann always made it a point to balance the victims' stories and their family's heartache with care and dignity. Both Casey and Ann cared about people, not wanting to re-victimize loved ones, and became good friends with families and survivors. As Ann told interviewer Valerie Ryan in *Publisher's Weekly* "I get to know the victim so well that I can see and feel the pain that these people go through: the victim, the victim's family and the family of the perpetrator."

This was how Ann Rule transformed the true crime genre. I've read true crime books written by men in the late 1960's and 70's. Their work is grittier, focusing or glamourizing killers, with much less research on victims.

Instead, Ann and Casey prioritized the lives of the people, mostly women, who suffered. For instance, some of the hurtful, gory details, and photos of Ted Bundy's crimes are so disturbing that Ann did not include them in the book *The Stranger Beside Me*. Instead, the reader learns more about the women's hopes, dreams, relationships and their heartsick loving families. Ann strove to consider her audience — who was reading this book? She constantly weighed two factors simultaneously: is the information or photo going to illuminate the content of her book, versus who it might hurt. She needed to tell what happened but didn't recite facts over and over by dwelling on the grisly. Ann never believed in showing ugly blood-soaked photos either. While other authors hoped these photos would attract more readers – Ann relied on solid writing for that.

If Ann thought a detail might be damaging, she either left it out completely or gently approached families for permission. Those were her ethics against gratuitous violence. Ann's more sensitive treatment attracted Kathryn Casey. Casey found a generous kindred spirit, a trailblazer, an author who'd been there, done that, "She was a really good, steady person to talk through problems with," Casey said. "She had been through everything before I went through it. I don't remember that I ever broke any new ground by telling her about some problem I had that she hadn't already experienced."

Once when Casey talked to Ann about abandoning a book because another author told her the case was *hers*, Ann told her very firmly that would be the wrong thing for Casey to do, "Throughout her career, she'd run into a lot of competition," Casey said. "And she told me to stay. *And* it was a really good case."

Rule explained to Casey that both writers had every right to be there and do their best, "So I did. I stayed."

The book they were talking about is *She Wanted It All,* about a Texas millionaire whose wife orchestrated his death and is now serving two life sentences for capital murder. Casey was glad she followed Ann's advice and didn't pack up her tent and go home, because the book still sells well to this day.

One of the first "cozy up to the killers" books on my shelf is by Truman Capote. A literary masterpiece, his 1966 non-fiction book, *In Cold Blood,* Capote immersed himself in the life of one of two men executed for the quadruple murder of the Clutter family in Kansas. The "nonfiction" journalistic reporting provides realism, with the imagination of a novel to build emotion and suspense. When I told Ann my opinions on *In Cold*

Blood back in the 1980's, Rule told me she thought Capote was too mesmerized by the suspects. She loved Capote's writing but found the book sickening for its sympathy toward the two killers, not the Clutters (Herb, his wife Bonnie and their two teenagers were brutally murdered in their own farmhouse).

As an author in the same genre, Rule picked up on the imbalance right away. And this was eye-opening for me. The book was so spellbinding that I hadn't even noticed. As she explained her point of view, I quickly recognized the omissions. Ann completely rewrote the formula on true crime to provide balance and empathy for victims. Victims in Ann's books are recognized, seen, and heard, letting readers know them as people, not mere numbers on a squad room cork board.

However, the old guard took issue with Ann's new approach. True crime author Jack Olsen, who passed in 2002, spoke harshly about both Capote and Rule. "…I know fakery when I see it," Olsen told Michael Hood in his *Conversation with Jack Olsen* in 1998. "Capote completely fabricated quotes and whole scenes" but Capote still insisted it was all true.

The book made millions, selling 100 million copies as a first of its kind.

Olsen's comments, quoted in *Esquire* magazine, brought a snappy retort from Capote.

"Jack Olsen is just jealous," Capote said.

Surprisingly, Olsen admits that it is true: he was jealous. His publisher Harper & Row apparently assigned Olsen to write the book until they discovered Capote and Harper Lee already had a six month head start in the case. Then the publisher pulled the plug on Jack Olsen. And perhaps Olsen's skewering of Capote is the same reason for his criticism of Ann Rule's work?

In 1998, Olsen announced that true crime was dead on arrival. He told interviewers the genre failed to stress accuracy and allowed authors to be too much a part of the story. It seemed he was hinting at Ann's involvement in *Stranger Beside Me*.

Insiders often referred to an "Olsen/Rule rivalry" as a long-running feud between the two. In retrospect, this rivalry looks more one-sided. Olsen took a thinly veiled swipe at Ann's writing style in an interview with Amazon books. "I enjoy authors who write seriously about crime—non-embroidered, non-embellished true crime journalism," he said.

Others allege hearing him saying this with Ann's name attached. But you never heard blowback from Ann. She always said, when interviewed, she stuck to the facts and that "people do such interesting things there was no need to make anything up." She advised up-and-coming writers that if they novelize, "keep your facts straight." Ann was legendary for her near-encyclopedic memory of names, times, dates, and miniscule details included in her books.

As true crime friends, Kathryn Casey said Ann spoke to her privately about Olsen. According to Casey, Ann would ask "Why does this guy keep on coming for me?"

Ann and I had the same conversation one night on the deck of her beachfront house on Puget Sound, when the criticism had grown from Olsen. Casey saw, well, some old-fashioned sexism at the core, "A woman was telling these more emotional stories…is 'soppy' the right word? True crime had been a real guy thing until Ann."

Casey noticed right away Jack was dismissive toward Ann. "It was disappointing when I realized he was being closed-minded" about Ann's success and standing as a pioneer bringing in millions of female readers. "They were both wonderful writers, and he should have been bigger than that," Casey said.

Ann never went there with Jack and his feud. And when he passed in July of 2002, she opined to the *Los Angeles Times* and others that Jack "was a brilliant writer who had a strong narrative style." She praised him as a major talent, but conceded "He was also extremely combative…He wouldn't not suffer bad reviews gladly. He was always in a battle."

Professionally, Ann wasn't criticized often by the media, especially compared to some other bestsellers. She was polite, accommodating and treated reporters with the same respect they afforded her. Ann's name was a go-to in their address books as a source for stories.

After her death in 2015, though, a backhanded compliment

came out in *The New Yorker*. The writer took jabs at *The Stranger Beside Me* while assessing Rule's dominance in the true crime genre. In the article, "Too Close To Ted Bundy," the reporter cited Rule's book as "perhaps the most unnerving true crime book ever published" and "consistently ranked as one of the most significant true-crime books ever written" as well as "suspenseful, chilling." But thirty years after the book's publication, the writer found fault in Ann's retelling of her friendship with Ted. In the book, Rule describes her devastating realization the friend she volunteered with at the suicide hotline was also the same serial killer she'd been hired to write about.

In my interpretation of the article, Ann was called into question on three counts.

First, not figuring out sooner that Ted Bundy was the killer in a timeline involving years of friendship between the two. But, in the summer of 1974, Ann called a Seattle Homicide detective when she saw the killer's composite drawing in the newspaper. She willingly gave Bundy's full name. She doubted he had anything to do with the murders, but she was bothered by the resemblance, and the fact witnesses had overheard the suspect tell victim Janice Ott his name was "Ted."

In the panic of the time, women were turning in their neighbors, their boyfriends, and their husbands. Countless people were positive they knew the culprit's identity. His own girlfriend called the police. But without a crystal ball, no one could have known Ted Bundy was responsible for the missing women. Perhaps it's easy for critics to say after the fact it was obvious who the killer was, but it's something very different to experience the long quest yourself, as Ann did.

Second, the writer takes a cynical view that Ann suspended judgment too long about Bundy's guilt in her firsthand account. This was a book she was contracted to write, no matter who the killer turned out to be, before anyone knew his identity. The difference here is that when Rule's suspicions about Ted Bundy grew, she contacted the major crimes unit *again*. Detectives told Ann that Bundy was one of 1,200 people they were investigating. Weeks later, when Bundy was finally arrested, Ann's narrative trajectory turned directly toward him.

I'm also puzzled by the writer's criticism of Ann not

admitting the "profitability" of her close relationship with Bundy. Ann always acknowledged Bundy made her career and that she made millions on the book. When reporters were brave enough to ask the question, Ann would admit to making money in true crime writing but also told them she suffered a great deal of guilt about it, too. Ann wrote books people wanted to read. Ann never denied the books made her rich, but she never walked away from her discomfort with the territory, either.

Third, *The New Yorker* article took issue with Ann's claims that victims' families urged her to write their books. The magazine writer saw this, as perhaps, disingenuous.

Families *did* approach Ann. I remember her talking about crying with them. And sometimes, she helped surviving victims or families monetarily. In my experience, parents often want their loved ones remembered as people with accomplishments, hopes and dreams, and not a victim of heinous crimes. Susan Powell's parents asked her to write *Fire and Ice: The Powell Family Tragedy* included in *Fatal Friends, Deadly Neighbors: Ann Rule's Crime Files Volume 16,* and Ronda Reynolds' mother convinced Ann to write *In the Still of the Night.*

Every Breath You Take: A True Story of Obsession, Revenge, and Murder is a perfect example of Ann's books written at the behest of a family. Before the victim, Sheila Blackthorne Bellush, was killed, she told her sister: "If anything ever happens to me, promise me that you will see there is an investigation, and find Ann Rule and ask her to write my story."

Ann's dedication says, "This book is for Sheila. I owe her a voice when she no longer has hers."

Ann told audiences at her crowded speeches, "I always care about my people. And if I didn't, I wouldn't be doing what I'm doing."

Sure, as a superstar author, it's no wonder Ann's work is scrutinized. What's heartbreaking for me, as her friend, is that she really didn't get a chance to defend herself.

Chapter 13
Rule of Generosity

Ann Rule could be a penny pincher when it came to herself. She seldom bought new clothes or anything else, but she'd open her wallet at Value Village. The excursions were a treasure hunt for her.

"OH! I remember this!" she'd exclaim to me. "My mom (dad, uncle, grandparent…) had one of these!" This woman worth millions might have been misunderstood shopping at donation stores, but this was a fabulous hobby for her. And this was a long time before shopping "the bins" became trendy at Goodwill. Ann said she never needed much for herself, but loved Value Village stuff. A child of the 1930's Depression, with plenty of love, support and encouragement, she knew material things wouldn't fulfill her. Writing did.

Ann always lived very simply. This was something that surprised her all-time favorite celebrity Peter Van Sant, a native Seattleite and CBS 48 Hours television correspondent. The two had such affinity for one another that they often joked they were secretly coupled.

Van Sant was, after all, just Ann's kind of man: successful, intelligent, tall and blue-eyed. A perfect secret crush, she told me privately while in her eighties. He was the correspondent she hoped would someday produce a documentary on her life. There was, indeed, such a friendship spark that I asked him to speak at Ann's celebration of life in 2015, and he graciously accepted. Meeting him, I instantly understood why the two had such a fondness for each other.

"I can't really describe the connection," Van Sant told the crowd. "But we both felt it. I knew what it was like not to have any money…to chase a dream and actually hold it in my hands…Maybe that was the connection."

When Van Sant, an uber fan of Ann's, went to interview her four years before she died, he'd expected her to be neighbors with Bill Gates or Howard Schultz. He remarked, "In my thirty year career, I've been to some ostentatious homes of the rich and famous," but when his crew pulled into *her* driveway, Van Sant was puzzled to find merely a modest ranch-style home. He mistakenly thought perhaps he had the wrong address.

CBS 48 Hours Correspondent Peter Van Sant and me at Ann's memorial in 2015. Author's photo.

"After all she had sold millions of books…She was THE rock star of True Crime writing!" Instead, he found a down-to-earth place, much like where her fans might live. The house brought back memories of Peter's childhood home in the University district. It was packed with furniture he believed Ann may have had since starting her career. Van Sant said, "That moment told me so much about Ann…What was *really important* to her. She didn't really want to talk about herself. Ann talked about her children."

In the scant time left between the keys and the keyboard, Ann sought meaningful connections, because money comes and goes.

One of the best stories I heard about the lean years when Ann was a single parent writing to pay the bills, was about Ann trying to save money by buying hot dogs on sale. Now, these were not your regular hot dogs. The dogs were discounted because they sprouted little "*arms*" along the rounded edges, places where the meat stuffing burst out of the skin encasement. Perfectly good, she said, but shall we say the hot dogs were unusual shapes, with little nubbins all over. They just didn't look, well, appetizing. Cutting them up and serving them (maybe with chili?), her kids *seemed* to eat them willingly.

But when the Rules finally moved out of their ranch-style house into a bigger house, Ann found those desiccated knobby hotdogs hidden under the couch. That dinner hadn't been eaten at all. No more discount hot dogs no matter how lean things got. Always good-natured, Ann laughed about the case of the missing dogs found under the couch.

If you were a loyal friend, Ann Rule was too. Her schedule prevented many conversational deep dives, but when I was with her, she was completely present. We'd waggle our tongues until the wee hours.

She was especially generous with fans. Even with lines snaking out the door of bookstores, she'd sit and sign each book, talk to people by name and sign books, and sign books, long after the rest of us would have buckled from hand cramps. She'd sign every single book. And her generosity didn't stop there.

Once, while visiting a Fred Meyer store (a local shopping chain in Oregon and Washington) in Burien, Ann went to purchase her items. Ann was popular there, she was a frequent shopper and many people talked to her by name whenever she stopped by. The cashier in the check-out line was a young woman who was having a rough day. The checker started pouring her heart out to Ann. "My car died, I don't have the money to get a new one. I don't know what I'm going to do!" Who knows, maybe this stream-of-consciousness checker blabbed about paying the rent, the price of diapers, what have you.

Having been penniless before, Ann felt compassion for the young woman's struggles.

Ann paid for her purchases and then, before leaving, wrote the girl a check for $10,000 to buy a new car! Ten.

Thousand. Dollars.

Okay, so you might expect if you were handed a check like that you'd be shouting for joy that this famous author, a regular in the store, just gave you thousands of dollars, right? There'd be a clean up on Register Two if it had happened to me. Apparently, that wasn't quite the case. When Ann gave the bank draw to the checker, the woman did thank her, but that was the end of the story. Ann had hoped to hear more.

Long before Oprah put car keys in cute boxes under seats of audience members, Ann put wheels under the feet of probably a half a dozen people.

Case in point, one of her son's girlfriends had been out of town for a while and was arriving home from the airport soon. For whatever reason, the girlfriend didn't have a working vehicle either. Ann and her son conspired to change that. Ann really liked this smart, kind young woman dating her son. The couple hung out at Ann's Des Moines ranch-style home quite a bit and Ann took a shine to her, mentioning her in acknowledgements of future books. After picking the girlfriend up together at the airport, Ann and her son took her to an "undisclosed location" somewhere along the road on the way home. The Rules drove up to a shiny new car. They stopped and parked. The girlfriend had no idea what they were up to. They both laughed and handed her the keys to this brand-new car! Imagine the surprised look on *her* face. This woman gave thanks profusely. Knowing her, she probably sent a Thank You card too! The girlfriend continued to have a relationship with Ann after she and Ann's son went their separate ways and continued visiting her. I met the girlfriend at Ann's place in 2015, and she still raved about Ann's car giveaway that changed her life.

Understand, too, that Ann gave to causes she felt passionately about. She often helped out friends and relatives. Ann gave generously to animal shelters because she was a huge animal lover. She recoiled at the sight of television commercials showing mistreated animals in cages, or tied up, hungry, with their eyes full of bugs, and scabies on their skin. Rule had written about men who tortured animals and grew up to be serial killers. Her money went to animal causes to save mistreated or abandoned cats and dogs.

Ann and Willow at her Puget Sound home. Photo Credit: Leslie Rule.

Her dog pal Willow was a big lumbering dog whom she loved beyond comparison. I can still hear her calling for Willow to come to dinner, or go outside. Truth be told, Willow was a bit, well, rotund, as well as spoiled, hairy and extremely affable. She *did* slobber, I gotta say. But Willow was precious, so kind-hearted and Ann's closest friend.

Ann's cats also meant everything to her. And she had many over her lifetime. Her cat Poppy followed me around as I replanted the next season's garden for Ann when she became unable to do it herself. Poppy passed the rainbow bridge long after Ann's death. Daughter Leslie, a cat lover extraordinaire, adopted Poppy and loved her just the same as Ann.

One night, in the spring of 2014, I was planting Ann's garden again because she was in a wheelchair and couldn't complete the task alone. I planted most things in taller pots to allow her to reach, water, prune and care for the flowers. She loved watering daily, and deadheading the old flower heads to bring on yet more flowers. I reveled in the thought of seeing her outside tending her new garden. On the last night of my trip, I was running out of time so I stayed up all night to get everything planted: moving pots and furniture for wheelchair accessibility before heading home the next day.

Ann went to bed. We said goodnight. I was determined to surprise her the next day with a new spring and summer garden, complete with a fairy garden for her grandchildren next door. Earlier that day, we had shopped for plants together at Fred Meyer. No $10,000 checks were written that day. Just a few hundred dollars to make a lush display.

I was humbled when Ann, a lifelong gardener, let me make new plant suggestions in her garden. I had moved out of the dark newsroom as an anchor and reporter and into the sunshine of my acre garden by then and had an Emmy award winning garden show at 7 p.m. Saturday evenings under my tool belt. And Ann had already seen my own acre garden by that time, saying, "You said you garden Anne, but I never imagined anything like *this!!*" The remark made me very proud.

Her favorites were tobacco flowers (Nicotiana *sylvestris*) with their long tubular nodding white flowers and heavenly scent, dahlias of all sizes and shapes and geraniums. I suggested newer varieties of the annuals she loved, adding multicolored, constantly blooming African Daisies, and brought my *amazing* lily bulbs I loved from my favorite source "The Lily Garden" outside Vancouver, Washington. The lilies were something to write home about and scented her yard (and home when the windows were open). Ann had lovely shrubs and trees in front of her home. I still keep strips of brown peeling bark showing bright green from the trunk of the tree alongside her driveway. It was a Stewartia. The bark reminds me of renewal and Ann's love of gardening.

Ann's garden during one of my 24-hour planting sprees at her house in Normandy Park, Washington. Orange shovels at the ready. Author's photo.

During my all night planting escapade, outside the back sliding glass doors, I heard Ann calling "Poppy, Poppy, c'mere, kitty." When I ran inside, Ann asked if I had seen Poppy.

Oh dear, I didn't remember where I last saw Poppy, but I made sure to round her up and deliver her to Ann before 10 p.m. And thank goodness I found her, because I don't think Ann would have slept a wink without her kitty snuggling beside her.

Ann was proud of her daughter Leslie's efforts to care for rescued animals. Her daughter lovingly established her own shelter where she housed, fed and watered seventeen cats and two dogs for the rest of their lives. Both women loved animals for the living beings they are. Deserving of love, care and respect.

Ann often helped survivors or families she wrote about. She sincerely wanted to help but knew her contribution could never compensate for the terrible losses they endured. Rule also championed their cases when names of the horrible killers came up again.

Ann gave many, many of her own books away. Her handwritten signature added value to each and every copy. She sent free books to people, and donated books to charities. Seattle-area fans often sent their purchased Ann's books back to her asking for a signature or dropped them off and picked them up *at her house* if they weren't able to attend signings at lectures.

Once while I was visiting her, I answered the door to a stranger, a woman, who said she'd come to pick up the books Ann signed for her. This woman hadn't just dropped off her most recent Rule book, but an armful. Ann remembered the woman's name and came out to greet her personally. No big deal for Ann; she always loved meeting her fans and that woman was over the moon meeting her favorite author. You know that nervous talk we do when we're well, *nervous?* It was very cute, you could tell the reader desperately *wanted* to have a conversation with Ann but every time the woman asked a question and Rule started to answer, the petite woman in her mid sixties would be talking three steps ahead with no room to interject. Ann went into listening mode and enjoyed the conversation. Just by being herself, Ann made the woman's day.

I'd see books from readers all over the country and Europe sitting on her table for signatures and special dedications. This was never a chore for her: she enjoyed it.

Charities for homeless children or children of trauma were also great causes for Ann. Her donations enriched their programs, "We have to take care of the babies otherwise we are growing the sadistic sociopath a decade down the line."[9] Every child deserves a forever home, but in the meantime, Ann wanted to improve their quality of life.

Another important cause to Ann were domestic abuse shelters. As a defender of vulnerable women everywhere, Ann hoped her contributions would give the women escaping violence a safe place to rest.

Ann gave $5,000 monthly to a hometown food bank for years. A Des Moines food bank once held a "Thank You" lunch for 75 people at the Windjammer restaurant near her home to honor Ann's giving, always, from the heart.

When Ann was growing up, her parents often took in wayward boys. I sometimes dropped Ann off at the home of one of these men. The Stackhouse family took him in as a teenager, and I met grateful young men at Ann's memorial service that she helped, too. I had no idea Ann continued this family tradition, beyond the one foster son who lived with her as a teenager.

Ann also paid for friends' facelifts. Now here is a taboo topic. So I won't name names. But they all looked fabulous and benefitted from Ann's largesse.

Sometimes, Ann's giving went south. Author and friend, Kathryn Casey, told me that she remembered at one point "there was somebody on [Ann Rule's website page] who said that she had cancer and had no money for treatment."

Ann wrote back and forth with people on her website guest page whenever possible, until it became overwhelming. Casey admired that "after all she had seen, she was still able to really identify with this woman and believe in her. *And* be moved enough to want to help her. You know?".

---

[9] Guardian Books, Ian Katz, December 19, 1994 "Ann Rule, a high life of crime" - archive, 1994

Ann ended up sending money for the woman's life-saving treatments. The topic came up between the two bestselling authors during their phone calls, "She was upset about it at the time, I remember. And I don't know how much Ann sent her, but she sent her some money. And then she found out later that the woman did not have cancer." Ann opened up to Casey about her disappointment. "I think she was upset with herself because she had seen so much in life and experienced so much. And here this woman had been able to take advantage of her. I remember telling her at the time that I thought it was actually a testament to the fact that Ann was really a good person. I mean, Ann had seen so much after so many years. You just see so much evil and you see so much bad." It was natural to want to help. Ann's heart, Casey agreed, was in the right place. But Rule always wished she hadn't opened her pocketbook when she learned of the scam.

Ann and I used to have debates about whether people were inherently good or bad. She didn't believe in the notion of a "bad seed." However, she did believe that, perhaps, serial killers were predisposed to violence and wondered if they had a defect between the frontal cortex and limbic system. In 1998, she told a *Times Leader* newspaper writer "I find that the people we're fascinated with are the cruelest, because we just can't understand why anybody would choose to be this way. And do they choose? Or is it something genetic, something psychologically wrong with the brain? Nobody knows the answers yet. But that's what I explore."

New technology studying murderous minds lends more credence to this argument. In 2019, long after Ann's hypothesis, a University of Chicago neuroscientist compared brain scans of more than 800 killers.[10] He found these brains have less gray matter, and the circuitry is damaged in key spots. The study looked at ten years of MRI scans from men in eight prisons in Wisconsin and New Mexico. Photos of the scanned brains look like the Swiss cheese of troubled minds. The brains show abnormally low activity at the temple behind the eyes, the center for empathy, judgement and violence.

---

10 University of Chicago. Citation: "Aberrant brain matter in murders." July 5, 2019

In my debates with Ann, I leaned toward some people being bad but working to be good, especially after decades in a newsroom where I reported on a constant barrage of the scraping, money grubbing, and the selfish side of human nature. Unfailingly, Rule would lobby for the good, saying she'd met far more good people than bad. Ann kept her phone number in the public telephone directory for tips and because, she said, "Most of her readers are very nice people." Ann got all sorts of messages. Some, about 2% she'd say, were off-kilter people afraid they'd become serial killers. The rest were nice folks. Several times, when I was there, Ann picked up the phone and chatted with women wanting to report a frightening experience.

Ann's author friend, Kathryn Casey, felt the same, "We do see a lot of good, you know. I mean, I always tell people that for every true crime book I've written, I've met probably two or three really bad people. But the majority of people I meet are really good people…it would be easy to get a really jaded view of life and of people doing what we do. And Ann never did. And I thought the fact that she sent the woman money and wanted to help her showed that. You know, she trusted her. You know...It's just...It's really easy to think the whole world's bad when you do what we do…I don't feel that way, and I know Ann never felt that way."

Ann re-established a rule for herself: "Believe, but verify."

Ann kept a tight writing schedule, her lifelong routine. For years she wrote seven days a week, although she did hope to cut her schedule to five later on. But the draw of the story she was engrossed in always lured her back to the computer screen. I don't think I ever heard of Ann taking a vacation longer than a couple of days or a weekend. She took working vacations, going all over the country to attend trials for her books. She loved the research, but most enjoyed being home writing in her office with fellow author and office manager, Donna Anders. For twenty-six years Donna faithfully kept the Rule Enterprises books squeaky clean, answered the phone, counseled and traveled with Ann. They often made book appearances together.

All of these things Anders does for her regular salary in the spirit of friendship no matter how long they were away at trials or book signings out of town.

Ann with Donna Anders, her best friend, bookkeeper and travel companion. Courtesy of Leslie Rule.

Ann finally invested in a couple of cars for herself after hitting pay dirt. But she never went for expensive chi-chi cars; she needed something practical for traveling to speeches and trials in the Northwest or to the airport. Her 1991 Toyota Celica was the perfect practicality for the tasks. She always kept a shiny small pickup truck to haul gardening supplies or larger items like furniture and such.

Ann allowed herself a few extravagances, but her 1990's home on the shore of Puget Sound was the first large purchase of her lifetime, after she became a millionaire from *Small Sacrifices* and *Stranger Beside Me* book sales and garnered her first half-million dollar book contract for *If You Really Loved Me* and *Everything She Ever Wanted,* which stayed eighteen weeks on the *New York Times* Best Seller list. Rule loved that house and its high cathedral ceilings. She'd never dreamed of affording such a luxury before, living in a tract home in the suburbs before making it big. The new house, accessible only by way of a lumbering tram up and down a steep hill to the front door, also had that writing cottage to the side. It was best to hold on tightly for your ride as the metal tram would pitch and yaw at times on its trek up or down from the driveway above. I remember watching her balance on the tram like a sailor with good sea legs, the ride unremarkable to her, while it felt like a zipline to me.

Although the home looked larger than it was, with floor-to-ceiling windows facing the water and a wide deck, there were few bedrooms. One large master bedroom for her and a smaller room for overnight guests. Once when I visited, I ended up sleeping on a mattress in Ann's closet. Yes, her large closet, (quite cozy, I might add), because her granddaughter was staying longer in the second bedroom. Kind of comical when I think back on it. But Ann always made room.

Every morning at nine, I could hear her flipping through the pages of *National Enquirer* and other tabloids to keep up on pop culture. Ann was skeptical of some of the articles, but she said the tabloids often got at the truth of celebrity dalliances and big murder cases faster than mainstream media because they paid for stories while legitimate news outlets didn't. She said the rags also helped her relax before writing for the day. The tabloids, although pooh-poohed in more highbrow circles, held a great power and a big piggy bank to pay sources. Their stories were often cobbled together with speculation, innuendo and outright guessing, which *sometimes* proved true. They were delicious reading for Ann. She relished her favorite newspapers as they hit the stands each week.

Coming from a journalism background, I found this peccadillo of hers rather charming, harkening back to her early days writing for detective magazines, mostly for the pleasure it gave her every morning. Did I start reading them? I did not. But sometimes Ann would read aloud details of some curiosity tucked inside the covers and we'd laugh out loud.

Throughout her life, Ann never lost her hometown touch with real people. Although she had celebrity friendships, her pals from college and the connections she made in Seattle were closest to her heart. As her friend, you could count on her as a calm, steady, listener who rarely interjected her own opinions.

When asked for a personal appraisal on any given situation Ann would often say "well…I don't know, really" and keep on listening. Unless, of course, she really had an opinion. Then her thoughts came with gentle but sage advice. In most circumstances, Ann steered clear of giving very personal advice, as she realized life's complexities often made it difficult to see a clear path forward. Ann's down to earth outlook made her an extraordinary friend that you could count on to talk through your worries whenever necessary. Even after a long stint between chats, our friendship would pick up right where it left off, like no time had passed.

I always thought of Ann as a girlfriend my age, with similar interests and really fun to cackle with. I know Ann was in her fifties when I met her as a young woman in my twenties, but I pegged her around 42 years old. She understood so much. For most of our time together, she'd share her growing up years, as I did mine. Although different, our upbringings meshed in some key areas. Most of all there was laughter: inappropriate, subtle, outlandish laughter. I still see her smiling a closed-mouth grin almost from ear to ear, with her shoulders thumping up and down when something tickled her fancy. She had a throaty laugh, mine; loud and uproarious. If you ever attended any of Ann's appearances, you *know* what I'm talking about. We were easily amused. In some weird way, we were kindred spirits. Ann called me her funniest friend. Of course, her love extended far beyond the gift of laughter with me.

Part III

Chapter 14
Hidden Truths

I hadn't heard of Ann Rule in May of 1983. *The Stranger Beside Me* was the first book of Ann's I was aware of just before I met her, and nobody had heard of Elizabeth Diane Downs until the morning *after* the hellacious crime on May 19th.

I remember the morning well. I was putting on my pantyhose for work. A toehold in one leg, ready to stretch and shimmy into the next, when I heard a radio news report: "A Springfield woman and her three children were shot last night on Old Mohawk Road in Springfield. One child is dead, the other two are critically injured at McKenzie Willamette Hospital."

I was stunned.

Something seemed so strange with the story, but I didn't have enough information to put my finger on what it was. No one could, at that early date. Must be someone the mother knows was my first thought. Maybe domestic violence?

Honestly, I wondered if the facts were straight. How could a woman with three children be shot, one killed in their car, late at night with no witnesses?

Sitting on the edge of my bed, pulling up the other leg on my nylons, I vowed to myself, "This woman, her children…It's terrible. I'm going to figure out what happened and who did it."

I decided right there and then I would own that story, even if it took months to win the assignment.

I kept pressing at work to get the Downs case, tracking it behind the scenes until it was mine. You wouldn't think the case would be a difficult get in a newsroom steering clear of "if it bleeds, it leads" in the newscast. But nailing down the case wouldn't be a cakewalk either. Fortunately, there were only a few reporters in our shop who might have wanted it.

Driving to work, another news bulletin asked listeners to be on the lookout for a long-haired man on Old Mohawk Road in Springfield who flagged down the woman's car, shot her in the arm and attacked her children. I wondered: why would this woman named Diane Downs stop to help a lone man on a country road after dark with kids in the car?

By the time I get to work, one of our best reporters was already out the door and on the scene early that morning. Seriously, I know there wasn't a snowball's chance in hell I was gonna get this assignment, but I lobbied for follow-up stories.

I guess everyone who was anyone in our newsroom was busy when the next plum assignment came up, or perhaps my pitches were getting through. Diane Downs, the injured mother and her family were holding a press conference. I was ready to go and jumped at the chance. I checked my sources before going.

When Downs got home from the hospital in the spring of 1983, news stations were called to attend the news conference by her parents, Wes and Willadene Frederickson.

I was glad to be there, but gotta tell you, back then I hated news conferences, indelicately called "gang bangs" in the news biz. They were impersonal meetings that allowed reporters to "share" their information. "Sharing" meant you as a reporter could ask all the tough questions, then every other reporter (whether they ask a question or not) could use your answers on their airtime. What really good reporter wants *that*?

A personalized sit down with a suspect was more intimate, less overwhelming for the person being interviewed, *and* other reporters couldn't use *your* breaking news. From Frederickson's point of view, and his daughter's, they saw this press conference as an opportunity to stop their phone ringing 24/7 asking for interviews, and to answer a gaggle of reporter questions all at once. Their goal? To get the public's help to find the man.

By the time we sat down for the conference, Downs' two surviving children had already been taken away by the state, and were in foster care together.

That first meeting didn't go as the family planned.

At their 50's style ranch-style home in Springfield, Downs was sitting on the family Naugahyde black couch, in front of wood paneling. We were in the living room, finally about to hear personally from this victim of a horrible crime, a woman who wore a lavender cotton short-sleeve top, with white lace tied demurely at the chest. Downs' lower left arm was in a bandage from fingers to elbow, after a metal plate was surgically implanted to shore up her shattered forearm where she was shot.

The room was stuffy, but flooded with lights from television light kits. I surveyed the scene, which was now filled with photographers and reporters and their microphones and camera gear whirring away. The atmosphere was tense, with each of us wondering how candid Downs would be. She was not yet a public suspect in the case but police chatter behind the scenes indicated there might have been holes in her story. And I found a big hole.

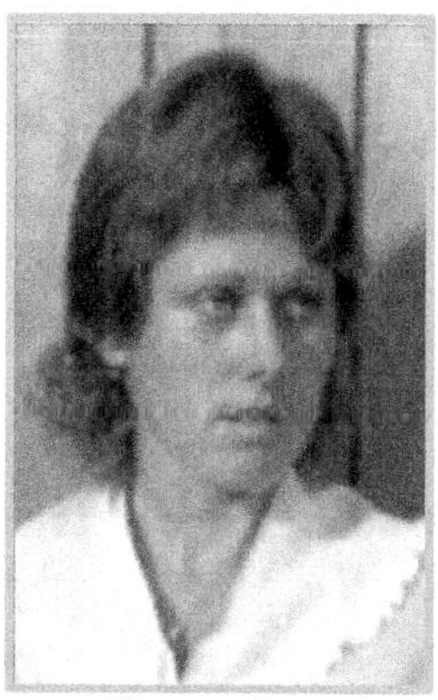

Diane Downs at her first press conference I covered as a reporter in 1983 after the shootings.

I sat across from Downs. Her eyes were sunken, almost hollow. Her face gaunt and sallow. She hadn't been out of the hospital for very long. Her lips appeared white and parched, almost non-existent, looking more like a sixty-year-old woman than in her twenties. What little light was available, before the artificial camera lights clicked on, was as dark and sickly as her. Her prominent chin was tilted down, accentuating her sad, sad eyes. I noticed more of the white under her iris was showing, as if her eyes were half-moons beneath the upper lid. The Japanese call these yin sanpaku eyes, which face readers claim suggest emotional instability and self-destructive behavior. Perhaps coincidentally, in my childhood, and in my career, I've seen this looking into the eyes of other killers.

I was anxious to hear what she had to say, after promising myself I'd try to get to the bottom of how she and her children were shot.

Other reporters, mostly males, gently asked questions, "What happened? How did you all get shot? Do you know how your children are doing?"

We all listened intently as Diane recounted the details she remembered: An unknown man flagged her down in the middle of the road as the family was coming back from visiting a friend's horses in Springfield. Diane got out of her car, and the man tried to take her keys.

"He wanted my car," Downs said. "You've got to be kidding," she reportedly told the assailant as she fought back. Then, he shot through the open driver's side door of the new red Nissan Pulsar and picked off the kids one by one with a .22 caliber Ruger.

Seven-year-old Cheryl was shot and killed first in the front seat, and in the backseat, three-year-old Danny was paralyzed and eight-year-old Christie was slumped over, critically wounded. Downs claimed to fight the intruder off, but got shot. She then wrapped her arm in a towel to stanch the bleeding as she rushed them to the hospital.

Out of the blue, I asked her, "Where was the towel?"

A few reporters looked at me, wondering why I'd made such an abrupt left turn in the questioning.

"In the trunk," Downs replied.

And here's where things get sticky.

I pressed on. "Diane, the police believe you shot yourself."

Her vehement denial came like, well, like shotgun blasts,

"If I had shot my own children," she said, "would I not have done a good job of it?"

Her speech pattern accelerated, becoming more staccato. "Why would I then immediately have rushed them to the hospital with two children still living? Christie woke up, and as I say, she may be the only one to get me out of this. Would I have brought her to the hospital? Wouldn't she be the one I'd make sure was dead, then cried crocodile tears? That's insane. To think I would do such a thing and then bring the witnesses in against me?"

Her voice calmed at the end of her diatribe, when Downs said, "That's crazy,"

This was the soundbite everyone's been waiting for.

But ohhh boy.

This did NOT sit well with Downs' dad.

Wes Frederickson, who was standing behind the line of reporters and cameras to my right, was red-faced angry. "You'll all have to leave, NOW!" he shouted. "This is over! Diane has been through a terrible ordeal and your question is disrespectful, uncalled for."

Whooooosh! All the air is sucked out of the living room as stunned reporters gave Wes Frederickson confused looks, but started putting their notepads away. My colleagues weren't too happy with me either, getting us kicked out during our first opportunity to speak directly to the victim. If we packed up and left, I'd get the stink-eye outside from reporters, or be given the cold-shoulder, believe me. But if we left, we wouldn't walk away empty handed: Diane's soundbite was the outstanding "get" of the day.

I didn't move.

I kept still for a heartbeat. Then, turning my body away from Diane to address Wes Frederickson directly, I said to him calmly, "Mr. Frederickson, these are all the questions police, and viewers, will be asking. I'm just doing my job."

Amazingly, this seemed to calm him down. Downs' father said we could continue but warned us to stay off that line of questioning. And the reporters breathed a sigh of relief.

Nobody asked any more important questions.

My story ran on the 5 and 11 o'clock newscasts.

Leaving the Fredericksons' Springfield home that day in 1983, I started obsessing about a new topic: that *towel* Downs wrapped her arm in. I was then on a quest to figure out why Diane wrapped her own wound first, without tearing the towel into strips as first aid for the children. I was thinking that tending the children first was what any mother would do. I know I would.

It would take months before investigators could finally put together enough evidence to arrest Diane Downs. In the meantime, maybe I could decipher the towel, and so much more.

I knew the towel might be an important new clue. But I just didn't know why. There'd be five more months of poking and prodding to figure it out. But there was a bad wind blowing my way.

Chapter 15
Night Terrors

Not too long after meeting Downs at her parent's house, there were rumblings that a very successful author would be covering her case to write a book about the crime. Just *which* author was kept under tight wraps. I wasn't surprised the case was garnering such big attention from well-respected unnamed authors, but I didn't think much about it. I kept my ear to the wall, finding more facts about Diane along the way.

In the meantime, reporters at other stations were breaking stories about Downs here and there. In one, Downs claimed to have been a surrogate mother, although later reporting said Downs had failed the psych test. Perhaps she had a private contract with the surrogate parents.

In another news story, Downs expressed her sadness about not being able to see her children. Her letters, birthday and Christmas cards were returned unopened because she had lost custody. And, of course, we all covered the story about her arrest on murder, attempted murder and assault charges in February 1984.

That's when the court's slow grind hit high gear, and Elizabeth Diane Downs would stand trial in May, just days shy of the year anniversary of shooting her children.

What other reporters, law enforcement, prosecutors and the public did not know right away in 1983, was that I had an explosive interview with Downs already in the can (meaning already shot, but waiting to air.)

I had clandestinely gathered important facts that no one knew and decided to finally ask Downs to come talk to me at the television station, after practically ignoring her for months. Other reporters seemed to be on speed dial, but I purposely stayed away until I could really get some nitty gritty about how and why the crimes occurred. Oh, and yes, that towel.

We'll get back to what Downs said a bit later, but my station management and I both knew that the short ten second snippets of Diane Downs that had been airing didn't tell the whole story. You had to see Diane to believe the way she was. My special *Elizabeth Diane Downs: In Her Own Words* wouldn't air for months. And for good reason.

Meanwhile, I was busy behind-the-scenes on the documentary, but Downs and her father were starting to worry about why my interview hadn't aired yet. They knew reporters wanted to get their stuff on television as fast as possible before other print or radio reporters beat them to the story. It must have been getting under Wes' skin that a television station had Downs' quotes in the can, but he'd have to wait to see it with everybody else.

Frederickson's anxiety was growing, thinking, "WHAT has Diane said? And will her words sink her at trial?" My estimation proved correct about the family's building frustrations. The Frederiksen's aren't alone in their passion about the videotaped interview.

After hearing that now the prosecutor is interested in *subpoenaing* the tapes for trial, the tapes were locked in a vault downtown. I work on the half hour story at KEZI's lawyers office.

The court case trudged on. There were lots of nuts and bolts to be figured out before the case hit the courtroom. The judge held pre-trial hearings to talk about what evidence would be allowed in the courtroom in May. I was there to keep tabs on the story.

The pre-trial courtroom was smaller than others. Rich, nicely stained wood, the hallmark of Lane County's timber money, lined the walls. The effect was austere, and the canned lighting was low without windows. Rows of benches lined two sides. Instead of walking into the courtroom and walking up the aisle between the two divided rows, the pathway from the public door was on the side, not in the center of the room. You walked along the back of the courtroom to find a seat, or made a sharp left inside the door to reach the aisle. I sat close to the door, thinking I might have to pop out to file my evening news story. I saw Downs' family, father and brother in the front row on the benches on the other side, to the right of the judge. Downs was in jail a few blocks away. Only the lawyers would be arguing to keep or jettison the evidence they had.

In this courtroom, thoughts of the crime started messing with my mind.

All this time later, I can't for the life of me even remember what evidence was talked about. But the judge's ruling did not land in Downs' favor. The judge ruled the evidence, whatever it was, could be used by the prosecution in trial. Downs' father, with his son beside him, flew into a rage.

Wes jumped up, red-faced and steaming mad. He swiveled his head around, his beady eyes trained right on me. The hair on my arms bristled. How could that evidence have anything to do with me, I thought? Our documentary about Downs hadn't even aired yet! Of course, I had nothing to do with it, and Wes' anxiety about that unaired interview had gotten the best of him. Wes was blowing it.

I couldn't make out most of his angry spewing because Wes was in front of the courtroom and I was in the very back, but I heard him clearly call me out. "This is because of Anne Bradley [my maiden name]," he said. Then he made derogatory comments, blaming me for something and threatening me.

This was the *second* time he'd attacked me publicly. Once at their home and now in the courtroom. But there was more to his machinations, as I'd come to realize.

At this court hearing, Wes' son (Downs' brother Paul), was trying unsuccessfully to stop him from saying any more. Paul tried mightily to make his father sit down and shut up. Dear Lord, this seemed to enrage him more, as he continued shouting and pulling away from Paul's holds on his shoulder and arms. From the back of the courtroom, I still couldn't make out everything being said.

I clenched my jaw and narrowed my eyes straight at Wes.

At that moment, I saw Downs' investigator, Doug Welch (whom I wasn't friends with at the time) stand up *slowly* from the bench in front of me, but slightly to my right. And by taking a stand purposefully, as if in slow motion, Doug was blocking Wes' view of me. I was relieved this lead investigator, whom I barely knew, was there to keep the situation in check.

Doug, the first time I met him in court, as the lead investigator of Diane Downs' case. Courtesy of Doug Welch.

Doug was staring him down. The standoff managed to finally cool Frederickson's jets, as he realized he could be joining his daughter in jail, for contempt of court, if he didn't get a handle on it.

He also knew Welch carried handcuffs and a concealed weapon.

The entire episode was over in less than two minutes.

I didn't have time to stick around and figure out what Frederickson said. I had to get back to the office. The hearing had run longer than I expected.

Internally? I was shaking. I'd dealt with many angry people in the news business, when I was forced to neutralize passionate opinions to ferret out each side of a story, but this seemed more ominous.

After that hearing was the first time I formally met Doug Welch. He walked me to my car. I guess he'd been wondering if Wes would try to catch me unaware outside, and pick up his diatribe again while I was alone. Doug's support then was a welcome graciousness I learned to count on later in life.

When Doug and I discussed the hearing in 2024, he didn't remember much about the saga, but told me, "Yeah, that was his style, his M.O. He needed a male to stand up to confront him because I think he always felt like, you know, he can pretty much dominate any situation, especially involving women." Frederickson's wife, Willadeen, was seldom present and never called on. She and Diane called each other "Sis," (as in sister).

Doug didn't remember the specifics of what prompted Wes' outburst either, but did recall other outbursts, many directed at him. "It was clear from early on that Wes did not like me," Doug said. "He didn't like any of the investigators, but there was something about me that really irritated the hell out of him."

After one particular hearing, Doug said, "I remember making eye contact with him, and he just seethed. His whole face was red and then he called me 'pond scum.'"

Of course, a couple of other guys in the Sheriff's Department heard that and teasingly nicknamed Doug "pond scum" for a while.

But Wes' anger was real and on display like a volcano, threatening much worse at that hearing.

So Doug knew, as well as I, that Downs' daddy was a grenade ready to pull the pin in a heartbeat.

My adrenaline gave me prickly heat from the incident, and my :30 story on the hearing was due on the 5 o'clock news. I remember sitting at my typewriter, my head like a pressure cooker, trying to pound out the results of the court session quickly. I was having a full on panic attack and didn't even know what that was. My head was swimming. Unable to synthesize my thoughts, with half an hour to airtime, I decided *not* to include Wes' maniacal chiding of me. Awash in anxiety, I noticed the front receptionist delivered an enormous bouquet of flowers in spring colors to my desk.

I thought, "Well isn't this beautiful, after such a crappy day? Who would be sending me flowers today?"

Then I opened the card. *Oh dear*…Awful. I read and reread the card, in essence it said "Sorry about what happened in court, - Paul." Downs' seemingly nice brother had signed the card, not Wes. My stomach turned. I'm woozy thinking about it, even now. Feelings, I realize, are time travelers. I felt — I still feel — sick knowing the family tried to manipulate me like that.

At my desk, I picked up the phone and called the

Fredrickson household, asking for Paul.

I asked Paul why he sent the flowers. Let me tell you, poor Paul stumbled and stammered. It became obvious this charade had not been his idea. Finally, as if someone on the other end of the line was directing him close by, Paul said "My family hopes there are no hard feelings about today." I felt like hanging up, understanding that Paul was Wes' patsy, whom I've just taken to school by virtue of my phone call.

Manipulative Wes, thinking women swoon over flowers and forgive, made his son sign the card. Ugly. I ended the call quickly. Looking at my watch, there were only fifteen minutes before airtime. I did not have time to deal with that mess right then. My anxiety was racing again. And I was supposed to be calm and collected - anchoring an hour's worth of news, including my story.

Outwardly, I didn't let on that the courtroom scene that day shook me to my core. To me, the flowers might as well have been a stink bomb sitting on my desk.

The Frederickson clan watched my story at 5:00 p.m., feeling smug that there was no mention of Wes' atrocious behavior. I bet the family felt they'd won.

But perhaps some context is necessary before I move on? Reporters were not supposed to be part of the story; we were expected to state the facts. Journalists didn't insert themselves in stories, and I didn't either. I focused on getting the story written, without any mention of the drama about me. I thought to myself, "That's okay, Anne, just keep chipping away at this story. Keep it simple, keep it clean, and keep your eye on the prize." The goal? Getting that half hour documentary on the air in less than two months.

But trying to shutter my feelings during the day made them pop up in dark hours when I was alone.

And in terrifying technicolor.

After finishing the news that night without time to process my true feelings, I started having nightmares.

Part of those nightmares were sparked by my trepidation about Wes Fredrickson's hair-trigger temper. The other was placed subliminally by Diane's horrifying details that I exposed during the documentary interview I was working on.

In writing and viewing the videotapes over and over again, while trying to write my first half hour documentary, Diane's painful words took their toll.

"What haunts you the most about the night of the shootings?" I'd asked her. Diane said that she could see "Christie reaching out to her," with blood gushing from her mouth.

Words not easily erased.

This vision hijacked my subconscious and scared the daylights out of me.

Over and over, night after night, those dreams came. I never admitted it to anyone in my life, but I was terrified by this recurrent nightmare:

I was suspended behind the back window of Diane's red car on Old Mohawk Road, the scene of the crime. Hovering there, as if flying behind the car, I'd see a child's hand reaching, pawing and staining the back window in blood before me. I didn't see the child, only the red blood smeared fingerprints clawing at the rear window to get out. I can still see it today. And it feels almost as intense now as it did then.

The nightmare continued. I never knew if or when another bad dream would hijack my sleep. Even focusing on other pressing news didn't quell them. Sometimes, I'd go weeks without seeing the visions. Then they would pop up again on auto-play.

One night during one of these night terrors, the window next to my bed shattered into pieces. It was loud and frightening, pulling me out of a deep fretful sleep. I sat up, stick-straight, shaking and sweating. I ran out of the bedroom, racing to call my nice neighbors next door, Pat and Antigone "Tig" Brown.

"Pat!" I shouted. "Someone broke my bedroom window! I think someone tried to get in!!"

Pat came over with his flashlight. He found no sign of an attempted break in. In fact, he said that the window looked like it had been broken from the inside.

"You mean somebody was inside here while I was sleeping and tried to get out?" I asked him.

The thought was terrifying. I had no recollection of what happened.

"I don't think so, Anne," he said. "A guy trying to escape would have launched straight through the entire window or used the door, not just broken the window right next to your bed."

I told him about Diane's father threatening me in court and at the media conference. Angry Wes Frederickson was my first thought!

"Couldn't somebody have thrown something at the window from outside to scare me?" I said.

Again, Pat stated he was sure the window was broken from the inside.

I was completely undone trying to figure out what happened – how or why? Pat patched the window up with plywood. Thankfully, his wife, my friend, Tig, invited me to sleep at their place next door for the night. She couldn't understand the circumstances of the window breaking either.

The next day, standing outside my home on McKinley Court in Eugene, I was reassessing the broken window, when I suddenly came to grips with what happened. I remembered that the awful nightmare had come to me again. This time, however, instead of never being able to get close enough to that rear window of Diane's Pulsar, where the children were, I was finally able to *reach the glass*. The terrible vision played like a film strip in my mind. I almost hyperventilated, overwhelmed by the power of the subconscious mind.

Back then I did not have time to process or come to grips with the visions. I certainly had never told anyone about the night terrors building in my mind. It seemed crazy.

In the daylight in Eugene, I was outside my broken bedroom window when slowly, I raised my hand up to my face, trying to match the recurrent memory with those crazy dreams. Knowing I bruised easily, I looked closely at my right hand, searching for cuts, scratches and marks. Nothing. Why hadn't the glass drawn blood? That's when I remembered sitting up in bed and walloping the window with the back of my fist with all the force I could muster. *I* broke the window.

Did the nightmarish bloody handprints and the real

breaking glass finally break the spell? Had I rescued the children?

I don't know. But I never had the nightmares again. Thank goodness.

But there was more to come in May of 1984. Downs was sitting in jail, awaiting trial, and my documentary would soon hit the airwaves.

Chapter 16
Stop the Presses

For six months my documentary special *Elizabeth Diane Downs: In Her Own Words* was ready to air, but didn't. This caused turmoil.

Based on the anger coming from the prosecutor's office, our station worried that the District Attorney would try to get his hands on the interview tapes. Before it aired, DA Pat Horton believed our interview would be sympathetic to Downs and ruin his case against her, and he was dying to know if she had contradicted any previous police statements. Horton was visibly *pissed, and vociferously* said so at press conferences. The District Attorney ranted to all the reporters about our KEZI interview. This was the first other reporters had heard about our unaired exclusive interview. We said nothing.

Indeed, the district attorney wanted to subpoena the tapes. Instead, the DA's office sent investigators over to *ask* if the station would hand over the tapes voluntarily.

Our News Director Bob Kerns told them emphatically *no*, the tapes were protected by the state's shield law, which protects reporters source material from police seizure. If by chance the prosecutor's office took on the station, legal litigation would start a court case. The trial might be long over by then, and all the facts out in open court already. The way prosecutors liked it. Horton knew he couldn't win but kept up the heat.

We still said nothing. But the threat of the television station being raided rang all kinds of alarm bells for us. So the vaulted KEZI tapes were driven back and forth to the station for editing by our photographer, then returned to the corporate lawyer's office for safekeeping.

The D.A.'s office wasn't alone worrying about the

documentary's potential consequences. The D.A. and Downs' family were both hand-wringing about preferential treatment: prejudicial in *the other's favor!*

From May 1983 to spring of 1984, reporters were doing sympathetic or at least empathetic stories on Downs because:

a.) Downs hadn't been charged or arrested yet.

b.) The sheer fact she and her three children were shot and she was living with the death of her middle child.

c.) The real nitty gritty damning evidence the prosecutors protected for trial hadn't come to light yet.

That changed the day our special report was slated to hit the airwaves in May, Wes Frederickson, who then worked as the Springfield postmaster, wrote one letter to our station General Manager, and sent another to our News Director, Bob Kerns. In the letters, CC'd to his attorney, Wes lobbied hard to keep the program from airing.

The letter read:

> *We feel that the contents of this program could be harmful to Mrs. Downs' position in court as well as a threat to the safety of our family.*

But there was more. This letter we're talking about sent up a couple of red flags for me. Reading between the lines, I began to understand why Diane's daddy had seethed at me in court. I got a clearer picture of why Wes felt so threatened. Although he began the typed letter with concern about his daughter's case, he got to the real point at the end:

> *The final consideration in our request is that the material might well impact my position…with future consideration for advancement within the Post Office.*

There it was. He was worried about himself.

Wes, near retirement age, was fretting about promotions at work while his daughter faced a long prison sentence for murdering his granddaughter, paralyzing grandson, and wounding his eldest grandchild.

Amazingly, the thought of his daughter being the shooter

had already crossed his mind. But he was firmly behind her now. Wes' was the first interview you saw in the documentary.

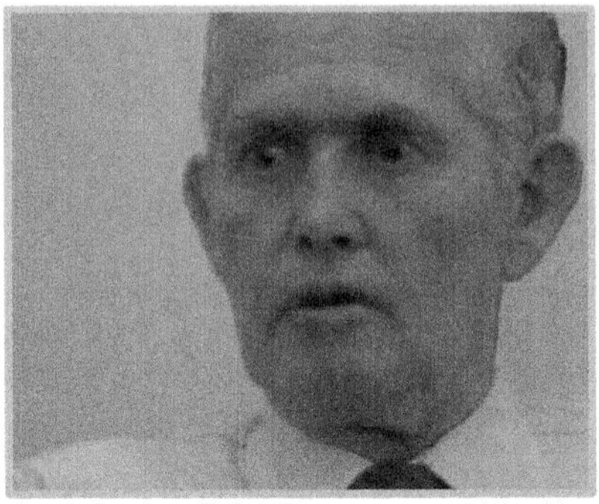

Diane's father, Springfield Postmaster, Wes Fredericksen voiced his suspicions about his daughter in my documentary.

"Was there ever a time, from the beginning, when you first heard, that you had any doubts about her innocence?"

"The first night, as a matter of fact, I had doubts," Wes said. "I saw at one point that Diane had been shot in the left arm, and she is right-handed, and I made the comment at the police department there that night: 'It looks to me like Diane did it, because the children had been shot in the chest and Diane has only been shot in the arm."

"And I said, it really looks like she did it."

Wes went on to tell us he was a very open person, "If I think somebody did something— I'm not about to hesitate to say they didn't." (A double negative Freudian slip perhaps?) "You know I'll tell them, if I think they did. I would say the same thing again if I believed it. I have followed through and I know my daughter didn't do it."

That was Fredricksen's staunch belief before and after the arrest warrant against her in February 1984.

What a turbulent year.

In May of 1984, a month to the day of the shootings and murder in 1983, we came full circle. The trial was finally underway in a room on the third-floor of the courthouse. Court was presided over by Judge Greg Foote, a tall, slender blonde man.

One after another, each possible juror was questioned by

both the prosecution and defense.

"Can you be fair and impartial?" they were each asked. Some were sent home. Fewer stayed. Finally, the jury was selected.

My bosses, News Director Bob Kerns and Assistant News Director Rebecca Force, decided the time was finally right to air the interview. They'd made the edict the special would air after twelve jurors (nine women and three men) were chosen, and the day finally arrived.

Waiting so long to air the startling details of the crime in my half hour report is an antiquated consideration now, but management really cared about not "tainting" the jury pool before they were seated. And I agree. But it wouldn't be done today. I'm still proud of their ethical decision. And that my groundbreaking work kept so tightly under wraps held the test of time. In the opening segment of the special report, we explained the program was delayed because of the sensitivity, graphic language of the subject matter, and that we waited for the jury to be chosen. But trying to keep my source of my information safe was another dance, entirely.

Chapter 17
Downs' Changing Stories

The evolution of my interview with Diane has quite a story. The source for my information came from the ranks of the District Attorney's office itself. Not the big guy, Pat Horton, and definitely not the prosecutor, Fred Hugi. Getting anything from them was like squeezing blood from stone. My source was a friend deep within the trenches, someone who knew the forensic scientist, Jim Pex, and other main players in the Downs' case very well. He knew all of them. Still, I knew the whole time that Ann's sources, at the very top, would have blown mine out of the water. I never asked, and Ann Rule would never tell. When *Small Sacrifices* came out, readers learned the wide expanse of her journalistic skills. Ann dug up twists and turns I hadn't heard of. Her writing made the book suspenseful too, even though we already knew the ending! I'm in Chapter 30.

My source told me *the* most important blood evidence in the trial would come from Pex's testimony. Not only about the *direction* of shots fired and *height* of the shooter, but how close the barrel of the gun was when shooting the victim's bodies. Evidence proved the children were shot, not through the door as Downs explained, but from deep inside the car. In fact, Pex did testify in court later that the .22 Ruger pistol was fired approximately nine inches away from both Danny and Christie. Danny was shot in the back, near his spinal cord, and Christie was shot twice. The barrel of the gun was less than two inches away from the hand she put up to protect herself, the other shot went directly into her chest.

Diane's shot landed six to nine inches from her left forearm. She was right-handed.

Cheryl was shot twice. Once through her right shoulder

when the gun was fired from about the same distance as Diane's. The second time, the barrel of the gun was held against the skin on her left shoulder, as the seven-year-old tried to escape the car and fell out onto Old Mohawk Road. Pex found high velocity blood spatter inside the *open door hinges* and outside the car. In court this forensic scientist used charts and graphs to explain the facts, and a mock up of Diane's Pulsar with lifesize canvas dolls of the children, and dowels which illustrated how the shots penetrated their bodies. The prosecution hoped the dolls would show the viciousness of the wounds, but suspend their imaginations about the real children *enough* to intellectually grasp the full scope of the crimes.

The evidence from my source was most intriguing to me when I learned about it far before Downs' arrest because it contradicted Diane's version of events. Downs said the children were all shot in the car. Pex proved Downs was deep inside the car, kneeling on the driver's seat to shoot Cheryl, who was so frightened she turned away from her mother's gun to escape. And here's how it happened: The first shot tore through Cheryl's right shoulder. Then, Diane lunged in from the driver's seat, arm extended to deliver the contact wound, the killing shot, in Cheryl's left shoulder as her child pushed the door wide open to run but landed on the roadside. After the shooting, did Diane get out of the car, walk around the vehicle to pick her bloody child off the gravel, then callously toss Cheryl back inside on the passenger floorboard? It sure looked that way. Either that, or Down's picked her up by the clothing on her back and threw her inside. Cheryl's mother wanted to make sure she was dead.

In addition, there was plenty of evidence, my source told me, that Diane had a .22 Ruger in her trunk, where Diane retrieved the towel for her arm. Before the crime, Downs once used that .22 semi-automatic weapon to threaten suicide, but fired her shot at her ex-husband threatening to kill him instead, while the family was living in Arizona.

I also found out Diane was changing her story. First, she'd claimed the family was shot by a lone gunman. Then it was two men. Next, in a hardball interview with lead investigator Doug Welch, Diane got flustered by the difficult evidence against her and stomped out the sheriff's office saying SHE KNEW who the murderer was and she was going to find him herself.

"Fuck you guys!" she said to the investigators.

I heard these critical facts from my source. He was not part of the investigation but close enough to each of the central figures to give me a deep dive. He gave me detailed information that allowed me time to process and question the veracity of it. I moved in the circles of Assistant District Attorneys, attending some fun parties. More information trickled out from my source as we built a trusting friendship and I didn't do news stories on any of it.

I knew 90-second-long stories, the average length of a nightly news report, with Diane's reaction to the evidence would not be long enough to explain details on the evening news. Double-checking my facts as I went, I kept quiet.

So, I've got all that in my back pocket while I'm waiting for the right time to call Diane Downs.

What changed to make me finally need to see her?

I heard a big break in the case was coming. And soon.

The timing was tricky.

Here was the dilemma: if Diane was arrested, as I suspected she would be, I'd lose my chance to record her reactions, to surprise her with facts nobody else knew. No cameras were allowed in the Lane County Jail. On the other hand, if I could time our interview right, no other reporter would have access to her in jail to follow up on my investigative reporting. Facts only law enforcement and prosecutors knew.

This all added to the exclusivity of my interview, *if* Downs would agree to talk to me. That was when I decided it was time for a private interview to confront her with all the damaging facts I'd compiled.

It was GO time.

Chapter 18
Killer Interview

In the fall of 1983, I called Downs to ask her to talk to me. I let her know she was free to bring her lawyer or come alone.

"I'll meet you at the station this weekend," she said.

I was surprised she'd talk to me at all. She hadn't seen me since that contentious media conference at her folks' house.

There was a real possibility she'd bring her lawyer. But then again, I had a hunch she wouldn't even tell him, knowing he would never allow her to sit down with a reporter. Her attorney knew she was a loose cannon.

On the afternoon of the interview, a Saturday, I asked one of our news producers, Janice Salvador, who was a mother of a small adorable child, to let Downs into the building. The doors were locked on weekends. Thinking ahead, I asked Janice to greet her at the door, hoping to cut down on any chatter from Downs about my questions beforehand. Janice agreed to let Downs in and bring her to the newsroom while the photographer and I set up in another room.

Of course, as a news producer, Janice *knew* about the shootings and murder. But she'd never come any closer to Downs than seeing her on the large banks of television sets on display, where the show director switched between videotapes for live news broadcasts. I admit that I never considered the stress meeting Downs might have on Janice. It just didn't occur to me. After all, we had newsmakers in the station all the time, this seemed no different to me. Truth be told, it was Diane's father that gave me the willies, and he wasn't invited.

Janice and I have talked here and there about her first and only experience meeting a woman suspected of murdering one child and shooting the other two. But all these years later, I asked Salvador to give me more detail about why she felt caught on the front lines. "I remember feeling frightened," she said. "Maybe even a bit terrified. While she obviously had not been arrested at this time, we had our suspicions about what she *may* have done. And *if* they were true, I was sitting in the newsroom by myself with a cold-blooded killer."

Janice made some quick observations about Downs while opening the heavy, locked front doors. "I immediately noticed her nylons were ripped," she told me. "Her dress or whatever she was wearing was a sketchy-looking ensemble of something she probably threw together to go out the night before. It seemed obvious to me, she probably hadn't been home, or at least perhaps just didn't bother to change…That rather surprised me." Surprised her because Downs liked the spotlight so much.

Downs was regularly spotted at Foo's, a singles bar across the river from the University of Oregon. People saw her drinking whiskey and water, even though she was pregnant, and writing for hours in her diary. And sometimes, Downs slept in a car when things got tough at her folks' house.

Me? I didn't notice the torn nylons Janice talked about when I met Diane that day, but I *could see* the relief on Janice's face as I swept into the newsroom and whisked Downs into the back conference room. My favorite photographer, Gary Kahne, and I are set up and ready to go.

I'm delighted Downs was alone. No lawyer.

I pinned the lavalier microphone on her cobalt blue and white pregnancy top. (The same one she later used for protection while scaling over the razor wire fence for her two week escape from prison in 1987.) Diane's hair was shorter and much lighter blonde. Her face was fuller; she appeared healthier.

Her pregnancy was starting to show. There was speculation, that she seemed to believe that if arrested, no jury will convict a pregnant woman.

The microphones were checked. Sound was good.

The camera focused on a head and shoulder shot of Diane's face. She seemed pleased and comfortable.

Looking at Gary, I got the slight nod of approval.

We were ready to start the strangest interview of my lifetime.

My initial reaction to watching the interview now, and seeing the two of us again, is that I'd forgotten how young we both were. I was twenty-four, headed for a career in broadcasting. Diane, twenty-seven, faced the rest of her life in prison.

I'm in my sixties now, watching us again. From the onset of hitting the play button, I am frightened of witnessing myself in Downs' orbit again. I know perfectly well the effect on me, so I haven't re-watched my interview until now for this very reason. I can intellectualize the experience in small snippets. But now the feeling is quite different. Between the taping of the interview in 1983 and when it aired in May 1984, I knew I'd have to transcribe her words and create a script with video timecodes for Gary to put the piece together. I'd find myself drowning in this task, only able to stomach it for about a half hour at a time. Then, I'd shore myself up for the next session putting the script together, and take a break. More ugly, ugly words and thoughts. But all this would come long after listening to Downs' trip down a lonely country road, headed for hell and back. If you watch my documentary *"Elizabeth Diane Downs: In Her Own Words,"* you should know that the story was edited so the answers to my questions appear in a different order than they were asked at the time.

I decided to start with easier topics, like her pregnancy. She was pleased about this.

Diane, knowing her cycle, slept with a young man and got pregnant right away on the night of October 13th! In our interview she wouldn't say who the father was, a secret she has still never divulged, but talked openly with me about having babies.

"I got pregnant because I miss Christie, and I miss Danny and I miss Cheryl so much. I'm never going to see Cheryl on earth again, and I just...*you can't replace children,* but you can replace the effect they give you. And they give me love, they give me satisfaction, they give me stability, they give me a reason to live and a reason to be happy, and that's gone. They took it from me. But *children are so easy to conceive.*"

Sitting with Downs, hearing her words, had an emotional undertow. You probably feel it yourself, through this interview or when reading Ann's *Small Sacrifices.* I mean, for starters, who says something like that? She was clearly replacing children for what they give *her,* not the reverse. A sinking sickness permeated the very air Gary Kahne and I breathed with her in that small conference room. Each tape held twenty minutes, and Diane would talk her way through two tapes, maybe more as we continued. I planned, researched, wrote and rewrote my questions over and over again to answer my fundamental question: How did the murder and the shootings *really* happen, and why? I wanted to give viewers insight into the mind of this mother suspected of terrible wrongs. I never dreamed we'd still be talking about this true crime forty years later.

The videotape in Gary's camera kept turning, and my interview had only just begun. Downs explained what happened that night:

"It's very hard, it's very tearful, there are a lot of memories that— I don't know, a lot of people if something traumatic happens…they suppress it immediately. I kept those memories because I knew I was the only person that could be able to tell them what happened when we went to the hospital."

Here she seemed to have forgotten the two other witnesses in the car. One was eight years old, the other was three. And there were more damning, incontrovertible facts coming up that would be harder to dodge.

When the documentary aired, we broke the news about forensic evidence in her case, which came from my source. I was especially curious what she might say about that. I asked about high velocity blood spatter found on the *outside* of the car, despite Downs' statements all the children were shot *inside.* This was revelatory. This was the first time Downs' found out anyone outside law enforcement knew about that blood evidence. Evidence that clearly questioned Diane's version of events. Just that quickly, she punted.

"The District Attorney has come up with this idea that someone (Cheryl) was shot on the outside of the car," Downs said.

"Well, you were," I interjected.

"I was on the driver's side of the car when I was shot," Downs insisted. "And…I'm going, it was planted…I mean it can't be real…because they talk about blood spatter…I think of something being shot out. Like the blood spatter in the car, you know it was so uniform, it was so regular, same size droplets evenly in a pattern. It's *drops…when they take Cher out of the car and it's blood droplets.* It's when they picked the kids up and carried them over the threshold, this is blood dripping down the side of the car."

I thought I had prepared myself for what was coming in that talk with Elizabeth Diane Downs. My sensitivities could be a real mind game then; I was feeling her words getting under my skin. Even now, I notice those old buried feelings aren't so buried. I realize, throughout my life covering killers, the soft spot of my soul isn't really immune to the consequences of listening. From the project's inception, my approach with this story was to ask the hard questions, give the facts, and let the viewers draw their own conclusions. I would not be stating mine. That was not the purpose, nor my job.

In order to sidestep the feelings evoked by her words, and stick to the facts, I used a couple of strategies back then. Most on-air journalists read, and reread, a script or questions until they are able to present it cleanly without emotion. I did this too. However, by taking some air out of the words, I was able to be analytical about what was being said, breaking it down into bite-sized pieces in order to be a critical thinker, using logic and reason to cull out the most important parts of the interview and ask follow-up questions. I know Ann did this too. Although she wrote about heinous acts, she was a master of switching into critical thinking and police training to draw conclusions in her books. Still, Ann never became jaded, or lost her ability to feel and voice the humanity of people, the victims, that she wrote or talked about in interviews. Her speech was soft and reassuring, even when delivering terrible news. Perhaps this is what's called "breaking it to you gently" like an aunt, or sister, or parent would? But at the time I was working on this project, it was easy to get sucked into the sinister imagery in Downs' head. She repeated her visions so often to me. And whether Downs committed the crimes or not, her recollections were mind boggling. Never, and perhaps to this day, have we ever heard such gut-wrenching details from inside the savage shootings of innocent children by their own mother.

The viewers would have to decide how convincing Downs was about the blood evidence. It was clear to viewers that there was a conflict between her story and the prosecutions. If you didn't know better, her explanation might have made sense, but Downs' version was fantasy. The explanations were chilling and pure manipulation, which became clear when the facts came out in trial.

High velocity blood travels at 25 feet per second, and makes a pattern that looks like hairspray. Blood under the tremendous force of a gun sprays mist, which experts saw in and outside Downs' Nissan. This spray proved Cheryl fought her way of the car. Experts could tell this because blood spatter shows a clear direction and angle of the shooter. High velocity blood stains are elongated pin pricks. The stains of this fine mist were tiny, around 0.1mm in diameter. It covered the threshold and metal panel *outside* the passenger side door, where you get in and out. There was no denying it. Cheryl likely took her final breath on the gravel road outside.

ABOVE: Crime scene photos of shooting reenactment shows a doll representing Cheryl as her mother reached over the passenger seat of this car to kill her daughter. BELOW: String pinpoints high velocity blood spatter on Downs' car inches away from Cheryl's body. Courtesy of Doug Welch.

Blood droplets on the other hand, as Diane claimed, are caused by gravity and are much larger circles. Cut your finger and it will drip until you find a band-aid. Sadly, the children probably did drip blood as they were rushed out the car door and into the emergency room to save their lives. But that blood is much different than aerosol spray.

Physics dictates the difference between high, medium and low velocity blood spatter. This was cutting edge science in 1983 and '84. This brand new and revelatory science blasted a wide hole in Downs' story itself and this spatter might have been completely missed, had Jim Pex not traveled to the FBI school teaching this class at its academy in Quantico, Virginia. In the midst of the investigation, Pex got off the plane, drove to the crime lab, and scoured every inch of Downs' car again. There, to his amazement, were previously indecipherable blood spatters on the door jam just waiting for him to read them. Now Pex could prove Downs was lying.

In our interview, Downs spent quite a bit of time talking about her history and her thoughts about men–especially her ex-husband.

It was common knowledge from police reports that the children were shot with a .22 Ruger. Her ex-husband, Steven Downs, said he once owned a Ruger, and her former lover told authorities Diane kept it in the trunk of her car. The gun was never found.

Trying to find out more about the gun in the interview, I asked about a story I'd heard about Downs and a .22.

"Was there ever a time you thought about taking your own life and..." I started to say.

Downs interrupted, stating, "Oh *yeah.*"

I continued my question, "And (you) went into the bathroom with the gun?"

"Yeah...this is true," Downs said. She said Steve had the gun. "I took it from him, I swiped it from him and hid it in my house."

The two of them had a wild, out-of-control fight, and then she grabbed the gun and locked herself in the bathroom.

"I considered shooting myself," she said. "But it was a .22 handgun and Steve says you can't kill anybody with a .22. *Surprise.*" She said smiling facetiously, about the fact Cheryl is murdered with a that caliber weapon. "Then I thought...my kids need me – I can't *die*!"

"The gun went off?" I asked.

"Yes, I fired it to scare the hell out of him. I WANTED him to know...if he kept doing this...someday perhaps that gun would be pointed at a person. *Not now, but someday.*"

Not now, but *someday* still makes the hair stand up on the back of my neck. Downs foreshadowed her rage and what she did when blinded by anger. Her rage, like the clock on a time bomb, was set to go off, *not now, but someday.* On this occasion, her anger was vented on her ex-husband and she was telegraphing to me her inability to protect her family from herself. I thought of witnesses who testified they saw her neglected children running around her neighborhood in Arizona, hungry and dirty, with no more than diapers or shorts to cover their small bodies, as they asked for food. I think of all the madness the children saw in their mother's world.

About that *someday* shot...in the early days of the case, Doug Welch and Paul Alton traveled to Diane's trailer in Arizona where the shot was fired through the bathroom floorboards. They spent a day searching inside and underneath the trailer in absolutely scorching heat for the bullet. They believed both or either would match those found lying in Downs' car or on Old Mohawk Road.

Welch used an old coat hanger to poke through the bullet hole in the floor. The wire traced the possible path of the bullet. Talk about a needle in a haystack. As luck, or good police work, or a handy old stick-straight hanger would have it, Alton found the bullet!

There was only one problem. The bullet was so deformed it was of "no ballistic value" meaning the metal was so mangled that forensics couldn't figure out if it was fired from the same .22 Diane used to shoot her kids. It was a bust in Arizona heat so hot that Doug nearly burned his fingertips turning on the ignition of his rental car.

However, a search warrant of Downs' Oregon apartment would later find bullets which *had* been placed in that .22 Ruger, the murder weapon. Under a high power microscope, the scratch marks on the bullet were like fingerprints, called 'toolmarks.' The fingerprint toolmarks were a direct match to the bullet cartridge found at the murder scene. Bingo. All of this, however, wouldn't come out until much, much later, during the trial that's months away.

By the time of our interview, Downs was obviously getting feedback about the shooting from other people in her life. The woman was still delivering mail to homes, thanks to her prior experience and her father, a postmaster.

"Everyone says 'You sure were lucky.' Well, I don't feel very lucky. I couldn't tie my damn shoes for about two months! (Downs laughed here) It is very painful, it is still painful. I have a steel plate in my arm."

She continued, focusing on her wounds instead of the bullet holes which shredded her children: "The scar is going to be there forever. I'm going to remember that night for the rest of my life whether I want to or not. I don't think I was very lucky. I think my kids were lucky. If I had been shot the way they were, we all would have died, except maybe Danny."

There were a couple of times during the interview that I needed to reorient myself. This was one of them. Twice, my mind wandered into dangerous territory that threatened to throw my questioning off. I knew by her strange answers that I was likely sitting with a child killer.

My feelings, even now, are undeniable. Visceral. I recognize her malice, making you gasp and come up for air as quietly as possible, as if not to alert the assailant, and in order to escape unharmed. Did her children feel the same way?

While listening today, I found my mind wandering into old territory. I needed to stop the documentary playing on my desk in front of me. I was distracted, thinking back to three absolutely stunning moments in trial. First, about that towel Diane wrapped around her arm. I'd been curious about the significance of that towel since the day I met her. I finally found out the devilish details in court one day. Instead of using the towel to stop her children from bleeding to death, Diane folded it in a methodical pattern ahead of time, proven by the blood stains through the folds, like a t-shirt tie dyed with crimson blobs soaking through. She had it ready in the trunk, for her own wound, not theirs. Her surviving daughter remembered her mother stopping the car that night, and seeing her pull the lever to open the trunk. Christie didn't know why–yet. The towel sat next to the gun.

We know the men in Downs' life told detectives Diane kept the Ruger gun in her trunk. The pre-folded towel to wrap her own arm sat nearby, waiting for *someday.*

I think back to the day in court when the prosecutor proved Diane could not have had her car keys in her hand, as she had claimed during the shooting. They were not in her hand, and the stranger didn't wrestle them away from her either. Christie remembered being shot while the Duran Duran song "Hungry Like The Wolf" played in the car's tape deck. The big hole in Diane's story? The tape deck won't run unless the keys are in the ignition, *not* in her hands playing keep away with an unknown shooter who wanted her car with three kids inside. I also think about a recent talk with Doug about the ringing in our ears from that song. Neither of us can hear it today without remembering the children. In stores, we both walk out. On the radio, we change channels. We can be anywhere when the song plays and instantly snap back to the 1983 shootings and the murder.

And finally I think about being back in court, listening to the testimony I heard directly from Christie Downs on the witness stand. Prosecutor Fred Hugi spoke with a tenderness few knew he was capable of, while gently sussing out the truth.

"Do you know who shot Cheryl?" Fred said.

"Yeah," said Christie.

"Who was that?"

"My mom."

"How do you know that?"

"I watched."

"Were there any strangers there? Anybody you didn't know?"

"No."

"How about with Danny. Was there any stranger there when Danny was shot?"

"No."

"Who shot him?"

"My mom."

"Who shot you?"

"My mom."

"Do you know that because you saw her do it?"

"Yeah."

With all these past memories swirling in my head, I realize I'm way off task. The video remains on pause. A brave little girl facing down her mother in court, the towel, the music. The suffering. A knot builds in my throat too hard to swallow. I can be *watching* Downs again in my Special Report, but my mind's eye is seeing so much more. I'm not sure if I found it all more shocking now or then, but I feel my hand covering my mouth to protect myself from the next utterance of completely vile words coming from Downs. Watching this is not a catharsis. This is an old wound Diane Downs inflicted on all of us who care and lived through it–and we're not the real survivors here. It makes little difference to the whole scheme of the case, I guess, if I still hurt for her children, who are now adults. After all, Downs' brutality inadvertently got them into the loving household they so justly deserved. After the trial, that same prosecutor fell in love with Christie and Danny and gave them a new stable home where they thrived. I'm thankful for this turn of events. They were safe, loved and nurtured.

Back to my desk, the video, *trying* to push the play button.

The most telling scenes come after I asked Downs what haunted her the most about that night. I am shocked at how cogently she talked about blood and watching her children being shot. No tears. No sniffling. No red puffy face. No flushed neckline. How could any mother openly express such terrifying memories, whether she shot them or not?

> "What I see the most is the blood coming out of Christie's mouth…because that's what I see. I can't see Danny and I can't see Cher."

Downs continued, as she moved from sight to sound.

"I can't hear anything but gunshots…Driving to the hospital I can smell blood. I can not hear Cheryl, Cheryl is not making a sound. Danny is just crying real, real soft…and the fact that Christie is choking. Just…and then I'm yelling at her, and screaming at her too, to roll over onto her face, because I was trying to keep her from choking on her blood. And it just didn't dawn on me that she was shot in the chest and the blood was coming (up) from her chest.

But the thing that really, really, haunts me the most…is not the sight and the sound, I mean the sound and the smell are fading. But at night when I close my eyes, I can see Christie reaching out her hand to me while I am driving, and the blood just keeps coming out of her mouth."

Downs' face should have shown fear… real terror, anger, confusion to match her words. But there was none of this. She can't mimic genuine emotions, nor hide her lies. I remember feeling woozy hearing about bloody children. A murderer has never publicly admitted all the terrifying scenes of a shooting from a mother's perspective. Viewers heard Downs talk for close to half an hour.

Now, again, I prepare myself for what I will hear and see next.

I know what's coming. I braced for it.

The closing video is still unbelievable to me. I wonder if I'll feel the same way today as I did back then.

"And that, maybe," Downs said, "will fade with time, but I don't think so. That's what haunts me the most."

This was the exact moment Downs stopped talking, but her face broke out into either a smile or smirk on camera.

Is Diane Downs smiling or smirking after talking about all the blood gushing from her children's bodies? See the full interview: Diane Downs Most Disturbing Interview, Diane Downs TV on YouTube.

This was the closing scene in the documentary: Downs' gleeful reaction after giving us horrendous stories of her children's demise. I've been asked about this closing shot of Downs' face many times. Never has one look been so terrifying. This was her reaction after hearing me say, "I feel sick," when I was off camera with the microphones off.

And the blood.

The blood.

Those innocent children.

All of this still haunts me.

Chapter 19
In Her Own Words

Shocking as the special was, viewers finally saw the Downs interview in its entirety on our ABC station, which broadcast it in Eugene, Springfield and within about seventy-five mile radius of Eugene in 1984 but not much bigger than that. It would take eons for the national news magazine ABC's 20/20 to draw a much wider audience and attention to this project that long ago consumed me for thirteen months. My documentary held its secret power for more than 25 years until it was picked up nationally. Before the first 20/20 episode aired in May of 2010, the story went cold for years.

Then, 20/20 came back a second time in 2019. Doug Welch and I were interviewed both times, Ann was included the first time. It's been a popular rerun. Anchor Elizabeth Vargas, who interviewed me at my home, said in the 2019 broadcast, "The Anne Jaeger interview really helped Diane Downs dig her own grave."

Me, being interviewed at my home for my second appearance on ABC's 20/20. Author's photo.

Back in 1984, we had no idea what the public's reaction to

Downs would be. However, once the special aired, viewer reaction to the documentary was favorable. One or two people wrote letters saying the program "made Diane Downs look guilty," (even though our interview, although thorough, made no speculation about guilt or innocence). It was, after all, *In Her Own Words.* Others wanted copies.

"You provided viewers with a very comprehensive and interesting piece of journalistic work…" read one letter. "Seldom has such a half hour of local TV been so watched or talked about. It was graphic and yet not condescending, a real balanced piece…It may offend some who turned in, but the vast majority of us watched, on the seats' edge and wouldn't have missed it for anything."

The Eyewitness News Special Report aired on election night for the primaries, not long after the anniversary of the shootings. No, I did not have the night off to savor my accomplishment and see it in the luxury of my own home. I was at a restaurant, the Oregon Electric Station, interviewing Eugene and Springfield politicians.

That was the year that Ronald Reagan won the 1984 Republican presidential nomination. Democrats picked former Vice President Walter Mondale, with Rep. Geraldine Ferraro as his running mate, the first woman VP candidate. I covered their rally in Eugene a few months later.

On May 15th, 1984, I was doing our live shots with local candidates. As 10 p.m. rolled around, we finally got a break. Our election night coverage ended when races were called locally and nationally in the primary.

The photographer and I raced into the news car to watch the documentary on a small television monitor. The TV in the car was tiny. *The Eyewitness News Special Report: Diane Downs In Her Own Words* aired. We watched from start to finish, not considering its content, which we knew by heart, but that the special ran without a glitch. That's what reporters do after stories are in the can. Mission accomplished, we headed home, never thinking beyond its airing what the viewers might have been thinking. How could we have? There was no social media instant feedback loop. There was no way to judge whether we would be vilified by Diane Downs supporters or lauded for a good, solid piece of journalism.

In the transitory world of television news, which is here one day, gone the next, my head was finally clear after seeing the half hour special done and put to bed. I knew *where* I'd be tomorrow: in court, seeing Diane Downs.

Entering the courtroom the next day, I noticed that people were eerily quiet when I walked in. They seemed to turn and look at me. I joked to myself that maybe my zipper was down? But no, they'd just witnessed Diane in her own words and were astonished by what she'd said. Seeing her at full throttle must have been mesmerizing, bewildering and startling. And this was the first time they *saw* her at full tilt until she got on the witness stand. The jury was sequestered in silence.

We, the reporters, had been sitting through *voir dire* (jury selection, often dry and unspectacular) when the author we'd been hearing about showed up in court. By now we knew it was *Ann Rule*. What we didn't know was that this author had an agreement with the Sheriff's Department to view notes and audio recordings after the trial was over. She was also very dear friends with a former Springfield and Eugene police chief Pierce Brooks who was consulting on the case. Ann had earned credibility and trust in local circles. But that was on the down-low. No local news reporter would ever get that access, only a trusted national author like Ann. Her news would come out later in *Small Sacrifices*, ours was immediate.

Hometown reporters had been on the case all this time and all of a sudden, there were two more bodies in a tightly packed courtroom: Ann and her daughter Leslie. There were no seats left in the courtroom for late reporters, such as me, for opening arguments.

As you'll remember, I encountered Ann Rule under these rather unusual circumstances when I tried to steal Leslie's seat! Fortunately, no one had to get up, as Ann and Leslie fit me in the crowded row. How do you explain a friendship forged by a meeting like this, except to attribute it to the open-mindedness and graciousness of the people being slighted? I don't know why Ann gave me the time of day, frankly. Somehow, even after this rather tense first meeting Ann and I became fast friends during the trial. We chatted during breaks, with me poking fun at myself in different (made up) voices mimicking my "you'll have to move" remark. This made her laugh.

In court one day, the judge called recess. I asked Rule if she would like to see the documentary on Downs, which had aired before Ann arrived in Eugene. I couldn't tell her interest level by the expression on her face, which seemed rather noncommittal about the prospect. We didn't know each other very well yet. After all, the author would get almost everything she asked for behind the scenes anyway. Finally, she said yes. In fact, Rule was excited at the prospect of getting together and seeing the half hour doc. "I've heard about your work, Anne," she said. "I'd love to see it."

Okay, yes, I was relieved.

I promised a private viewing the next day.

Ann drove from her hotel to the TV station and we watched the entire half hour in the very same conference room where Diane talked the year before. I tried my best not to stare at Ann to gauge her reactions. Who wouldn't be curious what the Queen of True Crime thought about their work? Rule was taking notes and watching so closely it was as if no one else was in the room. Ann had tremendous concentration, probably learned while writing with four kids in the house.

I could see, with my brief glimpses of Ann, that she was fascinated. Which made me extremely proud. Ann had already seen news clips of Diane on her Seattle news stations, but this was the first time she witnessed Diane's real verbal vomit. Ann loved her children dearly and could not conceive of a mother talking like this about the brutal slayings of her own children. Whether Diane did it or not.

Rule called my work "*THE* seminal personality profile on Diane Downs."

We were back in court the very next day, Ann, Leslie and I.

That was the start of a burgeoning friendship.

When Ann's book *Small Sacrifices* came out in June 1987, we had a publication and book signing party for her at the Eugene Hilton.

Ann in her Eugene hotel room before guests arrived to celebrate publication of her book.

The party ran until 2:30 a.m. for us die-hards. Of course, I asked Ann to sign my book too. Ann wrote to me more personally on the first page, "Anne, you have been such a part of this book. Thank you! Thank you! for your insights!" Then publicly in her book acknowledgements, she called me out more formally, "with special thanks to Anne Bradley Jaeger of KEZI, who shared her insights regarding the videotape of her exclusive interview with Diane Downs."

In her recommendation letter, she mentioned referring to my material several times a week in writing the book. I provided a transcript for her to work with. All this was high praise. Outside validation that photographer Gary Kahne and I had done our job. *Small Sacrifices* became Ann's very first national bestseller. *The Stranger Beside Me* and *Small Sacrifices* are her two most popular books to this day.

Chapter 20
Verdict Rules

Circling back to June of 1984, we were all on pins and needles waiting for the end of the trial. Closing arguments were in, the jury was out. Ann showed up every day for three full days while the jury decided Diane's fate. I was amazed she had time to hang out and wait because she was juggling so many projects in the hopper. She had sat through court, and would be getting the full transcripts, so Ann could have written this trial's ending at any time. But by now, the hook was set and Ann wanted to find out the verdict in person as much as we did.

With no more trial notes to take or interviews to dig up, Rule talked to all the reporters on jury watch. We were a small cadre of die-hards. Ann was friendly, talkative and well-liked by this time. Reporters gathered outside the courtroom from the time the jury clocked in to the time they called it quits. No matter how late.

There would be no early nights. I now admit to feeling anxious about the verdict, but gabbing with Ann was fun and lighthearted. Except, of course, when it came to the subject of WHAT the verdict might be. I couldn't see how any member of that jury could find Diane not guilty, especially after all the evidence and seeing Christie testify. Other reporters believed an acquittal was possible because it was taking the jury so long; overwhelming guilty verdicts often come back fairly quickly, while not guilty decisions take more time in long cases. Even Ann began to wonder if the jury was deadlocked. Were there hold outs for Diane's innocence? Every single juror on the panel would need to vote for the murder conviction. It had to be unanimous. Nothing less.

I did live shots outside the courthouse telling viewers the

jury was finally deliberating after six weeks of trial. Finally, the jury went home close to 10:30 p.m. the first day. Day two was even longer, they started early and finally called it quits at about the same time of night. They'd put in about 22 hours over two days.

We were getting a bit rummy on the third day, June 16th, 1984, since we'd been there all day, every day. Dinner time came and went, still no word. I asked Ann to cover for me as I went to buy us some grub. I have no recollection of what we ate, but I suspect the food was not good for us. By nine o'clock when the sun finally set, it was still almost 70 balmy degrees in June. The fluorescent lights flickered with a bluish tinge in the third-floor hallway outside the courtroom where we were sitting. By 11 o'clock it was almost as if we were all caught in suspended animation, but ready to hit full tilt with adrenaline if a verdict came.

At midnight, when the jury reached its decision, trial watchers suddenly came out of the woodwork to press into the packed courtroom. Everyone, including me, found a seat. The room was silent, but there was a creepy electrical current…a static electricity ricocheting off the walls. There were no sounds of spectators wiggling in their seats, opening purses, unwrapping mints, no one seems to move an inch. The courtroom was mesmerized as the verdict was read: **GUILTY** on two counts of attempted murder. **GUILTY** on two counts of assault. **GUILTY** of murder. The trance was broken when a new reporter jumped to his feet, elbowing people to get out of his way, *stomping* to the door, and hitting it at a full speed. Loud, jarring and rather frightening. That broke the spell.

My deadline had long passed for breaking news. But there was still work to be done. Interviews with spectators, and Downs' attorney–who said he expected the verdict. Then trying to get Downs' reaction as she was led through the sallyport (a back hallway for transport vans) back to jail.

I sent my photographer for sallyport shots, while I took a shot in the dark: I wanted to try to get an exclusive with the elusive prosecutor, Fred Hugi. I knew just where I could catch him. I ran to the street where the jail van would come out. I'd see Diane leaving, but knew Hugi parked his car in the lot across that street. The moon was nearly full, as I was standing smack in the middle of the street when I spotted him. Fred was less than a quarter block away, crossing. I moved toward him. He would be my dream interview that nobody else would get. Most prosecutors would be delighted to give interviews after a conviction. Not Hugi. He saw me, looked right at me, put his chin to his chest, looking down. With a slight move of his right hand at his side, he waved me off. I was the only reporter out there.

Ann and I kept up by phone after Downs' conviction. We'd chat in between her writing. I knew she'd watch the Price is Right, and Let's Make A Deal (she loved Bob Barker, an animal advocate) before starting to write about ten in the morning. On the hardest days she'd commit to four hours. When the juices were flowing, she might triple her efforts. Ann was a *fast* writer, as you can tell by her contract to submit two books a year. But *Small Sacrifices* would take her three years to write. We didn't lose touch, but because of her schedule, it was usually me calling on her for catch up sessions, support or advice.

Ann knew the steps I took to safeguard my Diane Downs interview through 1983 and early 1984, to keep law enforcement and other reporters from hijacking my interview. She had experienced the same struggles with other authors while protecting her work. She knew which authors she could trust and which she could not.

And it was during this time I leaned on her more closely.

Especially when my revelatory interview was used by another reporter, formerly at KEZI, who apparently decided against covering Downs early on, then dove back into the case after Downs exposed so many inner secrets to me on video.

I talked to Ann about feeling used and disregarded by this other journalist we both knew, after Downs' sentence of 150 years in prison. "Ann," I said. "I just heard he won a prestigious New York film award based on my interview without ever mentioning me, by name, as the source of the interview, in his project." I was completely cut out.

Ann commiserated with me, knowing how painful it was when others seemingly took credit for your work.

"That's awful," Ann said. "How did that happen?"

She remarked on the unfairness that such a thing could happen. Ann felt bad for me.

This was a disappointing time in my career. One Ann helped me reconcile. She knew the feeling. I explained to Ann this perceived slight was painful given my newsroom dealings with this reporter, who was far more respected than I, who I considered a friend.

Ann told me, "Just keep doing your work. You'll win out in the end."

This very same reporter, the first assigned the Diane Downs story, allegedly realized that I was the one supplying him with inside info on the case. I found out Christie lost so much blood in the hospital that emergency workers had inadvertently given her the wrong blood type in her transfusion and she'd suffered a stroke from the trauma. It would take a long time for Christie to regain her speech. I passed the information to Rebecca Force on Assignment Desk, because it was the other reporters' story. At which time, I was told he decided to focus on his real news beat and bowed out on Downs. A coincidence, perhaps. But after he left for a new job, and saw my Downs special on tape, he dove right back in.

"And I did it to myself," I told Ann during the call. I was kicking myself, even though I had no idea how the events would play out. Ann wasn't sure what I'm getting at.

In the six months it took to bring the documentary to air, the reporter came back into town. He was still the top dog from our station even though he was gone by then. I thought, er, I knew, I wanted to show him I *did* have the chops after hearing rumors a few reporters thought I was hired for looks, not skill.

I offered to show him a rough cut, not a final, of my work in the same conference room where I'd interviewed Diane Downs. He said, "That's good, Anne." To be sure, not the accolades or reassessment I was reaching for, but a seed had been planted.

But not the seed I'd hoped.

His station bought the tapes.

With his penchant for ethics, my naivete mistakenly believed my work would be credited. We had no communication during this time.

To be fair, my documentary focused on allowing Diane Downs to be herself, the good, bad, and very ugly, and on breaking huge scoops on evidence viewers hadn't known before the trial. I'd worked on breaking *that* news. But crime news wasn't as respected as other journalism. His approach, afterward, was holistic. His use of this material took another tack, focusing on the effects of child abuse in families. No longer concerned with breaking news about evidence, his overview was stellar. The reporter made a great juxtaposition between Downs' crimes, my interview and her old college paper.

I'd never seen the community college report he tapped into, although I remember the prosecutor Fred Hugi holding it up and alluding to her paper in court. I got a copy later. Downs' insights were as tragic as they were prescient and showed the reflections of a young woman barreling toward disaster. Reading her paper for yourself might help you understand her explosive headspace. Here's a taste of her mindset in her college report.

> *The gruesome crime of child abuse not only destroys the lives of our children, but it usually brings terror into the lives of our grandchildren.... Abused children develop different personalities.... And, because the scars, pain, and memories remain...this scarred child, turned adult, has children of his or her own, these children (our grandchildren) are usually abused in some way.*

Diane was holding the mirror up to her own face, her words written here were drawn from her own life.

> *Many abused children die from wounds inflicted by their parents. And, if they die at a young age, they are lucky, because their torture is long over...*

Then her words became even more prophetic.

> *That brings me to the most common type of child abuse- - - the*

survivors. These children are broken, bruised, and bloodied, yet they live on. They continue their lives with the horrible memories of pain and fear. The last form of child abuse... is sexual.

Downs was clearly talking about her past struggles with a strict religious father that she accused (then recanted after the trial) of abusing her. It foreshadowed terrible retribution that would bubble up when she eventually had children all too soon.

And, some people abuse their own children because they have so much hatred for their parents, yet they are still expected to (l)ove (sic) and respect their own parents: so their hatred is vented on defenseless children. They can not make their parents scream and cry, but they have the power to make <u>someone</u> scream and cry.

Someone scream, and cry.

...When these abused children grow up, they will, in no doubt, turn to abuse their children. I wish we could stop this vicious cycle...

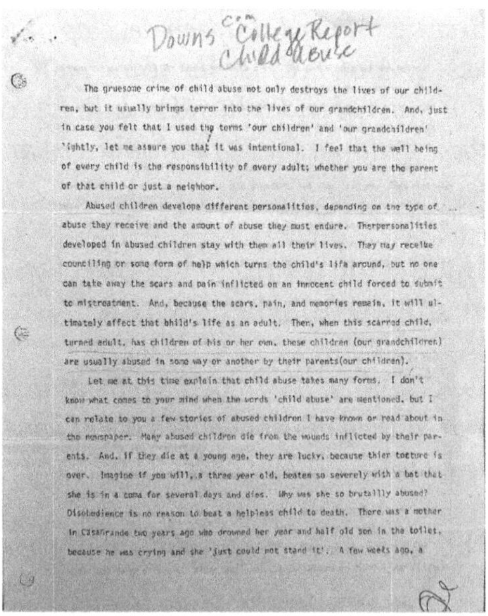

Downs Com College Report Child abuse

The gruesome crime of child abuse not only destroys the lives of our children, but it usually brings terror into the lives of our grandchildren. And, just in case you felt that I used the terms 'our children' and 'our grandchildren' lightly, let me assure you that it was intentional. I feel that the well being of every child is the responsibility of every adult; whether you are the parent of that child or just a neighbor.

Abused children develope different personalities, depending on the type of abuse they receive and the amount of abuse they must endure. Therpersonalities developed in abused children stay with them all their lives. They may receive counciling or some form of help which turns the child's life around, but no one can take away the scars and pain inflicted on an innocent child forced to submit to mistreatment. And, because the scars, pain, and memories remain, it will ultimately affect that bhild's life as an adult. Then, when this scarred child, turned adult, has children of his or her own, these children (our grandchildren) are usually abused in some way or another by their parents(our children).

Let me at this time explain that child abuse takes many forms. I don't know what comes to your mind when the words 'child abuse' are mentioned, but I can relate to you a few stories of abused children I have known or read about in the newspaper. Many abused children die from the wounds inflicted by their parents. And, if they die at a young age, they are lucky, because thier torture is over. Imagine if you will, a three year old, beaten so severely with a bat that she is in a coma for several days and dies. Why was she so brutallly abused? Disobedience is no reason to beat a helpless child to death. There was a mother in Casagrande two years ago who drowned her year and half old son in the toilet, because he was crying and she 'just could not stand it'. A few weeks ago, a

Downs' startling community college report on child abuse. Author collection.

Even with insight, Diane Downs was not strong enough to stop the cycle of abuse and violently pointed her weapon to maximum effect.

My doc was full of Downs' stories about her childhood and feeling "trapped by society" in a male dominated world, an "I fight authority, authority always wins" mindset. The reporter used our footage of Downs' vitriolic comments about men, her father, incest, and wisely interspersed her college report with the leading research about child abuse. He was not able to get his own interview with Diane.

After my special aired, the reporter's version was broadcast elsewhere, then won a big award. The reporter called KEZI to share his good news. I think his call had been transferred to me after talking to others? I could tell he really didn't want to talk to me, it seemed as if he were holding his tongue. He seemed stoic. I congratulated him.

After we hung up, I called Ann. She'd seen the reporter's documentary based on my interview but didn't have the heart to say my contribution credit was omitted and any sight of me was wiped clean. Ann thought the story looked as if he'd done all the work.

For the next thirty years, I'd hear "you covered the Diane Downs case, you should see the interview by *this* reporter," when I landed the fascinating interview. The perception stuck until 20/20 came calling the first time, after Downs' investigator Doug Welch informed network researchers that I did that interview. Only then was I asked about my groundbreaking reporting and credited fully. My work proved insightful in 2010 and again when 20/20 did another two hour special on the story nine years later. Seeing the material masterfully laid out and attributed accordingly was thrilling. I'd even forgotten some of the twists and weird turns that the Diane Downs' case took!

Today, with the benefit of hindsight, I wonder, if perhaps, somehow at the time, that reporter still held onto a mistaken thought. Perhaps his producers had insisted on running credits with "additional video courtesy of KEZI" and omitted my name? I don't know. I do know, there would be no story without Downs talking. And, perhaps, if my former colleague had felt strongly about including me, it would have been there.

By the time Ann wrote her shining reference letter for me to any future employers, she advocated for me. Ann drew attention to the other reporter's award in her letter of recommendation, never outing him:

> *In November of 1983 – five months before Diane Downs went to trial – Anne Bradley obtained an interview with Downs that captured the woman absolutely. Bradley showed the Eugene public a brilliantly psychopathic woman in a special that is so compelling that I refer to my tape of it several times a week as I write this book. Ann's taped material was the basis for a special done at a larger television station in the Northwest and which won second prize in the New York International Film Festival in the television documentary category.*

Rule knew the territory. Having been disregarded as a woman, forced to use male names for her books without recognition in her *own* name, and feeling discredited by another famous author for her hard work – it seems to me, she wanted to set the record straight if prospective employers saw my interview on another resume tape and didn't know the real source. I had no idea she'd put it in her letter. Ann later told me, that indeed, was exactly her reason for calling it out.

Ann knew the bitter aftertaste and helped me get over it.

Ann's advice was right: "You'll win out in the end."

I landed the more coveted 5 p.m. anchor position after these struggles. My belief in my work, now credited, has finally been put to rest.

Meantime, back in '84, I was working on another scoop about Diane. This one was steamy and creepy at the same time. And it was about another killer that Ann and I both knew.

Chapter 21
"Love" Letters Between Bars

Diane Downs, always searching for love, found it behind bars. In mid-June of 1984, she was pregnant, awaiting a sentence of life plus 50 years, and would soon be transferred to Oregon's largest women's prison in Salem, Oregon. Downs was being held in the Lane County jail until the birth of her fatherless child.

I knew something was up, after getting an out of the blue letter from Randy Woodfield, the subject of Ann Rule's bestseller *I-5 Killer.* Randy Woodfield was a murderer so incredibly vicious that you'd think Ted Bundy took a page out of this former NFL football non-starters playbook. Woodfield was serving life plus ninety years in the Oregon State Pen for murder, two attempted murders, sodomy, kidnapping and rape. Evidence links him conclusively to six killings. Investigators suspected many more. CBS called Woodfield "one of the deadliest serial killers in American history."

In a letter to me, dated July 16th, 1984 Woodfield said:

Dear Ms. Bradley,

I'm told you were a very good & competent news reporter for the Eugene area, so I have decided to ask you first about a possible story I think Oregonians would like to know about. ....I'm just in the stages of getting married, and when I do, there will be news coverage about it I'm sure...because the lady I'm planning on marrying will certainly make headlines her own self. (sic) ....Would you like to talk about this story?... ...please do NOT share this with others. I'm offering YOU this story.

Thank you,
R. Woodfield
#37376

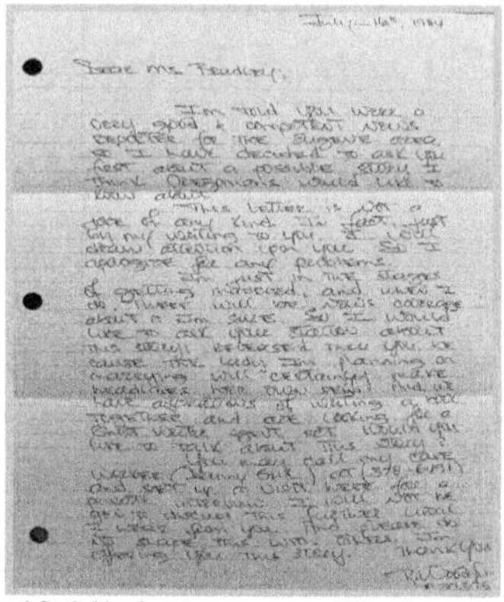

I-5 Killer Randy Woodfield's letter to me. His letter shows a manipulative "Mastermind" using Diane Downs to elevate himself into the spotlight again. Author's collection.

You could see this coming a mile away, right? The ONLY inmate with notoriety greater than his in Oregon in 1984 was Diane Downs. There's definitely a story waiting there, and I was thinking I had better get approval to do this story right away, because Woodfield might have been writing to every reporter in town. I needed to act quickly. Even though the station had long tired of Downs by this time, I got the go ahead.

I didn't call or write the *I-5 Killer.*

Immediately, I asked for an information release for inmate correspondence between Woodfield and Downs. Then, I set up a jailhouse meeting with Downs and headed there with the letters in hand. No audio or videotaping allowed, but I had a stack of letters two inches thick between the lovebirds.

Sitting across from Diane separated by glass, I took notes. I held up some letters, asking her, "Randy Woodfield's talking about YOU, right?"

Downs seemed demure, blushing.

I had picked up on the "relationship" so quickly, I caught her completely flatfooted. I broke the story about Woodfield's marriage proposals to Downs. She told me intended to marry him. But this story really angered Woodfield. At the Oregon State Pen the day after my story aired, Randy called a media conference, with cameras and reporters to ridicule me publicly. At the conference, Woodfield vehemently called me a liar, impugning my credibility over his cold-blooded killer lies in trial. The man serving a life sentence was upset because I'd wisely sidestepped him and gone right to the source, ruining his chances to parlay his relationship with Diane into some kind of a book or movie deal!

His letters were exposed.

If you've ever had occasion to wonder what star-crossed killers say to each other behind bars, I've pulled excerpts that these two Ann Rule killers wrote back and forth to each other.

Woodfield wrote under the pen name Michael Bethel or JUSTME in May of 1984, not revealing his real name yet, but sent Downs a photo of himself standing between two children saying "Me & my best friends! (I love kids!) -Jackie, Me, Jay-" from a Christmas photo five months before. So much for obscuring your identity, huh? But Downs didn't recognize the face.

Downs was in the midst of her murder trial when he reached out with more fictitious names, signing "Take Care, Love – 'Squirrely' (sic) Me.

Their letters went back and forth furiously.

May 5th, 1984.

Dear Di,

....I have read all about the bitch from Spokane [Ann Rule in Seattle] in her writing world. Crazy, huh? She sure is a leech on people!!! Making a living off peoples (sic) tragedies and lives.

Woodfield gives no hint he's actually the *I-5 Killer* Rule wrote about. And of course, he knows Rule is writing a book about his pen pal, Diane, too. *"You be strong and win your case to shut her up..."*

By page two, this sexual predator, killer, named 'Squirrely' gets to the point of his letter,

> *I will think of your soft tits & pretty face and stroke my cum out gently, thinking of you…You get your rest for the baby (s) and I'll write more.*
>
> *June 6, 1984*
>
> *Hello Sweet Friend,*
>
> *…My heart goes out to ya, your baby (Ian Randall?) will not be born until after your acquital, (sic)…You say you're very curious to know who this fellow is here [smiley face]..You will be surprised Im (sic) sure….Will you be mad if I've kept certain things from ya for important reasons?*

Then, Woodfield wrote more about marriage and children.

> *…Yeah, I'm open for adoption too. Especially if artificial insemination or surogate (sic) motherhood are out. I love kids THAT much. I bet our kid would be a beautiful baby!! Give 'em hell in court too!*
>
> *Love & Peace,*
> *"Squirrely" (sic)*

Five days before Downs was found guilty, Randy Woodfield revealed himself as her secret admirer.

> *June 12th,*
>
> *Dear Di,*
>
> *…I'm sorry I couldn't have told you all about me…You undoubtedly will be told crazy stuff and alot (sic) of it just ain't true!! But I will tell you everything soon. Take care my dear friend. I am pulling for you very much. Be strong now.*

Love – - Randall.

A week *after* the jury found her guilty of murder and the shootings: Woodfield proposed.

June 24,

Dear Diane,

...If you go OWCC (Oregon's Women's Correctional Center) Diane – then I will want your promise to marry me...I know this is a shock to ya, but why not marry me and visit me too? You can always divorce me later.

Night Di,
(XO) Michael

For some reason, Woodfield began referring to himself as Michael Bethel again. Maybe just another *charming* joke between lovers?

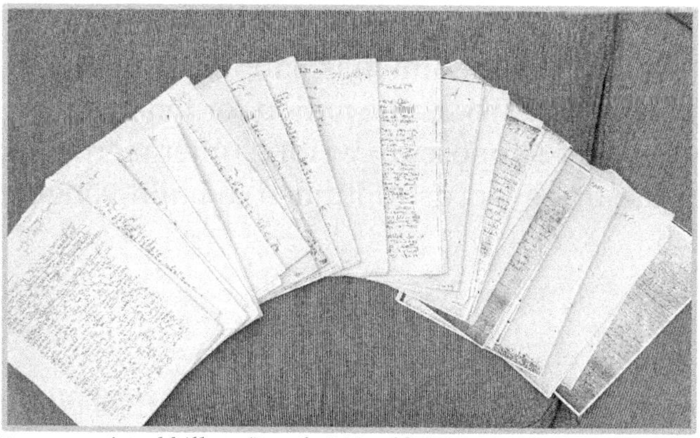

Stack of letters convicted killers Randy Woodfield and Diane Downs wrote to each other in 1984. Author's photo.

A volley of letters were written between July 1st and the 14th. Diane's letters sought connection, while Woodfield sought conjugal visits if he could talk the prison warden into it. He blames Diane for a stint in segregation for fighting and rails against Ann Rule again.

> *July 12,*
>
> *Are We Still Friends?*
> *I don't know – I've stuck up for ya the last time here. I'm in S & I (segregation) for fighting some dude...You've got to decide now to quit playing games about anybody you're writing here. ....That lady Anne (sic) Rule will only make you look like a cold-blooded killer too. Count on it Di. She wrote about me like I did all that shit!!!...Pure speculation by the bitch! I am going to sue her too... That author says I did crimes out of rejection and heartache??? (Ha) I was doing great & had a very beautiful fiancee' and girlfriends too. ...Even if I did believe you did that to your kids, I wouldn't hurt your feelings by saying so. But your (sic) innocent, like I am of killing & raping. I'm one "Helluva" Robber and the state used my past to say I grew into a worse criminal.*
>
> *Are we still friends?*
> *Hope So Di.*
> *<u>NIGHT.</u>*

Woodfield's fight landed him in isolation, not Diane, but perhaps he saw it as a romantic notion for females, and blamed his violence on her supposedly writing other men in lock up. Moreover, his strong words continued to build vengeance toward Ann.

> *July 20,*
>
> *Morning Blondie ...You can sense I'm hurt by all the slanderous statements & prejudice against me. I'm **<u>NO</u>** killer and that (Anne (sic) Rule) trying to paint a picture of "why" I became a murderer from just a flasher to woman rapist & robber. Well, I just get upset easy. Understand? Just like you want to forget about talking of your kids I too want to forget about my being a"sadistic" killer....a bunch of "B.S."*

Love & Peace, Randy XO

Once I got ahold of the letters, I called Ann to talk about Woodfield's threats against her. She'd already gotten copies but didn't know I had them as well.

"Have you seen the letters going back and forth between Diane and Randy Woodfield?" I said.

She laughed. "Yes."

We shared a few off-color jokes about these two killers (of all people) having children together. As usual, Ann said she wasn't worried about Woodfield's anger. But he did, in time, file a twelve million dollar lawsuit against Ann for libel *years* after her *I-5 Killer* book was released. Woodfield lost. The statute of limitations had run out in his case long before. Ann told the Statesman Journal, "He was suing me because I ruined his reputation." She added, "The matter of his reputation seemed not to be the strongest argument in the world" as a convicted murderer.

That was the last letter Woodfield wrote Downs before I broke the news story about his marriage proposals to her. And here's where this "love" story makes a decisive turn. I'd interviewed Diane in jail and told her, "I have all these letters of Woodfield asking you to marry him, is it true, Diane?" She said it was, not knowing he'd turn around and burn her, when he'd call both of us liars saying, "He'd never marry *her.*"

The story aired.

By the next morning Woodfield had orchestrated that full media conference at the State Pen with reporters.

I was jumping to go.

But the station said no, the public interest in Downs has worn too thin. And they found Woodfield repugnant.

They wouldn't let me cover it. There were plenty of harsh words spoken between me and management.

"We AIRED the story and now he's calling us liars," I told them. Not only was my credibility being questioned by a convicted killer but so was the station's.

Management wouldn't relent. I quit my job that day.

The station ended up sending another anchor, armed *not with the letters* but with information in the story. The anchor Ben

Lesser did a fine job being thrown into the mix last minute. At least Woodfield's "story" did not air on KEZI without rebuttal. Within a week, management and I negotiated a settlement and I went back to work.

And in the meantime our star-crossed lovers hit a breaking point. Their letters on July 27th coincided in the mail.

But Downs was too busy in jail anyway, about to give birth. At 4:30 p.m. my friend Detective Doug Welch was at the hospital with Downs. We recently talked about the whole experience. He remembers Downs was given the hormone Pitocin to induce labor as soon as they arrived. Detectives usually didn't accompany convicted murderers to the hospital, but the Sheriff's Department hoped, beyond hope, that Downs would relent and confess in the throes of labor even though she'd already been convicted. If she did, the sheriff wanted a detective there to record her words.

Downs hardly made a peep during delivery. Doug said Diane, now on her 5th child, popped the baby out quickly. No big deal, as she said in our interview: "children are so easy to conceive."

At 10:06 p.m. she delivered the baby she named Amy Elizabeth. It must have been a queasy experience for Doug to walk into a delivery room and see the killer holding an innocent child again. A murderer, who would be forbidden to be around children forever. It was a surreal scene: a convicted, but not-yet-sentenced woman who murdered Cheryl, paralyzed Danny, and wounded her other daughter, back in a delivery room touching a newborn.

After more than a year of taunting the lead investigator in her case, Downs told Doug, "Doug, you can hold the baby." The detective said he was shocked, but enjoyed the moment cradling the infant.

"I don't know why she would consider letting me, her arch-nemesis, hold that little girl," he admits softly, "but it was nice. A gesture that was unexpected, but it was nice." He instantly separated his feelings about Downs from the promise of new life, "She can be a stone cold killer, but that baby was as innocent as she could be."

Doug said she showed no remorse, regret or emotion

when the Children's Services Division was there to take the baby. During my interview with her Diane had told me "I'd like to see them *try* to take this baby away." But by now, it seemed Downs resigned herself to losing any rights to the child.

Diane was wheeled out of the hospital, in handcuffs, and arrived at the jail long before midnight.

She couldn't sleep, even after delivery. Instead, she was up writing. If the timestamp on Diane's letter was correct, at two in the morning, she'd had a come-to-Jesus revelation, not about her circumstances or her lost life and abused children, but about men.

July 27 Friday at 2:00 a.m.

Dear Randall,

I finally got my wish. I've been curious for quite some time about what your voice sounds like. Now I know. It isn't anything like I imagined. It's time to come to terms, Randy…When Anne Bradley [me] told me about your Letter…rather than let you look like a fool at O.S.P [Oregon State Prison] I openly acknowledged… that we had certain discussions (on paper.) My attorney yelled at me like you wouldn't believe, because I'm not sentenced yet, and they are trying to attach a "dangerous offender" label to me.

…Your presence doesn't help my case, but I wouldn't denounce you, because I knew I couldn't hurt you…
…Anne Bradley is mad because she saw what happened to me in the trial concerning Knick and Steve. Lies & deceit were used to destroy my character….I am now renewing my vow of 'hermit hood.'…I'm sure you'll find someone else to play with, but I'm beat. I just want to live the rest of my life in peace.

Good-bye Randy,
Love,
Diane.

She sent him eight Bible discussions along with her goodbye

letter. No mention of the brand new baby taken from her arms, hours earlier, a life changing event in most women's lives.

I *was* honest with Diane during our jailhouse interview, asking why she'd agree to marry a rapist and murderer. It is *the* question requiring an answer. Downs said she didn't know quite what kind of man (monster) Woodfield really was.

And the talk of her dangerous offender label? That was not a result of their relationship or letters. Two reports came into her case and they were not in her favor. One labeled her a 'psychopathic deviate.' The Defense had one report done by Downs' own newly licensed *psychologist* with no forensic experience. And a court ordered pre-sentencing report by a long standing licensed *psychiatrist*, detailed a laundry list of problems: calling Downs a sociopath.

As to why I'd be mad? I got more insight when I read her other letters telling Woodfield I was compassionate and nonjudgmental. I was not *sentimental* toward her. I still wished for her children's sakes, Downs had made other "choices," as we say in polite society. I always *tried*, as Ann Rule and her grandfather before me had, to treat criminals as people, with some veneer of dignity. Still asking the questions.

On the same day as Diane's letter, and the very same day of Woodfield's news conference to call both Diane and me liars, he took her to school. He didn't know Diane gave birth that night or lost custody of her baby.

July 27th

Dear Di –

....Why did you say anything to anyone just now? I'm really confused Di? I told you I was holding the 'Aces' and was going to sell a story of some kind to a mag. & newspaper & T.V. – – But now everyone thinks we're getting married and it's caused alot (sic) of unnessasary (sic) problems.

....You were to just sit tight and be "mum" and refer <u>them</u> on to <u>me.</u> It may have taken a while to find (an outlet) for all this publicity – ... But now I have to say our visit to meet was just a misunderstanding about "marriage plans." ...Please don't be angry. ....but now don't trust the "pigs"

who read our mail! OKAY? ...Please? Let me capitalize on what we do have here? Please?
I'm not playing games just covering my tracks right now. Let's try again...

I care Di,
Randy.

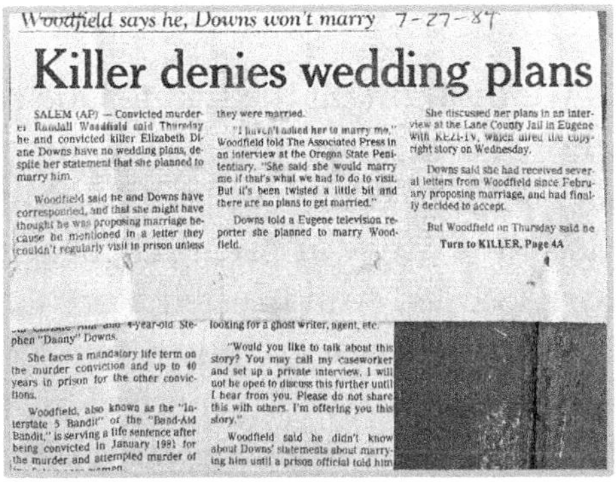

Woodfield says he, Downs won't marry 7-27-87

Killer denies wedding plans

SALEM (AP) — Convicted murderer Randall Woodfield said Thursday he and convicted killer Elizabeth Diane Downs have no wedding plans, despite her statement that she planned to marry him.

Woodfield said he and Downs have corresponded, and that she might have thought he was proposing marriage because he mentioned in a letter they couldn't regularly visit in prison unless they were married.

"I haven't asked her to marry me," Woodfield told The Associated Press in an interview at the Oregon State Penitentiary. "She said she would marry me if that's what we had to do to visit. But it's been twisted a little bit and there are no plans to get married."

Downs told a Eugene television reporter she planned to marry Woodfield.

She discussed her plans in an interview at the Lane County Jail in Eugene with KEZI-TV, which aired the copyright story on Wednesday.

Downs said she had received several letters from Woodfield since February proposing marriage, and had finally decided to accept.

But Woodfield on Thursday said he

Turn to KILLER, Page 4A

... 4-year-old Stephen "Danny" Downs.

She faces a mandatory life term on the murder conviction and up to 40 years in prison for the other convictions.

Woodfield, also known as the "Interstate 5 Bandit" or the "Band-Aid Bandit," is serving a life sentence after being convicted in January 1981 for the murder and attempted murder of ...

looking for a ghost writer, agent, etc.

"Would you like to talk about this story? You may call my caseworker and set up a private interview. I will not be open to discuss this further until I hear from you. Please do not share this with others. I'm offering you this story."

Woodfield said he didn't know about Downs' statements about marrying him until a prison official told him

Woodfield tries to wiggle himself out of a whopper of a lie. Author collection.

All that backpedaling must have gotten Woodfield's legs in a tangle. After newspapers, Associated Press, UPI, radio and rival T.V. stories picked up this jail time drama, Woodfield's machinations had definitely run their course and then some.

Still the two manipulative killers kept on commiserating by mail through August, maybe beyond, although the tone of Diane's letters were rather frosty after Woodfield's deceit. For his part, Woodfield's interest waned, realizing he could no longer monetize his infamy, nor hers.

Part IV

Chapter 22
Girls Trip

By the late 1980's we thought all the Diane Downs news had been put to rest. Boy, were we wrong.

After *Small Sacrifices* came out in 1987, Ann and I spent some much-needed time away at my folks' beach cabin on the Oregon Coast. Lord knows, Ann needed a break. She was in between books, but already researching a twisted 1985 murder in Orange County about a man who coerced his fourteen-year-old daughter and another teenager (his secret lover and his wife's sister) to murder his twenty-three-year-old wife. Ann would attend the trial in 1990 and write *If You Really Loved Me* about David Arnold Brown, published in 1991. But that was yet to come, along with a mini-series on *Small Sacrifices.* I made a point not to talk about Ann's work on the trip, unless she felt like it, to give her some breathing space.

Ann drove from Seattle to meet me in Rockaway Beach, Oregon at the 1920's cabin my father rebuilt by hand, from scratch. We had the woodstove going to send the shivers away from overcast coastal skies.

I had arranged with my parents to have the beach cabin to ourselves, making sure they wouldn't be there. Ours was a girls' getaway to laugh and discuss our lives.

Everything was going as planned. We were sitting in the living room, enjoying the fire and our day together, watching the waves roll in.

All of a sudden, Ann thought she'd caught sight of a man looking into the cabin from outside. He must have walked up from the beach unnoticed? How was that possible?

Looking out the window, Ann said, "Anne, someone is WATCHING us!"

I thought it was a joke, but it wasn't like Ann to be paranoid. I looked out the front windows toward the beach and saw nothing.

Ann directed my gaze. "No, look over to the left. Over *there!"*

I laughed, thinking she was trying to scare me or something.

Scanning the scene right outside the cabin again, I did see something (well, I thought I saw something) move. "Wait!" I shouted. "I see the top of someone's head in the seagrass!"

I popped up and ran to the beachfront sliding glass door to see better.

Feeling protective, I wondered if someone had seen us walking on the beach and followed Ann here to menace her. I mean, maybe this was somebody she'd written about. Who the heck would do such a thing?

Only then did the stranger reveal himself.

For goodness sake, it was my *father!!!!*

My mom and dad were great fans of Ann's and I had no idea my father was at the coast. I didn't know where he was staying. The cabin was his pride and joy, which he'd happily relinquished to us, on this alone trip together.

Dad stood up, realizing we'd seen him. He didn't wave at us…until we waved "hello" to him.

Our eyes were saucers, our faces perplexed. What the heck?

Obviously, Dad wanted to meet this famous author. And *this is the way* he decided to approach us.

At the time, maybe I was coveting my time with Ann, maybe I was reluctant to share her attention, or maybe I was just peeved at my dad for not calling and just asking if he could stop by to meet her. I'm not sure, but thinking back now, I'd fall back on the latter.

After acknowledging his presence to us, he left. We saw his back to us, as he walked back down to the beach.

You know how you laugh after being frightened? Well, that's what we did. This scare was a source of hilarity to us. Ann started calling it the time when Anne's Dad was "skulking in the seagrass." Another round robin joke between us for decades.

As for my father? He never brought it up again. And I didn't tell him he scared the daylights out of us out there in the tall seagrass. I guess I didn't want to hurt his feelings that he hadn't been invited inside.

With the seagrass skulker behind us, we talked about following up that excitement, somehow, in that favorite sleepy little beach town. We cooked supper and spent the evening chortling about this and that. Mostly, THAT! Anne's dad "skulking in the seagrass."

The next day we decided to visit some small stores nearby. We wandered into what looked like an old church converted into an antique store in Garibaldi. We walked through saying to each other, "Hey, remember this, remember that?" Or "what is this, or that?"

This and that, we found, was great fun. Ann loved junking.

When we finally strolled to the back of the building, to what looked like an old stage for religious pageants perhaps, we hit pay dirt. Ann found some very old ephemera and started reading it aloud. Suddenly, we were transfixed, reading postcards between lovers and friends from long ago Christmas, New Years and Valentine's and every other day between about 1890 and 1900. What a rush. We even found a sequence of old cards between one young man and a "girl" he had eyes for. He sent her postcards with fantastic old fashioned, lovey dovey flourishes on the face, with short notes on the back. Heck, there wasn't much space left on the back of a postcard for a note *and* an address, right? And of course, norms of the day didn't condone romantic sentiments handwritten on the back anyway. A young man knew a postcard could be read by not only the town postman, but also her parents, which would spell disaster for any future he was planning.

We spent more than an hour reading the postcards back and forth to each other, when we finally picked up the final postcard. Ann read it to me, and it said something to the effect of,

Dear Constance Mae,

I'm sure you remember Betty Lou Who from high school. We are betrothed and will marry hence, this Saturday. I hope you will wish us both well.

Best Regards of the Day,
Fred

Ann and I were crestfallen. Together, we imagined Constance Mae reading this and falling henceforth onto her fainting couch, hand over forehead, crying. I think I even re-enacted the event for dramatic effect in my chair at the antique store.

Yes, perhaps, this was welcome news to Constance Mae, maybe she was glad to be rid of Fred, but we suspected the contrary, especially as wise older women believing we could read the tea leaves of more than a 100 years ago! And how dare Betty Lou Who, from high school!?

We bought a few postcards with fancy embellishments, but NEVER would we even consider buying anything from Fred! Posthaste or otherwise.

We were on team Constance Mae!

I treasure my memories of Ann that weekend, and she did too. Ten years after the trip, Ann sent me autographed my copy of *Every Breath You Take,* writing on her birthday in 2001:

October 22, 2001:
For Anne!
From your old postcard reading pal! Here's some diversion – six weeks before publication! (Don't tell!) Hang in there!
Much Love,
Ann Rule.

I relished the book as I recovered from a life-threatening cancer that year.

That weekend shows there was always fun to be had when spending time with Ms. Rule. I remember after post-carding, we were driving back to the cabin and stopped at a local small grocery with thick old wooden floors, to pick up a few supplies for dinner that night. "Smells kinda fishy in here," Ann said. "Real fishy, like…bad fish." I noticed it too, but we were at the beach after all, and seafood can smell, well, fishy. The two of us got what we came for. Then, at the last minute, I decided to buy some large tail shrimp on sale. I bought a pound, and in the grocery bag it went.

In the car, Ann started ribbing me, "It *stunk* like fish in there and YOU buy a pound of shrimp, *on sale?"*

This was a sidesplitter for the two of us. I cried laughing.

In rebuttal, I told her, the shrimp were part of my evil plan to poison her and dispose of her body at the beach. No one would be the wiser.

Then Ann said, "Well yesterday's plot with *that man* 'skulking in the seagrass' didn't work, so what makes you think seafood poisoning will?"

Chapter 23
Quiet On The Set

In 1989, I went to the movie set of *Small Sacrifices* in Edmonton, Canada. Ann had been there since the production started. I was there to play myself, Anne Bradley Jaeger, in the movie. I was excited by the new adventure, but I didn't want to, or never could be, an actress. I love the immediacy and research of reporting. Acting requires different skills.

Farrah Fawcett and me outside the star's trailer on the movie set. Courtesy of Leslie Rule.

My goodness, there was a problem I discovered with the movie camera's rolling: I was all ready to go with my Best Actress stuff on the first take, but my stamina for the film business waned after that. Whether the error was self-inflicted or due to other players in a scene, the more rehearsals we did, the less interested I became, and every take had to look like the first one.

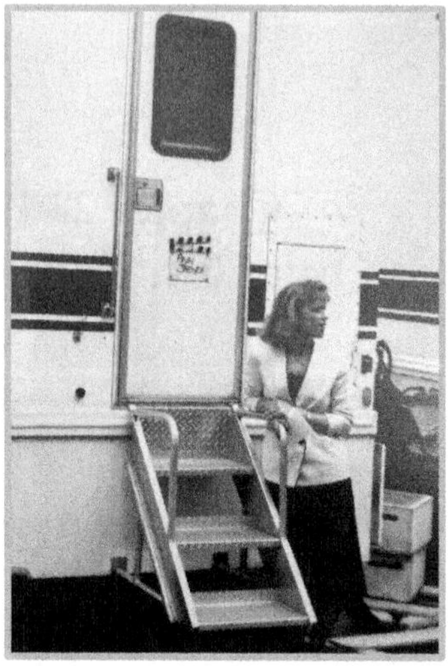

Me outside my very own trailer on the set of Small Sacrifices.

Circling back, right after my flight touched down on my first day, Ann met me at the sound stage before our dinner together. She wanted to show me something.

We walked to the back of an enormous dark sound stage together.

At first, I couldn't make sense of it. There was a red Nissan (like the one Diane Downs owned) hidden in a swampy scene with camouflage netting hanging from the ceiling like long tendrils. Imagine going through a dark car wash at night with its fabric enveloping your car and you're almost there.

"This is what I wanted you to see," Ann said.

I think there were bloody handprints on the rear window, too. I almost fainted.

I had asked Ann for secrecy about my old nightmare, but never thought about it after that. She had called me some time later, asking if she could tell Joyce Eliason (the award-winning screenwriter) about my dream. I hesitantly gave the okay, thinking, how could *that* ever make it into this movie script? Later, Eliason would win a Peabody award for her work on *Small Sacrifices.*

I didn't know, until Ann had the kindness to tell me that afternoon on the set, that the director, David Greene, planned on shooting the nightmare sequence that night.

Looking at the car, I didn't think I could live through seeing my nightmare brought to life.

"Oh Ann," I said. "I don't know what to say, this really bothers me, it makes me seem....well...crazy, unhinged." I worried about my reputation as a journalist.

Today, reporters and anchors openly acknowledge mental struggles publicly, especially after the COVID-19 pandemic. But that's not what we did back then.

She calmed me and said, "I'll get the scene taken out."

And she did. I'm still grateful for her sensitivity and kindness.

Ann watching her book Small Sacrifices made into a two part television movie. Photo Credit: Leslie Rule.

Ann held tremendous sway. She was a true crime authority in Hollywood and had spent a long stint there writing screenplays early in her career. Eventually, she bowed out of the screenplay business and went home to Seattle to write more books, because she was worried about the toll it was taking on her family. Her two sons were teenagers and she told me she missed them too much to continue in a "dead-end job," as she called it, facetiously. Swifty Lazar, the Hollywood agent for Cary Grant,

Ernest Hemingway, Madonna and Richard Nixon, represented Ann Rule at that time.

Watching *Small Sacrifices* on repeat frequently on cable, I don't know how I would have handled the bloody car scene, if it had been filmed. I'm still glad my nightmare wasn't included, but today, I'd probably face it quite differently. It took years to soothe the sting of conflict after my bedroom/Downs' car window broke. Ann empathized with that.

I do, however, have many very good memories of my experience playing myself in the four hour television miniseries, despite the subject matter. One of my favorites was seeing Ann Rule in her tall director's chair with her name on the back, the Hollywood stars paying deference to her.

Farrah and Ann share a laugh in-between shooting movie scenes on the Small Sacrifices *set. Photo Credit: Leslie Rule.*

I met Farrah Fawcett, who played Diane, Farrah's parents and her son Redmond, then a young redheaded child, during the filming. Farrah's parents sat in on the courtroom scenes, watching their daughter in action. Her dad, Jim, was a tall Texan and her mother, Pauline, a beautiful southern belle even late in life. Fawcett got her great looks from her mama, as they say in the South.

I wrote in my 1989 reporter's notebook about what was happening on the set:

1st glimpse of Farrah is scene confronting the prosecutor about the guard at her daughters' hospital door. FF playing the part w/a Texas accent. Shocked at first – since Diane is always so conscious of diction and has no drawl. But the more we listen… the more we become accustomed to this portrayal. (The "we" is Ann, me, two of her adult children and a few of her close friends.)

I wrote of a transformation I was witnessing on set: *FF does a chilling job of becoming Diane. Needy, then diabolically manipulative.*

Some days, Farrah felt ill on the set but worked anyway.

I wrote in my notepad: *Maybe FF is not leaving Diane 'at the office?' Is Diane taking her toll on Farrah now too? Just as DD troubles us… her actions/words must disturb FF.*

FF sick today. Unknown illness…but she is visibly upset. (We wouldn't find out what was bothering Mary Ferrah Leni Fawcett until a decade later when she died of colon cancer.)

For her role as Diane Downs, Fawcett would garner her second Emmy and sixth Golden Globe nominations. *FF is nervous when Ann Rule is around while she's acting. What actress wouldn't be? Not because of Ann…but because Ann WROTE THIS. It is through her that FF is getting in touch w/her character. (Some lines are right out of my doc!) And, what if the author doesn't agree with the portrayal? Ann is tickled with FF ability. But, Farrah doesn't know that yet.*

I also watched Ryan O'Neal, her partner, coaching her off set:

Ryan concentrates on her lines…

-listening at sidelines or w/earphones.

-he gestures w/hands in circular motion to himself when he thinks she should hurry up delivering her lines."

Farrah and her partner Ryan O'Neil, who played Downs' boyfriend Robert Knickerbocker in Small Sacrifices, *in a publicity photo.*

Farrah, quite to my surprise, called for me in her trailer one day. She asked about one particular event during Downs' trial. It was a jaw-dropping moment, true to life, when Downs was listening to the song "Hungry Like the Wolf" by Duran Duran which was being played loudly in the courtroom for jurors. The night of the murderous shootings on May 19th, 1983, this music played while her children were shot on that lonely country road. Her eldest daughter Christie testified the music was on when she was shot. The song, the prosecutor demonstrates, *could not have been* playing in her car tape deck *unless the engine was running*. IF Downs' keys were outside the car—with an unknown assailant trying to grab them, the music would not play. This proved Diane was not playing keep away with the keys as she claimed, because the stereo was playing as she reached inside the car and started firing again and again.

In the real courtroom in Eugene, jurors and the rest of the gallery were stunned seeing Downs actually enjoy the music in 1984; kicking her crossed knee up and down to the beat, her head bobbing side-to-side, back and forward. It was, hands down, one of the most bizarre, frightening things I'd ever seen in court. The jury looked baffled and perplexed too.

How did Downs explain her strange reaction? She said on the witness stand that she loved the song and it didn't hold any bad memories for her. Another lack-of-empathy headshaker.

When Farrah Fawcett took me to her trailer on the movie set, she wanted to understand Downs' body movements exactly. I sat down on one of the kitchen benches inside the star's motorhome to show her. She studied my movements, then asked me to do it again. She got it, quick. As an actress, she nailed it during the movie courtroom sequence. The jurors' reactions were spot on too.

Fawcett was also interested in how Downs spent her time in court at the defense table. I explained that she doodled on an 8.5x11" notepad. The actress wanted to see what I meant. I scribbled what I'd seen Downs draw as I sat behind her in trial. Downs sketched what looked like large veins, but without a human body, then very slowly morphed into a barren tree. Farrah put that to use, too, in the movie courtroom.

For my insights, Farrah Fawcett sent me one of her signed and framed hand-done lithographs of two faces facing opposite directions, which if studied long enough became three faces. Beautiful. Fawcett was a good artist. Was it the three faces of Diane?

Farrah's artwork for me, signed "Anne, For Your Support, With Love" Author collection.

I wrote Fawcett a thank you note for the hand-painted picture and sent her a copy of my Downs documentary. *Much of this was used in the book and screenplay,* I said in my note. *But you know what? You really don't need this, except maybe as a reality check, because* you *are right on target. I'm proud of the way you're portraying Diane. She doesn't deserve someone as good as you, but the movie does. Sincerely, Anne.*

In my reporter's notebook I also kept notes on various flotsam and jetsam around me, including Farrah's likes and dislikes. She ate oat bran cereal cold or McCann's Quick Irish oatmeal with 2% milk, a splash of pure maple syrup, dried apricots, with a wee bit of fruit sweetened peach yogurt on the side. My notebook said this woman drank papaya, fresh orange or cranberry juice, or Tetley decaf tea. For a snack, she had a few almonds, fresh fruit (no apples) and Quaker Rice Cakes with organic peanut butter. She'd eat chicken or tuna for dinner and drank lots and lots of Evian water throughout the day. I ate less than that and gained weight! Sure, it was ridiculous what reporters notice, but we never know what information the anchors back home will ask us about on the air!

I flew back and forth from Edmonton, Canada, where my cousin Diane Hutchinson lived, five separate times, a total of 10 days, in between working full time at KGW-TV in Portland, Oregon on the night shift 2:30 p.m.-11:30 p.m. (One of my first stories at the station was interviewing a woman with a pet possum in her home. I enjoyed the story until the lady fed the possum cheese right out of her mouth. Ewwww. I also reported on a story about car hubcaps. I suspected the "earning respect" curve was going to be a steep one at KGW.)

On one of my trips north, my mother came to watch the production. There was a very strict code on the movie set: No cameras and no photography. My mom smuggled a camera into the movie courtroom scene, well, not so much *smuggling* —she *forgot* it was in her purse. No sooner had the director called *action* for the scene where Farrah testified as Diane Downs on the witness stand, one of the most important scenes in the movie, when Mom's camera started rewinding its film loudly and automatically inside her bag. When Mom opened her purse and tried to stop it, the noise only got louder!

"CUT!" the director, the talented David Greene called. He looked at the gallery, clearly angry.

He heard the whirring from my mom's camera on Farrah's mic!

I looked behind me, where my mum was pretending to be a courtroom watcher and she was snickering in embarrassment. Everyone looked at her. Seeing her, I laughed. Now, we were both in trouble. It was then that I got the opportunity to introduce my own mother to the director, in hopes we both wouldn't get thrown out on our *keisters,* as they said in her time.

The next day, my poor mother almost got 86'd from the craft services table, the yummy place feeding the stars and crew on set. The food was so good that Ann and I were both gaining a few pounds. I happened to be close by when I noticed a ruckus, and walked over. The catering manager thought Mom was an extra trying to get free food. We made apologies all around and I think my mum (as they said in Canada, where the movie was being filmed) might have been just a little bit proud to be able to eat fresh berries and half a waffle with yogurt and nuts where her daughter was filming a movie.

Among other good memories are the dinners in Edmonton. On the second night during my first trip north, Ann, Leslie and I were invited to John Shea's hotel room for a private dinner. Shea was starring as Downs' prosecutor. He wanted to know all the mannerisms of the man he was playing. Leslie, Ann and I filled him in. Shea later had a five-year run on Gossip Girl, and then for 10 episodes of Agent X with Sharon Stone.

Me with actor John Shea talking about the next movie scene.

In my notebook I wrote: *Shea is a doting host. Jumps up and down to refill refreshments. He's fun. Serious about his work. Down to earth. Artsy person. Especially interested in Leslie Rule's courtroom observation of prosecutor "standing behind prosecution table, leaning forward, or rocking side to side with straight arms and fists resting on knuckles" just like Fred Hugi.*

The largest dinner crowd during one of my trips gathered executive producers, producers, the director, and president of Motown Productions—Suzanne de Passe, Ann, Leslie and me. This was a lively group of people, with decades of experience in entertainment. The banter was fascinating.

I was especially thrilled to meet de Passe, knowing she was Barry Gordy's creative assistant at Motown Records— she styled the Jackson 5's wardrobe and accompanied the band on the road. This Harlem-raised woman was legendary then and she's now President of de Passe Entertainment. I got to ask all my *pressing* questions about the J5. It was so enthralling that I didn't even take notes. Imagine me, no notes!

After long days shooting on set, Ann watched what the movie industry called the "dailies." These were the director's and photographer's favorite scenes they'd use in the editor's final cut. I accompanied Ann one day, wanting to see how the movie industry did this, because as a reporter, I time-coded and chose shots for my stories too.

The movie honchos were pleased by what they saw in the dailies, checking sound, lighting, and the best shots for actors. Ann enjoyed watching, but I wouldn't go back on days I'd acted, as I was critical of my own work, always thinking of all sorts of ways I might have done it better. This was fruitless since the shots were already in the can —there were no do-overs!

Small Sacrifices was the first of Ann's books made into a television series, an experience she quickly parlayed into executive producer credits for other movies.

Rule's writing stands the test of time, which leaves room for the *possibility* that other books could come to the screen, works that put you in the same room with murderers as their crimes unfold.

Chapter 24
Sitting With Killers

Ann wrote The *Stranger Beside Me* thinking she'd answer all the readers' questions about Ted Bundy and she wouldn't have to talk about him again. As time wore on, though, Ann found out she'd never really be free of him. As she told the Poisoned Pen Press in 2007, "I'll be in the home for old ladies and people will still ask me 'What was Ted Bundy really like?'"

I'm often asked the same thing about Diane Downs.

Have *you* ever wondered what it's like being in the same room with a killer? What would you say, if you could find your tongue, and how would you go about getting real answers for parents and survivors, viewers or readers when the criminal already knows the likely questions? Ann Rule knew this before she signed her book contracts. She didn't personally interview all the killers she wrote about. Rule knew there wasn't going to be that Perry Mason moment when the murder suddenly confessed to her in private, "Alright. Alright. I did it! I did it all!!!"

Ann wrote with the authority of already having investigators' notes, forensic files, and the testimony of scores of witnesses testifying in court right in front of her. Ann did her homework, attended trials, talked to families, and followed up leads on her own.

Rule did talk to Diane in the Lane County jail after sentencing and left within about twenty minutes, after realizing Downs would never tell the truth. Killers tell you what they want you to know, seeing you as just another ignoramus to publicize their threadbare story of innocence. She'd already sat through three-days of Diane's testimony in trial. Ann's jail interview went nowhere, so she left. Ann had trial transcripts of

Downs' testimony and my special report to rely on.

If you're going to be in the same room with a killer, you need to understand before going in, these people operate in an alternate universe. What comes out of their mouths is downright strange. Their view of the world is startling, to say the least, about even the most ordinary of thoughts or events. Your very human reaction could set them off, end the interview or piss them off.

Also, prepare yourself, because you're going to get an earful if you sit with Diane Downs. More than that, you're going to have to feel safe in a room with a sickly swirl around you. To do this interview right, you need to divest yourself from what you feel and concentrate on the facts.

Downs' aura permeates a room, *that* I can tell you. I've felt it every time. And so do others.

When Janice Salvador, the TV news producer, told us she was frightened meeting Downs the day of our interview in 1983, she hadn't just psyched herself out. I *do* know, all too well, what Janice was talking about. The strange *feeling* she got sitting alone in the newsroom with Diane. To keep from getting up and running out, you needed to deny an evil magnetic pull around Downs.

And then there was Gary Kahne, the photographer who shot the 1983 documentary. He knew a lot about empathy and death. He almost died in Vietnam, shot in the left leg by accident in friendly fire along the demilitarized zone. Gary limps sometimes. Honestly, after watching him pull up his socks one day, and I saw his lower leg, it was amazing he could walk. There was so little muscle left. "My foot was hanging at 90 degrees," Gary told me when I interviewed him for this book. "The tibia and fibula stuck straight out of the hole."

As his leg gushed blood, Gary tied his own tourniquet with his belt to save his life. He had watched many of his buddies die horrible deaths. At those times, he stood over them, worrying about families back home.

That's the kind of photographer you want in the room when you have absolutely NO IDEA what might happen with an unpredictable woman.

Seeing our documentary in its entirety for the first time

in forty-one years, Gary said, "Everything you got her to reveal shows the depth of her goddamn mental illness. She is a walking mental disorder, there's no question about it."

"Honestly, she's very personable," he said. "I felt like she was charming. I really did. And she wasn't stupid. She's very articulate." Diane played the room: A diagnosed antisocial/sociopath at work. Then, there's that sickening closing shot.

Did Diane smile? Or smirk after my last question?

Her expression came a heartbeat after saying, "The thing that really, really haunts me the most is not even the sight and the sound…But at night when I close my eyes I can see Christie reaching her hand out…and the blood just keeps coming out of her mouth"

And I told her, "I feel sick," which was my gut reaction to what I'd just heard. Would the average mother smile? Or did Diane smirk thinking "Reporter lady, you don't know the half of it"?

What did Kahne see or feel?

In retrospect, Kahne saw it as a smile of success: satisfied that she'd convinced me, and anyone watching – the people of Eugene and Springfield – and the District Attorney, of her lies.

Diagnosed with histrionic personality disorder, which quite simply means theatrical or dramatic to the overt extreme, Downs' responses came out of nowhere, expressing strong emotions in rapid fire. She claimed a strange man flagged down her car.

"When this man shot my daughter, my first reaction was to snap back to my childhood, to the pain that happened back then, my marriage, my entrapment by society, this man was bigger than me, he was stronger than me, he had more power because he had a gun," Downs said in our interview. "He was in control and I was not. There was nothing I could do and I stood there and I look at Christie reaching and the blood that just kept gushing out of her mouth and, what do you do? You just stand there trapped and then the gun kept firing and firing and firing…It was monotonous. It just kept going. It was like a slow-motion picture."

These were pure rehearsed theatrics told from a shooter's

perspective. We, the viewers, might have expected a woman, a mother, to snap into Momma Bear mode and fight like hell to save her children or die trying. Or at least give up her car to save her babies. But her histrionic behavior turned the shootings of three children into a soliloquy about herself. The words were difficult to make peace with. We witnessed an egocentric woman, searching for appreciation. So, yes, Downs was well spoken, theatrical to the point of histrionics.

Fewer than 2% of the population are histrionic. Like Downs, more women than men are diagnosed with this. Symptoms start showing by the time they're fifteen years old and last a lifetime. This was a hot brew waiting to happen by Diane's mid-20's, when the shots ricocheted around her car.

Ann Rule gave us the telltale signs of extreme histrionics and narcissism. "Diane takes what Diane wants, and she has demonstrated she will do whatever it takes to get what she wants," as she told KGW's Claudia Brown in an interview after Rule finished *Small Sacrifices.*

Another hallmark of Downs' disorder was manipulation. And as Ann wrote in her book, Downs certainly manipulated many people and situations to get her own way. The prosecution made a strong case for the motive that she needed to be free of her children *and* as I see it, get enough sympathy from her former lover to win him back. The lover was long done with Diane.

Gary, who had witnessed dozens of fellow Marines killed with semi-automatic weapons much larger than what Diane used, had a two word opinion for her explanation of high velocity spatter. He didn't believe a word Downs was saying at the time.

Gary walked away from our interview with Downs and said afterward to our News Director: "She's dirty."

Meaning: Downs did it.

Downs' antisocial diagnosis, which used to be called sociopathic, was another warning beacon on clear display in the interview. Her complete lack of empathy with no remorse was chilling:

"Everybody says 'You sure were lucky.' Well, I don't feel very lucky, I couldn't tie my shoe for about two months." She laughed. "It is very painful…If I'd been shot the way they were, we all would have died."

This was especially galling to Gary, knowing what it was like to be shot, even by accidental fire,

"Every time I hear that I just cringe, man," he said to me. "One kid is dead, one is paralyzed, and the other is critically wounded and you're worried about your fucking arm? Are you kidding me?"

As *you* know now, their pain was incidental to hers. A sign of antisocial and narcissistic behavior.

Most people have an instant reaction to Downs' words. They recognize the absurdity. Some people, well, they just don't. They know it sounds wrong, but not sure why, exactly. I've often tried, intellectually, to pinpoint how this lack of concern is so out of step with our behaviors at home when we empathize with the people we care about.

According to the experts, children like Downs usually exhibit their manipulative antisocial behaviors by the time they're eleven, right along with the lying, and constant overstepping of boundaries. Up to four percent of the population, mostly men, are diagnosed with the calculatingly disordered mind of an antisocial/sociopath. The National Institute of Health says family studies show 20% of these people have a close relative with the same disorder. Flashback to Downs' father, Wes Frederickson?

In the interview, Downs talked about how easy it was for her to get pregnant: two births, a surrogate child, her now-paralyzed son Danny was the result of an affair, and the baby she carried through trial. Gary described her explanation with his observation, "She wanted you to believe she is so into the creation of a child, and nurturing a child that she would be above any kind of a criminal act against a child."

Even though Gary and I worked together during his thirty-five years in television news, we never actually *talked* about our shared experience until recently, which may be strange to some of you. Once in a while when Downs' name would come up, we'd give each other a pensive, knowing look, and then keep on moving. That's just the nature of news and news people until we get older and start sharing *what-happened-when*, like old farts.

I found it heartwarming and so great talking to Gary about everything. He's been out of the biz for awhile, and we've both had time to reflect. He encapsulated the whole Diane Downs experience this way: "It's one of the most infamous murders in Oregon history. It resonated with people across the entire country. This was the biggest story I've ever worked on. And I was glad to be a part of it." Although Gary never got his due for bringing this piece of history to life and showing Diane Downs as she really was, the pictures and sound wouldn't exist without his expertise.

In 1994, almost a decade after Downs' conviction, I was working at KGW in Portland, Oregon with photographer Brian Robertson. We traveled to the nation's largest women's prison in Chowchilla, California to interview Diane. We're here to compare her crime with the then-recent case of Susan Smith, who murdered her two young boys by drowning them in a South Carolina lake.

I saw striking similarities between the two crimes. Both women:

- Were in their twenties when the crimes occurred.
- Took their vengeance out on children.
- Trapped children in cars to commit murder.
- Blamed their crimes on an unknown assailant trying to carjack them.
- Were rejected by lovers who didn't want children.

Brian, the very seasoned photographer I was with on the trip, didn't cover Downs' trial, conviction, nor sentencing in the 80's, so he knew only the hits, runs and errors. After our flight to California, Brian wanted to know what to expect when he met her. As we were driving to the prison, I suggested, "No matter what you may think, or what she says, or does, *do not* react."

"No problem," he said. The interview was not his first rodeo with a killer!

When we walked into the room where Diane was already seated at a table, I said hello to her, turned my head toward Brian (walking a half step behind me to my right) as I started to introduce them.

Diane had not moved, but, not only was Robertson *stopping* in his tracks, he actually JUMPED in the air. His feet left the ground. The metal light kit jangled loudly in the carrying case. Brian eyed Downs like he'd seen a ghost, transfixed.

I ignored him, and carried the tripod toward our subject, trying to block her view of him. We all laughed nervously. She had aged noticeably since I'd last seen her. Downs was wearing a cotton knee-length duster, a house coat women used to wear to do housework, hemmed up to look rather spicy above the knee. I saw hairs growing above her upper lip, and a bit longer from her chin. I immediately thought of her mother, Willadene, who had the same facial hair years ago, much longer and more plentiful, than Downs'.

Diane Downs in 1994, during our first interview in more than a decade. Courtesy of KGW/Tegna.

On that day, when I was interviewing her, it was almost eleven years after her crimes and Downs still couldn't be honest about the possible ties between her case and Susan Smith's.

"A man attacked me and my children and he has confessed," Downs said to us. "Susan Smith drowned her children and she confessed. I don't see any parallels to that."

To be clear, nobody confessed to killing and shooting

Diane's children. Period. Ever. Her trademark personality disorders were on parade again.

"What was her reaction to Susan Smith's children, [ages three years and fourteen months,] dying, gulping in water?" I asked her.

"I had no reaction. It wasn't part of my life," she said.

No empathy.

What came next was the first time in my career I openly veered off the facts and gave my honest reaction as a mother. I had a toddler at home.

"Diane, I was sick to my stomach," I said. "I cried and I didn't even know these children and you had no reaction? You *had* to have a reaction?"

Diane answered, "Let's put it this way; I had no reaction that I'm going to give *for you*."

The interview got rather testy then as I again brought up the blood spatter outside the car from Cheryl's murder. Would she finally come clean? I mean, here was the evidence again that disproved her story, evidence that she'd had a decade to confront, process, perhaps come to terms with. I asked her about this again.

In the 1983 interview, Downs had said, "It's when they picked the kids up and carried them over the threshold, there is blood dripping down the side of the car."

And here's what Downs said the day we interviewed her again in '94. "That came from the sweater that was draped over Cheryl…The sleeve dropped down and flung *blood up under* the car."

Downs didn't want to look at Cheryl dead in the car, so she hid the child's bleeding body from sight with her postal work sweater.

"Okay, well, let me refresh your memory back ten years ago," I said. "You said at the hospital 'it's when they picked the kids up and carried them over the threshold; there is blood dripping down the side of the car.' You don't talk about any of *these factors*."

Downs said, "I agree."

Agreed, but never conceded.

We left after seeing Downs handcuffed again, walking

down the hallway to her cell. Brian witnessed her making fun of a guard for allegedly being gay or lesbian. Remarks that didn't go over very well. As an openly gay man, he never forgot the flirtatious looks she gave him during our interview, thinking he was a man to win over. Today, Brian tells me he thought at the time, "Honey…I'm on the wrong team."

In the car on the way back to the station, I ribbed Brian about "not reacting to anything Downs' does." She hadn't moved or even so much as twitched when he saw her and jumped.

Brian then explained his leaping lizard reaction. As a photographer, he had covered wars in Kosovo and Iraq, was at 9/11 for the collapse of World Trade Center, in San Francisco for the earthquake. So you know, Brian had seen some pretty bad things, but said *Downs* was something new and raw for him. "I've never felt like I was in the presence of absolute pure evil," he said. "Like a cloud, or like a spirit, or something around her, it was almost visual to me."

I understood then, what he was getting at. I've always felt a low vibration in her presence, sensing a strong, malignant aura that made hair stand on the nape of your neck. Robertson said, "There was something that frightened me. That sounds absolutely insane, but the whole room felt like there was another entity…something that was giving off this sense of evilness and bad. That's all I can say. That's what I remember."

After the story aired back home, and we were back at the station, Robertson told his fellow photographers about the experience. "I told everybody," he said. "I grew up in a traditional Lutheran Christian community. We talked about evil and Satan but I never knew it was real until looking in Downs' soulless eyes." Until then, he said, "I don't think I really believed in evil."

If this has been the reaction of all these professionals who met Downs, who have forty plus years on their timecards, imagine trying not to jump yourself when meeting her?

That's what it's like sitting with killers.

Part V

Chapter 25
Stalked by Killers

Writing books about killers was dangerous. Fellow true crime author Kathryn Casey and Ann also talked about the fact that what they did could be a little scary at times. Casey remembered Ann once talking about the FBI visiting her because a prisoner Ann wrote about was trying to hire a hitman on the outside to go after her. "We had quite a long talk that day on the phone," Casey told me. "You know, she was concerned, but not afraid." The FBI got wind of the plot and foiled the plan.

Killers were known for keeping tabs on Ann. It took two decades to unravel the Green River Killer serial murders in Washington and Oregon. Some bodies weren't too far from Ann's Seattle home, one was close to mine. Ann's investigative work in *Green River, Running Red* followed the nation's second most prolific killer. Gary Ridgway murdered forty-nine female victims, revisiting their bodies to sexually abuse them postmortem. Ridgway said in court documents that he killed so many women, he lost count.

While he was still hiding in plain sight, still hunting women in the 1980's and 1990's, he paid at least two very public visits to Ann. It was well known that Ann had a long-standing contract to write *Green River, Running Red* long before the serial killer was caught, similar to *Stranger Beside Me.* According to Casey, when Ridgway was arrested, with his face splashed across newspapers and television screens nationwide, everyone finally knew what the Green River killer looked like. With the mask pulled off, Ann started putting the pieces together."I remember her talking about it," Casey told me. "I remember the day she called me, saying 'Kathryn, I knew this guy. I knew him the minute I saw him'" on the news.

Ann's daughter Leslie was first to notice Ridgway as a man who came to Ann's public appearances, never bought a book, but he just sat and watched her. Rule later found out from detective files from the prosecutor that Ridgway was even mentioning her *by name* to investigators during interrogations. This really upset her during the writing process, especially when she heard him say that he read Ann Rule books because he wanted to know how to act in trial if he ever got caught. Ann said it was plausible Ridgway stood near her in a grocery store line or sat in a nearby booth at a restaurant. A case of a killer and an author researching each other at the very same time.

It was too close for anyone's comfort, said Casey. He wasn't the kind of true crime fan either of them wanted, nor encouraged. But Ridgway, and other psychopaths, have an outrageous need for anti-social stimulation, their arrogance and narcissism drive them to take more and more risks to control women, or feel superior to authors and investigators tracking them. Casey said she jealously guards her privacy for this reason, not giving details about her family and location.

Ann and I both had a minor dust up with Bradly Cunningham, the *Dead By Sunset* killer. Even after being convicted of murder and serving a life sentence in the Oregon State Pen for the death of his estranged wife—who was found dead in her car on Sunset Highway in Portland, Oregon—Cunningham still professed his innocence.

The palatial home featured in the 1995 television miniseries based on Ann's book on Cunningham was less than a mile from my home. I visited Ann on the set a few times, her name even more prominent on a new director's chair! It was always a thrill to see Ann getting her much-deserved recognition.

Seeking appeal of his conviction, Cunningham called me at KGW-TV, asking me to do a story about how he was railroaded. "Send me your information, and I'll read it front to back," I told him. "But I can't promise you a news story."

The fat manilla envelope arrived a week later. I read through it, and left it on my desk for future reference, then forgot about it.

Finally, Brad Cunningham called back late one afternoon, nice and polite, asking me to take up his cause.

"I can't do that, Mr. Cunningham," I said.

"*Why*?" His tone started escalating.

"I've read your filing for appeal and the other documents professing your innocence, and I'm sorry to say I am not interested."

He was pretty mad by this point. "It's all there! I didn't kill Cheryl [Keeton] and I need people to see my case for what it really is! And you won't even do a news story about it?"

"I can't," I said.

"WHY!?"

"Mr. Cunningham, I see absolutely nothing *new* here."

I didn't tell anyone at the station about my phone calls with the ruthless killer, and I didn't pass on his high volume pleadings to anyone else either. He later lost his appeals.

After the newscast that day, I called Ann. "Hey, had a very unpleasant call from Cunningham today. He wants a news story about his appeal."

"Oh yeah?" Ann said. "He called me today too!" The antisocial, paranoid and narcissistic sociopath often called her from prison even after threatening to sue Ann's book publisher.

"What'd he call about?" I asked. Wondering why the killer who'd maligned her work in interviews would then turn around and call her?

Ann said that Cunningham called for help on his appeal, then started railing at her about some KGW reporter, whom he doesn't name, that wouldn't even give him the time of day either.

The light bulb goes off in Ann's head.

"OH! You must be talking about my friend, Anne Jaeger!" she said to him.

We laughed, realizing we'd both turned down the same man.

The two of us hadn't spoken about Cunningham calling before, nor mentioned the packet of information he was sending me. But Ann *knew* by his explanation of "that *bitch* in Portland" that Brad Cunningham was talking about me.

We chuckled about sharing the same killers, yet again.

Chapter 26
Escaping the Truth

Any news of Diane Downs had faded by 1987. She was locked away in Salem, an afterthought to the public. That is, until shocking news came that summer. I was at home in Eugene on a Saturday afternoon, hoping to visit my parents in Portland that day. Packing up to leave, I got an unbelievable call from my station.

I instantly made two calls.

One was to Ann. "Diane Downs escaped from prison, Ann!"

"*What?* No! How?" Ann said. "Are you sure? How'd she get out?"

I explained what our assignment editor had told me. "It's all over the police scanner, every cop in the state knows, they're searching for her now." My heart was racing at the possibilities, thinking of the consequences Downs' escape might have on her surviving children. My station was worrying about this too. As I said, Ann was my second call. We shared the stunned disbelief about the breaking news.

My first call before Ann, came without hesitation. I spoke with less emotion, was far more straightforward and professional.

I knew that the most important phone call I could make after getting the news was to the prosecuting attorney, Fred Hugi, who had adopted Downs' surviving children.

During the trial, I had become more acquainted with Fred Hugi, and found him to be a great trial attorney and human being. I think it was his first murder case- a whopper. Hugi and his wife Joanne adopted Danny and Christie to keep them safe and together in their rural home on the McKenzie River, outside Springfield. Without the Hugis, the kids likely would have been adopted into separate homes, because a traumatized girl and a paralyzed boy would have been a lot for most adoptive parents. The Hugis could not stand the thought of splitting them up after what they'd been through. Hugi was a man of deep conviction; having never been a father, he and his wife welcomed them gladly.

During the trial, I sat with Fred on a bench outside the courthouse a couple of times and shot the breeze. We never talked about the kids, the trial or Downs. I admired his intensity, his self-sealed thoughts, and his integrity: the way he put his case together, how he hammered at Diane's inconsistencies on the witness stand for days and the professional but kind way he spoke to frightened Christie Downs on the stand. He had a touch. Many people, including his co-workers, thought of him as a curmudgeon, cranky, and dismissive. I never did, I saw a genuinely nice reserved person.

At trial, Hugi plodded slowly toward gut-wrenching territory with 9-year-old Christie on the witness stand. He was able to elicit answers so disturbing that I ran to the restroom, and vomited, after seeing this nervous little girl, sitting across from her mother, bravely reply to Hugi's question, "Who shot you?"

"My mom," Christie said.

On the day Downs escaped from prison, after the newsroom called me, I gulped hard knowing that I needed to call Fred Hugi and make sure he had heard what happened. Kooky as Downs seemed, she might have been on her way to Hugi's house for the children. If she'd caught a ride in Salem she'd be there in an hour and thirty minutes.

Hugi's number was unpublished, but I had it, never crossing the privacy boundary.

"Hi Fred, this is Anne Jaeger," I said. "I'm so sorry to bother you at home, but I knew you'd want to know: Diane Downs escaped from prison minutes ago."

There was silence.

I thought Fred was about to hang up.

"Fred?" I said.

I was wondering — was he absorbing the information? Would he hear me out? Or slam the receiver down?

Hugi piped up and got right to the point. He wasn't angry at all.

"I'm sure she's still inside," he said quietly. "What information do you have?"

By law, relatives were supposed to receive first notification of any event threatening victims' lives. This was definitely a threat to their safety.

Fred had not been alerted.

"I'm sorry Fred, but the search is all over the scanners and cops are using her NAME *openly*."

He thanked me. We hung up. My stomach was in knots, imagining the worst possibilities.

Calling the station right back, and making sure my phone call with Hugi would not be used in any story, I told them Hugi thought it was a false alarm. I found out the station hadn't called pumping me for info about Hugi anyway, my colleagues were genuinely worried about his children's safety too.

By now, the assignment editor had already rerouted the weekend reporter to Salem and found out the prison did an inmate count and thought Downs *was* in her room the whole time.

On the second count, however, Diane was nowhere to be found.

She had scaled the eighteen foot fence in the recreation yard, using the same blouse she wore in our interview to hold the razor wire away from gouging slices through her skin, as she alley-ooped to freedom.

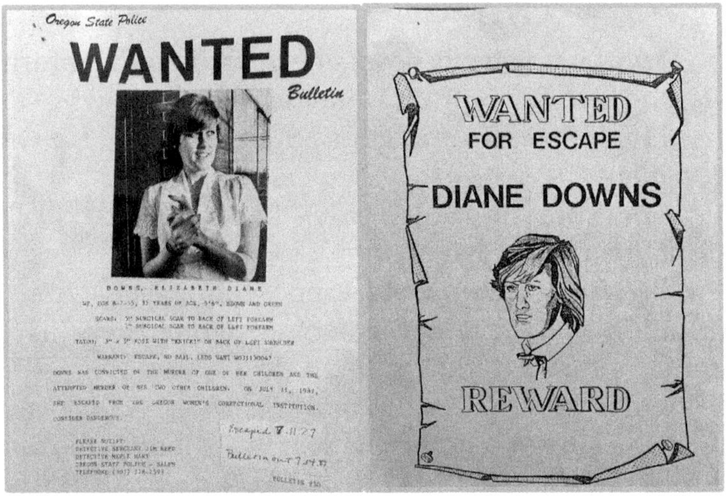

Oregon State Police Wanted bulletin during Diane Downs' escape in 1987. An artist also made a reward poster at the same time. Author collection.

A few minutes later, to my surprise, Fred Hugi called me back, "Yeah, Anne, the prison did a count and she was accounted for."

"Fred, we heard about that," I said. "But the first count was wrong. She's been out for about forty-five minutes, maybe longer." If determined, Downs might be on his doorstep soon.

That was the last time I ever spoke to Fred Hugi.

In *Small Sacrifices,* Ann wrote that Hugi sat in a chair with a shotgun on his lap until Diane was captured ten days later about a mile from the prison. She was living with another inmate's husband. He said Downs showed up at his door naked, so he let her in. They had sex and she never left.

After Downs' arrest, Ann Rule sent me flowers for my birthday with a note that said, "I arranged for Diane's capture for your birthday. But, hey! Here are some flowers too! Love, "The Real Ann."

The two of us were thinking that would be the last time Diane would bask in the national spotlight. She was in solitary confinement and transferred from the West to the East Coast. But she popped up the very next year on the Oprah Winfrey show! This time, live by satellite, from prison! Ann's book had just been published and Oprah flew her to Chicago for the program. Ann was wearing a turquoise dress with cheetah shaped dots (animal prints were in that year) and sat in a prominent spot on the set to the left of the beautiful Oprah, whose hair and earrings were big (it *was* the late 1980's). Diane appeared on a television monitor wedged squarely between them. The scene was incredible. Downs talked a blue streak, was well-spoken, smug, argumentative and interrupted Ann constantly. Ann played it cool, allowing the audience to take in the full measure of Diane's strange comments.

"A lot of people don't understand how a mother could stand by and *watch* her three children shot without being hysterical?" Oprah asked.

"Well, it wasn't like going to the baseball field and having popcorn and hot dogs," according to Diane.

The audience murmured, not knowing what to make of the woman. Downs then changed her well-worn story (that she'd told for five years) to claim she had *no memory* of the shooting. Implying she didn't know if she was hysterical or not.

But Oprah had done her research. "So you don't remember trying to pull the gun away from him [the stranger] fighting him, kicking him, screaming, yelling, anything?"

"No, I don't remember that," Diane said.

Ann interjects, "You remember now pretending to throw the keys [to trick the man]?"

"Yes," Diane said.

Downs was glib, openly taunts Ann, ridiculing her, trying to get under her skin. Ann remained calm, answering when she can get a word in edgewise.

The audience listened to Diane in disbelief, alternately with wide, frightened eyes, then giving her the side-eye and recoiling. They finally erupted in agreement with the host's next statement.

Jabbing her finger expressively into the air, Oprah said, "One of your children is now dead. And you tell this story like you're talking about going to the State Fair!"

Diane smiled, sheepishly.

The applause was overwhelming, as Oprah went to a commercial break.

The room had turned on Diane Downs. She'd lost them.

Chapter 27
Signed, Sealed, Delivered

Four months after Diane Downs' capture, Doug Welch was at work cleaning out the trial evidence locker. It was still 1987, and Welch had been told by court order to clear it all out: the bullet casings, fragments, bloody clothes, the towel, her diaries, her rifle, the Duran Duran tape of 'Hungry Like the Wolf" – every bit and piece left from a searing crime that was still held in the sheriff's property room.

This evidence used to convict Downs had been on the record since trial, every speck of it, and so the court released it all for disposal. Other than a few items, the evil was consumed by flames. Diane's red Nissan Pulsar was sold for scrap.

Doug called me as he was bagging the evidence up to ask if I wanted anything.

"I don't think so," I said. "But what if we save the brass unicorn for Ann Rule?"

He set the unicorn aside.

The District Attorney investigator, a liaison between the children and the D.A's office, got the canvas rag dolls used in court to simulate the bullet wounds they suffered. The dolls were on display in his Children Services Division office.

Doug was interested in a few bullet casings from the crime scene, which matched a bullet found on Downs' bed. All had been used in the same Ruger pistol.

By November, Doug and I piled into his family station wagon for our first ever road trip to Ann's house outside Seattle. Our plan was to pay Ann a visit together and surprise her with the brass statue. We thought she'd be delighted to have the Unicorn, which was pictured on the cover of *Small Sacrifices*. We thought that alone made it a gift nobody else could give her.

At the time, Ann's house was smallish and in the suburbs. I would stay in one-room, Doug was prepared for couch duty. We couldn't wait to see Ann and were pleased with the accommodations. At least I was, since I had a room of my own.

That night, after laughs and beer, we decided to show Ann what we brought for her: the unicorn that Diane Downs had inscribed for her children before taking them on her murderous excursion in 1983. The statue was signed by Downs to memorialize her love for them.

At first, Ann accepted the unicorn, rather hesitantly, but graciously. She seemed excited about it. We didn't catch on about her real feelings, even though only one of the pictures we took at the time showed Ann smiling. The rest were bewildered grimaces, at best.

The moment Ann receives the brass unicorn left in Downs' evidence locker for disposal. Courtesy of Doug Welch.

Overnight, the unicorn stayed on Ann's living room mantle. The same room where Doug was sleeping.

By the next day, Doug was green in the face. He reminded me about this turn of events in 2024 as we reminisced, "I was sicker than a dog, I felt like I was knocking on death's door. That was the night I got poisoned, remember?"

Doug had been fine one day, out the next. We were flummoxed about his illness.

Then, Ann told us she had let off a couple of flea bombs in the living room before our visit, right where Doug had been sleeping. We opened the windows wide to flood the room with fresh air immediately, but Doug needed more time to recover.

He was down for the count, so Ann and I decided to go shopping together.

Over at the Southcenter mall, Ann got her ears pierced for the first time in her life. She'd grown tired of clip-on earrings falling off. While we were there, we compared funny stories about societal attitudes about pierced ears. When we grew up, only "fast girls" had them! My mother didn't want me to have pierced ears either, even in the 70's. I saved my money, waited until my sixteenth birthday and then snuck out to get them done. I thought I would pass out after hearing the CRUNCH of the piercing. Not Ann. As I watched her, hoping she wouldn't have the same reaction, the ear punch made one, two holes and done. No big deal. Ann Rule was a tough one! We laughed, saying we were fast women together.

On the same shopping trip, Ann hoped to find some new clothes. This was really fun! She liked the trendy stirrup pants I wore at the time; the pants had an elastic band fitted over the arch of each foot which elongated the leg as it pulled down the fabric under flats or high heels. This was the mid-1980's, okay? Consulting together, Ann bought a few pairs, some tops and some flats, reminiscent of the 1950's, and we headed back to Ann's house.

That night, Doug seemed to be on the upswing.

The unicorn was still perched on the living room mantle. As I walked in the living room and checked on Doug, I caught sight of it again. I mentioned how unconscionable it was for the mother of three children to have planned ahead to buy a unicorn and have her kids' names inscribed for such murderous motives. A statue to replace Christie, Danny and Cheryl upon their death. The words of the unicorn chosen by Downs said "Christie, Cheryl & Daniel. I love you, Mom. May 13th, 1983." But the kids were shot six days later.

Doug brought up an earlier trip Downs made to the Oregon coast on the date inscribed. Investigators believed that trip was the original day she planned to murder her children, but then changed her mind. Waiting six more days to bolster her courage, the shots finally hit their targets on May 19th.

Abruptly, Ann said, "Let's go out for Chinese food

tonight and a movie?" Which we did.

Doug and I were not catching on.

As Doug and I left the next day, Ann had a package under her arm. There were hugs all around. Then Rule handed the parcel with the unicorn back to us.

We were surprised and obviously tone deaf—we just didn't get it. Why wouldn't Ann want this original featured on her book cover? Ann said it made her nervous, suspicious it would cause bad luck. As Doug and I drove back home to Eugene in the big old station wagon, we wondered what went wrong.

Revisiting the episode now, Doug said, "I remember when we were in the car, and we were like 'well, why wouldn't she want that?' I thought, gee, what a wonderful memento for her. It's on the front of the book…"

"I was kind of embarrassed after that, weren't you?" I said.

"No, no, I guess I was just...I was still a little puzzled."

Quite simply, we couldn't understand why this woman who wouldn't so much as kill a spider flinched while holding a symbol she viewed as the embodiment of death and destruction. We had a bad case of cognitive dissonance.

From our respective viewpoints, Doug and I decided we just weren't good very judges of such sensitive topics.

The statue found a new home at Welches' house. The unicorn held a very different meaning to Doug. The Downs killing was his first murder case as lead investigator.

"I go back to that fifteen-months of my life that, you know, was…it was difficult. I mean it was *tough.*"

He admitted to me, "I was a new investigator, it was stressful. I didn't want to make mistakes and screw up. And it took a toll on my family too. I was absent. Even when I was home, I was absent because I thought about that case constantly."

Luckily, Doug and Tamara have a marriage for the ages and weathered it together.

I would come to find out, again, this symbol of the unicorn spoke very differently to people. During the second ABC 20/20 episode on the Downs case, we met the daughter

Diane was forced to give up for adoption at birth. Rebecca Babcock mentioned she wanted it after seeing the unicorn in Doug's house. To Rebecca, it represented the siblings she never knew and had no contact with.

Today, the unicorn sits on a bookshelf out of plain sight at the Welches' home as a reminder of sweating bullets about every twist and turn Diane Downs made to avoid arrest and conviction. The year and a half investigators spent agonizing to make sure Downs didn't get away with murder.

Chapter 28
Far Away Freedom

I haven't kept in touch with Fred Hugi, but I have continued to watch Diane Downs. I've exchanged a few letters with Downs over the years. In one, she suggested I wear yellow when coming to visit her. I guess she wanted a good laugh. I don't remember asking to visit nor what to wear if I did. I didn't visit and haven't bought any neon yellow, like Big Bird.

After my interview in 1994 with photographer Brian Robertson, Downs wrote back two years later. Her case was up for appeal at the time. The letter was long, but here are some excerpts she wrote:

> *August 12, 1996*
> *Anne:*
>
> *When you were here in November of '94, I remarked that it surprised me to learn you ~~are~~ were born a Leo. Leo's are by nature the most honorable of beings, devoted to truth and justice. Yet you had spent 11 ½ years perverting the truth…I shudder to think a Leo could even sell-out for the illusion of power that accompanies the false praise of those unscrupulous people who would like to use you…*
>
> *To this you replied that you didn't sell-out, that you did believe in everything you'd said and done, and that if you ever found out you had been used by people who deceived you, that you'd be the FIRST to admit [it.] …You challenged me to prove Hugi and Rule are liars and then I'd see a change in you.*

This was Downs' version of events. I did say if incontrovertible evidence proved the trial evidence wrong, I would say so. I'd be the first to say so. To be clear, I still stand by my reporting and the facts. This, in essence, was the nexus of where Downs' truth veered so far off center.

And the business about me being a Leo? I'm still at a loss. Astrology doesn't dictate the facts, the *evidence* does. Her letter continued:

> *You already know (because I told you at the end of our meeting) that I welcomed you only so I could study you that day. I just could not fathom a Leo following and embracing such negative forces as Hugi and Rule. I still can't!*

My special documentary came long before Ann wrote her book. So did my reports and live shots, every single day. I sat in Downs' trial. I heard her testify for three days. I saw the evidence the jury saw, evidence as shocking and chilling as the day it came to light. But the evidence was and is straightforward for murder.

She wrote eight pages on the reverse side of what "appeared" to be a legal case history. A case history, which to me, looked more like a history of what Downs wrote for her Federal Public Defender Wendy Willis to petition the U.S. District Court. Eight pages. Not a thousand. Diane believed if she could talk or write long enough, we'd all see, we'd all understand the errors. I have no idea how much of this reconstructed "case history" was used in her appeal. I did talk to her lawyer when she called me in 1996. I told the young attorney I saw no wiggle room in the evidence that Downs shot her children. By herself.

I was of no help to her. She lost the appeal.

Nothing Diane Downs wrote to me was convincing. What did catch my interest were a few juicy tidbits she brought up in her case history printed on the back of her handwritten letter.

In a section called: C. STABBING

Diane said she was attacked and stabbed by an inmate in July of 1990. She said the stabbing came "*because of the Ann Rule movie Small Sacrifices."* Downs said the scar remained on her right rib cage.

In a chapter titled L. Prison Reality

Downs wrote: *[Statistically 92% of those condemned are truly criminals...but in this case Diane should never have been tried, let alone confined to prison.....She just feels it is important for the PEOPLE reviewing her case to know she is a PERSON too--that she is innocent--and that prison WILL be the death of her if the Courts do not intervene.]*

We also learned that after her Oregon prison escape and transfer to New Jersey that she had at least two uncomfortable trips in leg irons.

On November 24, 1987, Diane was forced to walk from one end of Chicago O'Hare to the other, and from one end of the Philly Airport to the other while wearing leg irons. By the time she arrived at the New Jersey Prison her ankles had swollen over the restraints.

On March 23, 1993, Diane was again transported in leg irons. This time chunks of her flesh were hacked from her legs leaving 8 ugly scars.

I'm sure guards pointed out to her that she's a flight risk.

Here was the biggest news of her letter, and this news just happens to be printed on the reverse side of paper she picked up to write to me in longhand. Downs said earlier in her letter that she agreed to see me in 1994 because she wanted to study me. Yes, a bit creepy, but I've never stopped watching her anniversaries roll by. I made myself a promise in 1984 that I would attend every parole hearing Diane Downs was entitled to for the rest of my life, or hers. If Downs is ever paroled, I want to know what she's done to earn that honor and write about it. I've kept my promise. Investigator Doug Welch has moved on from parole hearings. I haven't and make it a point to update him whether he likes it or not. Ann wasn't able to attend while she was alive.

Doug and I accompanied two jurors to Downs' first parole hearing, the foreman and a woman who'd gotten in touch after the trial. I called each of them to offer to take them to the hearing. After talking together, they agreed. And they had a story to tell me, on camera. Their main mission was dispelling the popular belief that Christie's testimony sank her mother.

"This isn't true, it's not her fault Downs is in prison for life plus 50 years, it's Diane's." The EVIDENCE convicted her, they told me. The jurors had had so many people asking them after the trial if Christie's testimony made them all vote GUILTY, they chose this parole hearing to speak for the first time, and set the record straight so Christie wouldn't blame herself.

I've wanted to make sure the parole board keeps Downs where she belongs. The next hearing is in 2025 and come hell or high water, I'll be there or at least listen again. The Oregon Parole Board does a stellar job of allowing interested parties to hear its sessions.

To be paroled, Downs must admit details of her guilt completely, get extensive therapy, and redeem herself in ways that serve society—so far, the board says Diane has failed on all counts.

And after witnessing all of Diane's hearings, she hasn't fooled the Board one iota.

In the last hearing, Downs talked about her escape attempts. I was surprised to hear more facts about her many schemes to get out. In addition to Downs' 1987 escape, there are more attempts on record:

- In May of 1989, after transfer to the New Jersey prison (after capture, and by the request of the prosecutor who feared Downs would come looking for her former children at his house again someday, only 66 miles from the Oregon prison,) she again denied the escape attempt. "I can't tell you why it's on my record, but it's a blight."

  Parole officials had tapes, letters, and transcript evidence right in front of them at the hearing, including Diane's list of what was needed to escape again in New Jersey.

Her excuses were weak and convoluted.

- In 1991, Downs was found with three yards of polyester fabric. New Jersey Prison staff said she intended to sew a navy-blue prison security uniform. Downs said it was a jumpsuit. She landed in segregation, but insisted "It looks legitimate, it's not. It's just not." Well. It was to the parole board members.

- In 1994, transferred to Chowchilla, the largest women's prison in the world, officers searched her room and found mortar and caulking missing around her only window. The sealant had been chipped away, piece by piece. "I told an officer immediately. That window is only three inches wide. Nobody's going to *fit through that,*" she protested. Diane said she was "too obese" to escape.

The board asked if those attempts were evidence of criminal thinking?

"Oh definitely, with my escape? Definitely," she admitted. "My appeal was denied. I lost without reason. The situation you're in has to be so bad you'll risk death. I was at a point that I didn't even care if I got shot going over the fence. I haven't felt that way since." The records show otherwise.

At these hearings, Downs often called me out as a reason she couldn't fully disclose the "facts" of her crimes, mired in conspiracy theories only the wicked could understand. She admitted to being paranoid about "these people" who were still after her. Diane warned the parole board with undertones of a threat. "I fear for you, not me. FOR YOU. If that makes me look crazy, I'm sorry. No, I'm not sorry. These people are powerful, they're important."
...Even Anne Jaeger is there (at hearing)." Was she concerned I was either tied to that criminal underground or my reports might put her in jeopardy? A board member asked if she was still fearful?

"I'm not fearful for me," she said, explaining the lives of *board members* were in danger. Not hers.

Her psychiatric report explained Downs was a low overall risk of violence to strangers, but she was an EXTREME risk to intimate people in her care. She refused treatment and therapy for her personality disorders. Diane strenuously refuted her diagnoses, and gave unusual reasoning why her COVID-19 mask proves she's not a narcissist, "If I was a narcissist, I wouldn't be wearing a mask!" she said. "It ruins my lipstick."

Downs complained that the prison psychiatrist "wants me to say that 'I shot my children.' I didn't. If I have to sit here, because I won't say that, so be it." This, she said, was the reason she had not sought mental health help, a prerequisite for her release. "That was the worst thing that happened to me in my life. I don't love myself. I don't know if I ever will or can. But I'm not going to denigrate myself to prove I hate myself."

Sometimes, I reported on the results of these parole board hearings, sometimes I didn't. In September of 2020, I did not. But....I got an inkling at the last hearing she'd listened to my words on the last ABC 20/20 appearance I had made in 2019. In it, I suggested if Downs really wanted to get parole then she needed to admit her crimes with no equivocation, with heartfelt apologies to the children. Diane went halfway there, saying, "I failed my children by not keeping them safe." The final part of that sentence should have said "safe from me" and given a full-throated admission of guilt. Instead, she rationalized, "I was stupid. I lived a foolish, careless life. We couldn't fight. They couldn't defend themselves. It was foolish to take them into my careless life."

Somewhere inside me, I still hope beyond hope Diane Downs will give up the ghost and tell the truth. Even though I know what Ann, and my friend Doug Welch and the prosecutor, said is true: her narcissism and antisocial/sociopathic personality will never allow it. What difference will it make anyway? I'm not sure, to be honest. The children, now adults, likely reconciled this long ago, but it would confirm a truth they know all too well. I do believe putting the dragon to rest is easier when your perpetrator finally acknowledges your pain, not their own.

The board questioned Downs' taste in men. They asked

why she was contacting another infamous female inmate. Susan Atkins, a trusted member of Charles Manson's "family" was serving a life sentence for participating in eight murders at Charlie's behest. At the time, Atkins was the longest-serving inmate at the same women's prison where Diane was housed. Downs wrote Atkins. Downs told prison officials she intended to marry Susan's former husband and wrote to find out more about him. Atkins back wrote to Downs, saying that her ex "is a con man." A board member said to Downs that with her experience, she should be able to discern that about people based on her past. And, that Texas man had married Susan Atkins after those murders! They wondered why Downs would agree to correspond with or marry such a man? Or even write another infamous killer, Susan Atkins?

Downs retorted: "I was not serious about marrying him. I wanted to know if the men writing to me were connected. I WAS PLAYING THE TEXAS MAN TO FIND OUT."

Diane Downs didn't marry Susan's ex. Atkins died of a brain tumor in 2009.

The most chilling admission during that hearing? Downs blurted out, "People who hate me, don't hate me because I'm a *'baby killer.'* They hate me because I'm famous."

So much for Downs' own innocence project.

Diane will come up for parole again in 2025. With Ann gone, I miss calling her with the latest updates. I tried to coax her to come with me for Downs' first two parole hearings. The first time, Ann was working on *Mortal Danger* and the second, Ann was promoting *In The Still of the Night* and still recovering from illness. Still, Ann was always on speed dial on hearing days. Reliving regurgitated, nasty details always brought us back to square one.

"Ann, Downs was denied parole again today."

She chuckled, saying facetiously, "Well surprise, surprise."

We laughed.

The mood shifted quickly when we both thought about the children. My voice dropped to a whisper, "I can't, even after all these years, get over how her children watched their mother shoot them one after the other. Cheryl took her last breath seeing the muzzle of the gun her mother was holding relentlessly fire at her."

Ann spoke quietly, her tone was low, but like honey, revealing her vulnerable side openly, "*I know…I know…*I've had four babies at home, and the thought of anyone killing them, kills me."

"What Diane did really shook up a nation of mothers," she confided. Collectively, the horrible details feel like a gut punch.

There was a pin drop silence on the phone line between us. We remembered together. The sting hadn't lessened.

The hearings were a Downs diatribe. After listening to Diane minimize, rationalize and offer a multitude of conspiracy theories for hours, the parole board denied her freedom. Diane Downs couldn't get beyond the bars. And in 2020, the coup de grâce: someone in the hearing room yelled, "Yoooo hoooo!" when it was over.

Post by Leslie Rule for *Ann Rule Fan Club* Facebook page.

Downs has been busy in the intervening years since her last parole appearance. Diane is trying a new tactic to be set free. She's won a rare court hearing about her sentences. After forty-two years in prison, Downs wants a new trial. Her lawyers say she was wrongly convicted of attempted murder and assault. And here's the background: her jury voted ten to two, not unanimously, on those charges. When Downs was convicted in 1984, juries didn't need twelve votes to be guilty of attempted murder and assault. All twelve jurors did convict her of murder. The courts have now ruled what they call *non-unanimous jury sentences* as unconstitutional. On her website, Downs writes "Lane County would have the option to retry me on Counts 2-5 [attempted murder and assault] if they want..." and claims entitlement to being resentenced for murder. Murder still carries a life sentence in Oregon. Lead Investigator Doug Welch wonders how a new trial would be possible. "All the evidence is in court transcripts, but physically, it doesn't exist. All that stuff is long gone."

At the time of this writing, Christie is married with three children and named her youngest Cheryl after her deceased sister. Danny, although paralyzed, still loves the freedom and buoyancy he feels in the water and loves to go fishing and work with computers. He's had some hard times lately.

In 2020, the Hugis' beloved home on the McKenzie River outside Eugene came within feet of being burned to the ground, as they and their neighbors were in the path of Oregon's most destructive wildfire on record. A time when the sky was red with acrid smoke for weeks, burned a million acres, and took eleven lives. The Hugis lived elsewhere while the fires raged.

I suspect this was another time when disaster made the family tighter. The resiliency Fred and Joanne taught at home would make them grateful for spending Thanksgiving together that year, wherever they were together.

Chapter 29
Rule Maker

Ann Rule didn't just write books about serial killers, she helped change laws. The Federal law Ann fought for, revolutionized the way investigators traced and captured violent killers across the country. Serial killers.

In the 1980's, at the same time Rule was attending Downs' trial and writing books, she became an outspoken advocate for a new and critical FBI program called ViCAP, the Violent Criminal Apprehension Program. She was great friends with Pierce Brooks, the mastermind of this anti-serial killer program. Brooks' knowledge was also instrumental to Ann's career. Their drive to understand psychopathic minds drew them together and strengthened their friendship with purpose.

Brooks' reputation as a "criminal profiler" started long before the two met. In the 1970's he tracked the movements and behaviors of serial killers all across the country, with only newspaper periodicals at the library to compare crimes. By the time Brooks met Ann, he was using the term "serial killer" instead of lust, spree or thrill killer, which were the previously used descriptions. Brooks was already famous for solving the 1963 "Onion Field" murder of a cop in California. Former LAPD detective Joseph Wambaugh wrote the bestselling book about Brooks' investigation to find the men who kidnapped the two police officers, killing one in an onion field outside Bakersfield California, that became a blockbuster 1979 movie. Brooks' hyper-attention to detail, evidence, and his understanding of the psychology of killers was phenomenal.

In the 1980's, Brooks was living not far from Fred Hugi, along the McKenzie River outside Eugene, when he was called to consult on the Diane Downs case, too. The sheriff's office brought him in to strategize on building an airtight case. I didn't meet Brooks back then, but knew of him. I'd invited Ann over during Downs' trial a few times, and she bowed out because of her plans with Brooks for the evening.

Apparently, he was nicknamed "Fierce Looks" in our newsroom for his countenance toward reporters. And I certainly remember the case he solved when I was an intern at KEZI in the late 1970's, years before I met Ann. The case demonstrated Brooks' ability to look beyond jurisdictional boundaries dividing cop shops, and his willingness to think outside of the box when looking at evidence.

I remember a ruckus in the newsroom. The upheaval was centered on the heinous discovery of a human thigh and breast in a dumpster in the parking lot near the 5th Street Public Market in Eugene, in February 1978. In my naiveté, I thought this crime would be a lead story, but I was just learning and I kept my mouth shut. The professionals in the newsroom, including two reporters who quickly left to launch Ted Turner's 24/7 brand new nationwide cable news channel CNN, thought quite differently.

Our News Director Peter Spear, who was then in his forties, and looked like aging hippie, would be calling the shots on this chilling murder. He'd made his mark in San Francisco television before coming to Eugene. Spear gathered the capital "J" Journalists, producers, writers and the rest of us together in the newsroom.

The journalists were arguing this case wasn't serious journalism. They didn't want to do the *"if it bleeds, it leads"* stuff. Plus, if ever there was a bleeding lead, it was body parts in a dumpster. The staff wanted to do real news about corruption in local government, crooked politicians, boondoggles, and taxpayer deceit. Not gruesome crimes.

Spear set everyone straight: this was a story our station would be covering–extensively. He doubled down telling a story from his career at KGO, a terrifying account of a penis found severed on the railroad tracks in San Francisco. Bob Kerns, our then twenty-four-year-old producer at KEZI, remembered hearing the story. "ABC7 was more tabloid then," he told me. "Pete

Spear believed bloody crime built viewership." Because it caused fear, and fear motivated people to watch. Our solid journalists wanted no part in getting higher ratings by covering gratuitous violence. And here was the kicker, Kerns said KGO reported the entire story leaving out one key detail: "The viewers didn't find out until the very *end* of the story on the 11 o'clock news that the penis came from a bull." Spear teased the heck out of the story during News Breaks before the 11 p.m. news without revealing the truth. The ratings were big that night.

In Eugene, Spear didn't want reporters to shy away from the thigh and breast in the dumpster. We were reporting on this case from start to finish. KEZI would cover this because people wanted to know the who, what, where, why, and how of this public crime. He saw the dumpster story as a way to answer questions from shocked residents and, as a way to apprise them of each step of the process to quell fears. Kerns didn't disagree with that reasoning but it was the manner in which the stories were reported that made the difference. Kerns worked hard to keep a line drawn between news and sensationalism, still he admits, with the boss's orders, "We overdid it."

Later, when Kerns took over the News Director's job, Kerns and Assistant News Director Rebecca Force stemmed the tide of gratuitous bloody stories.

Nothing even remotely like the dumpster crime had happened in family oriented Eugene, Oregon in the late 1970's.

Dark humor was whispered around the newsroom. Some called it the "penis on the railroad track story" in hushed circles, mocking the story for its bait and switch potential. As you might imagine, the facts of this murder only got worse. We'd come to find out the grisly details as Pierce Brooks and investigators put the horrible case together.

Pamela and Johnny Bruno, living in Springfield, were at Charles "Chuck" Haynes and Lionette Haynes' house in Eugene, smoking dope and drinking heavily in February of 1978. According to her husband, Pam Bruno agreed to group sex, then refused. Johnny Bruno confessed that's when the men took his wife in the other room and made sure she couldn't get away.

Lionette Haynes was in a rage seeing Chuck have sex with another woman. Even though Pam was tied up, restrained against her will, Lionette stabbed Pamela Bruno viciously. Then, she passed the knife to both men. Each took turns mutilating her body.

"We gotta do something about this now," Chuck Haynes said. Their choice was too sick for words.

They decided to hang Pam Bruno's body over the bathtub. And her husband, Johnny, helped. The body was dismembered—parts shoved in plastic bags then thrown in dumpsters.

Unbeknownst to me, but I would later come to find out from Ann, Pierce Brooks had by then relocated from Los Angeles, first as Chief in Springfield, then transferred to Eugene as Chief of Police in the 1970's. Brooks knew what both departments could do if they shared information to solve this crime. He got them working in tandem. Brooks also *knew* this approach could work nationwide and started working to see it happen.

All three were convicted. Johnny Bruno and Chuck Haynes got life. Lionette got twenty years for manslaughter. The men would be eligible for parole after twenty-five years. They didn't make it that long. Johnny Bruno and Charles Haynes both died in prison. Remarkably, the woman who took the first slicing cut, Lionette Haynes, was released in 1985, having served just seven years.

Looking into the Bruno murder again today, I realized a force of nature was working at the highest level to solve the case without DNA: Pierce Brooks. I had no idea what a big deal he was. But Ann Rule sure did.

Their philosophies were two sides of the same coin. Brooks threw out the "good cop/bad copy" police interview technique early in his career, preferring to treat suspects with dignity over derision. His approach got results for his detectives over the years. Ann had already learned this from her grandfather. They both used intellect *and* some imagination to explain and gain clues in crimes. As in Pamela Bruno's case, that practice got confessions and convictions. The old adage "honey gets more than vinegar" was a winning strategy.

After Brooks retired as Chief of Police, this analytical man, often called the father of criminal profiling, told Ann about a new idea he's pitching the FBI. The idea came years before any of us had home computers, cell phones, home security cameras, DNA or forensic genealogy. This was an era younger adults now can't possibly comprehend in crime fighting.

While Pierce Brooks was consulting on the Atlanta child murders, the Chicago Tylenol poisoning murder, and the Green River killings, he was also working behind the scenes to create a nationwide computer database to track "serial killers" to identify the same person, overwhelmingly male, with sadistic sexual tendencies, killing multiple victims over time.

A serial killer wasn't crazy, but was manipulative, seemed charming, and remained cool and collected in stressful situations, he liked kidnapping people and getting away with random murders. This psychopath killed, hunted, killed, then stalked new prey again. In the 1980's when Brooks and Rule joined forces to get this new FBI universal database program started, Ann had already written scads of detective magazine stories with detailed information on serial killer habits. As well as four books on the topic: *The Stranger Beside Me, Lust Killer, Want Ad Killer, and I-5 Killer*. Ann was the first major author to see a striking similarity in behavior patterns among these unconscionable men. "A serial killer strikes in waves," she told me. A serial killer might murder a woman, man or child once a year then take a break after the impulse was satiated. Then his obsession built.... and he killed again to release the rage, sometimes murdering daily or even twice a day as his confidence grew, Ann said. Psychopaths acted without remorse or guilt and were completely vicious.

In the 1970's and 80's, most serial killers weren't being caught. Their crimes seemed disconnected in time and space. In her appearances, Rule cited crime stats from the FBI's Uniform Crime Report that said in 1969, the majority of the 10,000 murder victims nationwide knew their killers while only 5.4% did not. By 1981, murders rose to 25,000 in America and more than three times as many victims (17.8%) were random and senseless. The computer database Brooks envisioned, and Rule promoted, would compile evidence of these crimes nationwide all in one place at the FBI. This was a groundbreaking concept. Before this, most departments didn't look outside their own borders or share information. With the advent of the computer, cities, counties, and states would be able enter crime reports to a central FBI repository. The FBI could step in or help local cops work together on the same crimes with seemingly similar facts, even across state lines. The states and Feds would collaborate.

On a micro-level this was exactly what Brooks did as the Chief of Police in Eugene while solving Pam Bruno's murder with the Springfield Police Department. At the time, the cops worked together with only typed reports and interviews to solve the murders *if* requested by a different agency–and it wasn't unusual for most cop shops to be so possessive over crimes that they'd only share cases grudgingly. But a computer database could combine all the evidence, complete with a psychological profile that included specific patterns of each crime in any jurisdiction. Brooks got a $35,000 government grant to research his brainstorm.

Brooks and Rule worked tirelessly on the U.S. Justice Department task force to get it going. Brooks started meeting with FBI behavioral scientists and computer experts. Soon, Rule and John Walsh, of television's *America's Most Wanted,* whose son was slain by a serial killer, made public appearances together.

The public and U.S. lawmakers took notice. Brooks and his task force gained traction.

And finally, hearings for stable funding began. Ann testified twice in front of the U.S. Senate Judiciary Subcommittee on Serial Murders, telling lawmakers a central database was essential because serial killers could travel as much as 200,000 miles each year, leaving victims in their wake. Rule had watched, researched and written about men using Interstate Five with its easy access to forested land from California to Washington as their killing fields. Brooks and Rule knew this was happening across the country too. Through her research, Ann told lawmakers that serial killers couldn't voluntarily stop killing, they either "aged out" (they got too old to overpower victims), they got arrested, or they died.

The Senators became believers thanks to the facts and testimony from Brooks, Rule, Walsh and others. ViCAP, the Violent Criminal Apprehension Program got the money it needed. In 1985, while Ann was writing *Small Sacrifices,* the FBI plugged in its huge ViCAP computer system at headquarters in Quantico, Virginia. Pierce Brooks was the first ViCAP director.

Now for almost forty years, ViCAP has been tracking serial killers, missing people, kidnappings, sexual assaults and homicide cases targeting random crimes with detectable patterns. The FBI helps investigators nationwide work together, or runs the show with local help. Just as Brooks had envisioned.

Ann doesn't often get credit for doing more than writing about crimes, but Ann was proactive, putting her insights, research, knowledge and reputation behind solutions. Her dedication to ViCAP's inception was instrumental.

She became a certified instructor to law enforcement officers in California, Oregon and Washington. She was a regular keynote speaker at annual law enforcement association meetings and taught a four-hour seminar on serial killers for the FBI at Sam Houston State University. She also spoke about women who kill and Victims' Rights. As the granddaughter of a sheriff, she herself became an expert in criminal behavioral profiling. With solid influences like Pierce Brooks, Ann Rule put her mark on a groundbreaking computer system, which tracks serial killers to this day. How many other true crime authors can you name who helped rewrite laws to catch the psychopaths they write about?

Chapter 30
Killer Coincidences

Ann and I both met killers in childhood. We talked about this bizarre coincidence between us. Ann was about nine when she met Viola, who taught her how to crochet while in prison for murder. I was about the same age when I met Charles Manson.

My brush with Manson came a year after the Summer of Love in the late 1960's, when I heard Charlie Manson sing his song "Cease to Exist" at a beach campfire.

Earlier in the day, my parents had parked our small travel trailer near the ocean, next to a psychedelic school bus in the summer of '68. We were near Santa Barbara, California. Other real campgrounds for families were full. This was how our vehicle ended up feet from Manson's, alone together on a secluded beach.

No camping signs were posted. But there we were.

We pulled up next to a bus. The bus doors swung open. Girls piled out, or fell out topsy-turvy, like the old Volkswagen advertisement "how many people can you fit inside a Beetle?" There were a lot of girls. Finally, one small, real scruffy guy with long brown greasy, unkempt hair launched off the first step, jumping into the air and FLEW, arms wide out. His legs together, almost Christ-like. All those girls giggled. No other men made an appearance. I'd never seen anything like it. The flying entrance, one guy and lots of girls, left an imprint on me.

I was lingering outside, watching Dad set up our trailer. Mom was inside. Dad kept bumping into me. It was probably hard to get anything done, because I was following so closely behind, completely oblivious to what he was doing. My head kept rotating like a satellite dish, mouth agape, staring at those people, as I stayed one step off his flank.

That night, Dad sat at their big campfire with them. I heard guitar music and wandered over. I sat next to Dad. The girls asked my name. The girls seemed nice, but their clothes were dirty. I remember a funny smell. Charlie stopped playing, and instantly he was passionately immersed in conversation with my father. He asked Dad if record companies would buy his songs. My father was a journalist, not a record producer.

I got up, left to find my mom. Something about this small man bothered me. But then, adults often bore kids.

The next day, one of the girls started walking toward our trailer. I was outside stalking Dad around the camper again. My eyes? Saucers. I froze, and in that second as Dad got to the other side of the trailer, unseen and unaware of the girl walking toward us. I demonstrated the nonchalant grace of a ten-year-old and started skipping, running to the trailer door.

"MOM!" I shouted. "A girl from over there is coming over here!" Standing just inside the door, Mom was working in the tiny kitchen.

Still outside, I pivoted to point my finger at THE GIRL. I nearly poked her. This was the kind of awkward moment that children are able to ignore, but mothers can't. The two laughed, exchanged greetings. I saw the girl held a light green coffee mug shaped like an ancient Polynesian tiki statue in her hand.

Honestly, the mug didn't look friendly. The face disappeared when I noticed the large chocolate Hershey bar sticking up above the rim.

The tiki mug given to me as a child from one of Manson's girls. I ate the Hershey chocolate bar dropped inside, and my parents kept the mug. Author's photo.

The teenager asked Mom, "Can I take your daughter for a walk?"

I tried to get Mom's attention without the girl seeing me. Because I didn't wanna go. I remember stepping slightly behind the girl doing some pantomimes shaking my head "no!" like a frightened rabbit.

Whether my mother saw me, I cannot say. Mom chimed in, "I'm sure Anne would love to go for a walk."

We walked away from the big blue ocean, toward the California Coastal Highway behind us, which is now Interstate Five. The girl scrambled up higher, between bigger and bigger round boulders. On top, we were cut off from the makeshift campsites. Our tiny travel trailer was so far away. I saw Dad in the distance, but the highway above us looked massive, like a background shot in The Jetsons.

The girl walked along. Then we sat. She asked me a lot of questions. Where was my family headed? Why were we here? What did my daddy do for a living? Did my parents have money? I didn't have much to say. The girl said, "Here, I brought this for you," and handed me the heebie-jeebie tiki mug, candy still intact.

For reasons I cannot explain, I didn't grab the Hershey bar, rip off the wrapper, and eat it in ten seconds flat. I must have hesitated, because the girl said, "C'mon, it's for you." I'd like to tell you I resisted, heeding the "something is not right here" jitters and waited to eat under the watchful eye of my mother, but alas, I did not.

Candy: gone in four bites.

Thus was the power of candy in the hands of a "kind" stranger.

I talked between swallows.

"My dad doesn't have a job."

"We don't have any money."

"We're living off clams…corn and…vegetables falling off the trucks." Unbeknownst to me, my parents saved every penny but did not spend them. Both products of the Depression. This picking up produce seemed like a game to me, vegetables fell, I jumped out to pick them up, throw them in the backseat as Dad slowed the car. This game was fun, I told the girl.

The girl said I reminded her of her little sister and I asked about her. The girl said her sister lived with her parents back home. I asked why she didn't see her sister anymore. The girl said she can't. She can't go back home. Why? I feel sorry for her, naively wondering why a daughter can't go home? I wanna know if she'd like to see or at least call her sister?

"I can get a dime for you," I told her. "You can call them." A dime was the cost of a telephone booth call back then. Ten-year-olds want to help. The young woman was wistful. Although we faced each other, she stared beyond me. This was my first experience of seeing someone view the past while looking into their eyes. She seemed touched, softened somehow.

Trailing back into camp, Dad and the guy, whose name is Charlie, were talking at the fire pit. Inside the trailer, I asked Mom, "Is Dad gonna grow his hair long like Charlie's?" She snickered because Dad was sporting a tightly clipped Friar Tuck hairdo, not by choice. I didn't want him to grow his hair long like that, even if he could have. I must have been worrying about how intrigued my Dad was by Charlie. The attention he was getting. Dad loved new ideas, drawn to offbeat "interesting" people. (Later, one of Manson's prosecutors would describe Manson's magnetic charisma like this: "When he would walk in the room, you could almost feel the electricity pouring off of him.")

My child's mind was baffled by the attention my dad was giving him, because I didn't want anything to do with these people. They seemed weird.

My mother asked me what the girl and I had talked about. I told her everything.

After nightfall, Dad was *still* out there. Mom was reading. I was watching TV on a tiny black and white. The antenna got one channel, which had special coverage of the 1968 Democratic National Convention. Policemen were cracking batons against teenagers' legs, arms, backs and heads. Brutally beating teenagers, in someplace named Chicago. This was fascinating to me. I could not understand why policemen were hurting people. The teenagers were chanting, "The whole world is watching." Mom looked up from her book, saw what was going on, and wanted to redirect me.

"Anne, why don't you go out, check on Dad?" she said.

"Okay."

Stepping outside, I saw the bonfire. Dad and Charlie were sitting across from one another. There were other people there too, the hippie girls and one or two young men. What we didn't know in the summer of '68 was that Manson's harem included Lynette "Squeaky" Fromme, Patricia "Yellow" or "Big Patty" Krenwinkel, Leslie "Green" Van Houten, Susan "Violet" or "Sadie" Atkins, fourteen-year-old Dianne "Snake" Lake, Mary "Mother Mary" or "Ooh" Brunner, and Sandra "Blue" Good. The misfit rainbow.

Charlie started singing again. Playing his guitar. They were talking about stuff that was way over my head, but I heard something about cops. I was wary of this guy. I was tall for my age, he wasn't that much taller than me, he was really skinny with excitable eyes. I didn't really know what to make of this guy talking about cops, but I'd just seen them on television smacking people with batons.

The talk turned to record companies again, and promises made to Charlie about recording these songs. In a 1969 newspaper article written by "Sadie" Atkins, she said Manson wooed her easily, "His voice hypnotized me— mesmerized me. When I saw him, I absolutely fell in love with him."

Dad encouraged Charlie to keep trying. I tried to be invisible as I headed back to the trailer. Dad, a lifelong musician and World War II Royal Canadian Navy trombonist as well as a journalist might have seen promise there, which, by the way, turned out to be sorta true. "Cease to Exist" was later watered down and recorded by the Beach Boys as "Never Learn Not to Love." Not a top seller–almost a non-seller. For me, all this adult stuff made me hungry and I trudged back home for a snack before bed.

I was asleep on the kitchen table that pulled down into a bed when Dad tip-toed in. The filament on the old Coleman lantern burned slowly on the countertop, leaving a soft golden light so I saw it was him. Seemed very late.

He slid in the double bed with Mom at the other end of the trailer. They were two or three feet away from me. The small bunk above them where I usually slept was locked in the "up" position. Dad whispered to Mom. His voice was high, fast, but hushed. Mom said something. She seemed alarmed. They must have been comparing notes.

Next thing I knew, I'd been moved from the table bed next to the only door in the trailer, to the bunk above theirs. Groggy, I heard them whispering again. I dozed off, unable to hear what they're saying.

I woke up to the dome light inside the car. Dad had carried me from my bunk to the backseat. I was grumbling. He told me to be very quiet. He also seemed kinda mad, but determined. Dad started the car slowly. Not a word was said. My dad made that car, hitched to our travel trailer, glide so easily over the beach, I don't remember even hearing the sand crunch under six wheels.

There were no sudden movements. I pretended to be sleeping in the backseat, wrapped in a blanket, but I was afraid knowing something was up, if we were leaving camp long before daylight.

Once we were on I-5 headed north, a gorgeous sunrise greeted us over the Santa Ynez coastal mountain range on our right. I finally slept very soundly on the way home. I would enter elementary classes again in a few days at a new school.

"Charlie's on the FRONT PAGE of THE PAPER! *CHARLIE'S* on the front page!"

Mom was running down the hallway, practically slipping on her finely-waxed wood floors. She was waving the newspaper's morning edition in the air. Dad was the Business Editor at the paper then. He barely roused. I was thinking "Mom's blown a fuse," but she got Dad's attention with this: "*Charlie's* in the newspaper for killing all those people in California!!!"

The big full-page splash detailed first-degree murder and conspiracy to commit murder for the deaths of Leno and Rosemary LaBianca, film actress Sharon Tate Polanski, Abigail

Ann Folger, heiress to the coffee dynasty, Wojciech Frykowski, Steven Parent (an eighteen-year-old visitor) and Jay Sebring.

I pretended *not* to remember who Charlie was. At the time of his arrest in December of 1969, I was completely immersed in school. And I didn't want to even think about it. After all, who wants to be known at that age as the girl who accepted candy from the Manson Family? But I *knew* who Mom was talking about. We learned Charlie's last name that morning after seeing his picture. We had slept feet away from them, shared campfires, and listened to *Charles Manson's* philosophy a year and a half earlier.

The troubling events of our travel trailer days on that California beach became an official family secret, a source of embarrassment or fear of what might have been. Honestly, I'm not sure why the three of us never talked about it, alone. We just didn't. I rarely talked about it anywhere with anybody.

Fast forward to when I was sitting with my ninety-three-year-old dad before he died in 2016. I finally thought to ask him, "Hey, Dad, what happened back there, you know, with Charlie Manson?"

Here's what he told me.

"After you left the campfire, Charlie wanted to use our toilet."

I told him even *we* didn't use our toilet.

"If I want something, I'll take it," Charlie said to him.

"You'll have to go through me first," my dad said.

Silence.

"I only hurt people who are afraid of me," Charlie said.

Dad stood his ground. Eye-to-eye, Dad never so much as flinched or lost eye contact. "I'm not afraid of you," he said. And I can assure you, he wasn't. At least not at the time.

Long after the stare down, Dad had told other adults about this dangerous dance the two men did, but he never shared it with me. He'd shrug it off, seemingly irritated whenever I'd ask. Until some fifty years later, I learned the truth. I put on my best *Anne Jaeger, Courageous Reporter* face, while inside myself I wanted to throw my head in my hands and wail. The feeling of being a child unable to defend myself came bubbling up again. Knowing my childhood instincts, although not fully formed, had been right long before the headlines screamed at us. I am still sick at the thought of ever having seen Charlie Manson, or hearing him sing in the flicker of a beach campfire, while my family was trapped in an aluminum box right next to him.

When I think of it now, I can't quite wrap my head around it. His cocky demeanor, penetrating eyes, lord of his female flies, directing murders so despicably brutal that they changed the zeitgeist of America. Based on those ruthless, bloody killings, what kind of savagery were Manson and his girls capable of—just to use a bathroom? Kill us? Steal money?

Recently, I asked my 95-year-old mom about the episode.

"Yes, I remember it," she said. Mom always thought it was "Squeaky" who gave me the mug and candy. I remember the young woman looking like Leslie Van Houten, who had a younger brother and sister her parents adopted from Korea, and she had told me about missing her younger sister. Fromme had one brother, no sisters. And to me, Squeaky's red hair would have been unforgettable.

But Mom got a good look at Lynette Fromme in 1975. The redhead served thirty-four years for pointing a loaded .45 Colt 1911 semi-automatic pistol at President Gerald R. Ford in an assassination attempt.

"What'd you think about camping next to Charlie Manson, Mom?"

"I think….I've blanked it out on purpose," she said.

"Why? Because it's too scary to think back on?"

"I don't want to bring it all up again."

Sometimes denial is a safe place for ugly feelings you have no more use for. I said we don't have to revisit it again, ever, and thanked her and Dad for getting us out of harm's way.

After Manson died in prison, I carefully lifted the lid on my memories. I discovered Manson had been released from prison not long before we met him. He'd been paroled, after trafficking underage girls over state lines for prostitution. One girl was only a few years older than I was at the time. He fathered a child with that fourteen-year-old we met. Could I have been caught up in that plan when my parents were disposed of?

I posted a truncated memory of my story on Facebook after Manson died in November of 2017. Pat Boyle, a morning reporter for a Portland radio station called as soon as she read it. Pat interviewed me for drive time news. Then, the ABC station in Portland talked to me about it. In the afternoon, Mike Benner of NBC, my old station, called for an interview. The conversation went live on KGW's website that morning, followed by a story on the evening news.

After the live feed on KGW, I went back to read viewer comments. A few called me a liar. One asserted I had fabricated the entire life experience. I was taken aback by the reaction, especially after holding my story cloistered inside for years. I had hid the story before, thinking it might be a poor reflection on my parents. Thankfully, the majority of viewers knew my track record as a reporter and anchor and empathized with my fear as a wide-eyed child and shared my gratitude that my family hadn't witnessed more. They lauded my parents for escaping danger.

My memories of this tied me closer to Ann. I miss our talks, especially when I remember the conversation we had when I finally confided my story in her, long before I spoke publicly about it. She wasn't surprised or doubtful in any way.

We were sitting in her Seattle home when the entire episode came tumbling out. Ann was wearing dark lipstick and prettied herself with makeup for my visit. She also had on a new pair of cute glasses. The frames were a wider cat-eye style, and really suited her face. We'd been catching up about our lives and kids when the topic came up. Our conversations bounced around a lot, as you can probably tell. I mentioned noticing parole had been denied again for Manson or one of "his girls," like Leslie Van Houten, and asked Ann's opinion on it.

"Do you think they'll ever get out, Ann?"

"Manson won't," Ann said. "They should serve all their time for those awful murders."

I remember thinking Manson broke the mold for mass serial killers, more like a mob boss picking victims then convincing devotees to do the dirty work in nine murders. (After Ann's death, Van Houten gained her freedom in July 2023. She'd been denied twenty times.) That was the trigger.

"Ann, there's more to that story, I haven't told you."

She knew the outline of my Manson meeting, but I hadn't filled in many of the blanks as I've done here.

"I know you'll understand in a way my family or few friends ever could." Then I added more from my personal perspective as a child.

Ann took a cube out of her glass and cracked it between her teeth, a long-time habit of hers.

She listened intently and seeing I had bottled up those memories for so many years, she said, "I'm so sorry this happened to you, Anne. Especially as a child." We both teared up.

Ann was a wonderful friend and listener; she didn't interrupt or question the saga I had lived through. She'd heard so many victims' stories in her life, and there was little that she hadn't heard before. But she had a calming demeanor of reassurance. I know the solace I found with her helped me untangle the scary parts and made me ready to share my story on television years later.

Today, I wonder if my friend offered her comfort as much for me as for herself, since she had walked away from Viola and Ted Bundy unharmed.

We both got glimpses of killer minds and survived to tell our stories to each other. In our conversation about our brushes with evil, Ann said serial killers wore a mask most of us never saw behind, "Ted never wanted people to see who he really was," she said. "The mask allowed him to be different things to different people." A liar. A manipulator. A bloodthirsty killer.

"He seems more covert than Manson, and without the cult followers," I offered. "Manson wanted his people to know his dangerous side and ruled them through fear and intimidation. Like he tried to do with my Dad. Which is hard to do when you're a small scrawny man like Manson. Wasn't Bundy more intelligent, well dressed, more, well, sophisticated?"

"Behind Bundy's mask he was a schemer, stalker, killer

and a liar," she said. "But he was also smart and showed so much compassion at the suicide hotline....and that's the only side he allowed me to see." Given the complexity of his crimes, it seems possible Bundy might have been willing to retaliate if he ever saw Ann as a threat to expose him. She walked a tightrope for years.

Daughter Leslie remembered the first time she met Bundy, in June of 1972. She was fourteen years old and had just seen the Rolling Stones with her two best friends. The concert ran pretty late that night at the Seattle Coliseum, so Leslie called her mother, who was working at the crisis clinic, to let her know they'd have to wait an hour for the bus. Ann worried about the girls being out on the streets that late, and took a short break to pick them up. Ann brought them back to the clinic where they would be safe with her and Ted. Her friends were gaga over him. But, Leslie remembered when she cast eyes on Bundy, he would not return her gaze. Leslie was clueless about what her friends saw in him. This was the first and only time Ann allowed any of her children to meet him, according to Leslie.

Ann never felt afraid of Ted Bundy, nor believed he would ever hurt her. Maybe not, since his chosen victims were a decade younger, with long hair often parted in the middle. More like Leslie's friends. But, Bundy didn't want to know anything about his victims; they needed to be anonymous to him. Anything more than a five minute conversation would snuff out his impending violent and brutal attack.

Early on, when Ann was still on the fence about Bundy's guilt, she wrote to him in prison and sent the occasional ten-dollar check to his commissary for food and essentials. She sent no more checks once she reached the conclusion that he was a sadistic murderer and had made those two separate calls to Seattle detectives about him.

They met when Rule was in her forties, while I had been a child when I met Manson briefly but vividly. The experiences were different, but both created feelings that resonated over a lifetime. Together.

"Ann, his eyes were so scary," I told her, about Manson. Although I didn't know how to explain it as a kid. "Manson's eyes were hollow, like there was no 'soul' inside. Then, when he'd get excited talking about music or 'the cops' his eyes would be wider than wide open, darting around wildly, like a maniac."

Ann understood instinctively, after seeing the many evil eyes stare back at her during her interviews with killers, or watching their trial testimony. And I'd seen those same empty eyes afterward in serial murderers that I'd sat face-to-face with during my career.

"I wonder if that Manson meeting was the catalyst for my interest in crime?" I asked Ann. "Seems strange that an episode that scares the holy hell out of me would lead me to want to interview criminals instead of running the other way."

Ann said, "I think our minds are looking for explanations about why these psychopaths can be so charming one second, and such brutal murderers the next. People go into professions all the time because a childhood incident had such an effect on them."

It certainly did in both of our lives. I still feel an eerie sense of danger every time I see the mug Charlie's girl handed me fifty-years ago.

That Tiki mug has never been used since the day I took candy from a stranger. No one in my family wanted to drink out of a green chalice of evil.

Chapter 31
Duck for Cover

Ann called and left a message on my work voicemail when she'd heard on television, out of the blue, that I'd been shot at while out reporting on a strange story. She wanted to know if I was okay.

Up until January of 1994, I'd never been shot at before.

The genesis of all this went back to a skating rink in Detroit, Michigan. In early January of 1994, a guy named Shane Stant, who lived with his grandmother in Portland, Oregon (where I worked), hit Nancy Kerrigan with a baton across her lower right thigh, hoping to prevent her from competing in the Olympics in Lillehammer, Norway. You likely witnessed Kerrigan's pain caused by this 'injury heard around the world' on the television or radio after the attack. It was swift and without provocation. Her rival, Tonya Harding, also from Portland, won the U.S. Figure Skating Championship that year because Kerrigan was injured.

It turned out that Tonya Harding pleaded guilty to felony hindering prosecution for taking part in a cover-up of the crime with her then ex-husband, Jeff Gillooly (who's since changed his name.) Harding's bodyguard allegedly hired Shane Stant and his uncle for less than three thousand dollars to injure Kerrigan that January to keep her out of the Olympics. Gillooly admitted guilt for racketeering, Stant and his uncle were found guilty of conspiracy.

But our story takes place under the veil of secrecy about the case before the suspects started yapping to investigators.

Our station, KGW, was the first to figure out where Shane Stant had been living with his grandmother in Corbett after the crime, a small town about half hour east of Portland.

Another reporter was assigned the story and was getting interviews. A photographer, Karl Petersen, and I were sent to get "real estate" or cover shots of Shane's grandmother's home on January 14th. Nothing more. "Just go out there. Get some video of the house and come on home," we were told. It was four days before my daughter's third birthday.

We were the only crew there. We didn't park near the grandmother's home but traveled above it onto a road overlooking the back of the house. The place was a ghost town. No other reporters showed up. Karl and I got out of the car, and he set up the gear to start videotaping the back of the house, while I got back inside the car.

With the back hatch of the car open, I heard Karl say, "Some old lady is coming outside with a gun." "What are you talking about Karl?" I asked. Through my glasses, but without a zoom lens, I saw nothing at first.

Then, Karl, the Vietnam War vet, started calling off the shots.

"There's one."

I heard the sound ring out, in disbelief.

"There's two…." Petersen was watching the woman's finger squeeze the trigger through the zoom lens, but I thought he was omniscient.

I radioed KGW and said, "Karl and I are being shot at by somebody at Shane Stant's grandmother's house. It looks like *her*."

This was the first and only time, I've ever heard before or since, that a KGW crew was openly shot at directly.

"Here comes three…" Karl said. Sure enough, he's calling the shots, seemingly able to anticipate each one. He sounded incredulous, but sure.

The assignment editor Molly Kretz calmly cleared all KGW radio traffic. No questions were asked. Our radios, usually abuzz with updates with the reporter/photographer's whereabouts, stopped abruptly.

Time seemed to slow. I asked Karl, "Where is she shooting?"

"In the air toward us," Karl said.

We *were* in the air, above her house on that old road!

I brazenly told Karl to "Duck, but keep on rolling," which later became a printed T-shirt at my old KEZI station in Eugene. He laughed, and never hit the camera off button.

Then I heard the woman shouting from down below.

"Yeah, that's me shooting," she yelled. "I'm a gun-toting, pistol-packing grandma!"

I couldn't believe what I was hearing.

"Here's another?" Karl questioned the next round.

Although we could hear the effects of the woman's anger as she pulled on the trigger, the camera's microphone didn't quite pick up what this seventy-four-year-old woman was shouting into the sky at us, but *we* heard her.

The whole situation seemed surreal. Not until I heard those words did I realize how naive I'd been and the danger we were actually in.

"Karl, pack up, let's go," I said. "This is madness."

When he got in the car, he said, "Nah, those were just warning shots." His blasé reaction somehow made me feel safer in his presence.

As we sped back to the station, I realized we hadn't reported back to KGW yet, so we told the assignment editor, "We're clear of the location. No injuries. Heading back."

When we arrived, nobody said anything. I surmised they knew we were on deadline and left us alone. I noticed a reporter from Seattle in the newsroom. He looked at me, and kept on writing. Then the News Director called me into his office, asking what happened and if we were alright.

"Yes, I'm fine," I said. "But you'll have to talk to Karl Petersen about the rest."

Then ESPN called, wanting an interview about the shooting. They used my interview on Breaking News. The Seattle reporter used the video in his story too. Our video also was also folded into the other KGW reporter's story for the 5, 6, 11 p.m. news. *Honestly, I was glad to be rid of it.* I never wanted to cover the Tonya Harding story, stayed away from it, and wanted no part of it, only glad to walk away unharmed. There was more than enough coverage already! And now the bizarre story of shots fired was making national news on all three national networks.

That's when I got the call from Ann. Hearing that Stant's grandmother had been cited for shooting at us with a .22 caliber Ruger, Ann left a message asking if I was still in one piece, both physically and emotionally.

"Well, you know Ann," I said. "As Diane Downs says 'You can't kill anyone with a .22 Ruger.'"

Karl and I had been shot at by the very same caliber and make of weapon Diane used to shoot her children.

Ann was happy to hear my voice when I returned the call. At first, I downplayed the episode, but I finally confided in her, "Really, I am pissed. My child's birthday is in a couple of days. I'm not even part of this Harding debacle and I'm not about to risk my life or Karl's for an effing 'real estate' shot. I've got a daughter to raise."

But despite our best intentions, we already had.

Chapter 32
Rule's Resilience

Over the years, I'd see Ann when she came to town for book talks. Or when she'd visit Leslie, who lived up the street from my house for several years. The proximity of our two houses was bit of serendipity that Ann brought to my attention before I moved from Eugene to Portland, Oregon for my new KGW job. Here was Ann's friend, and her daughter, living one long block from one another! What are the chances?

Leslie, me, and Ann on one of our visits.

One time, when the three of us were together in downtown Portland having dinner, I got distracted. It must have been the old Veritable Quandary (gone now), a very good restaurant and favorite of newspeople and newsmakers in Portland. I was excited to see Ann, but I started eavesdropping the next table over. I kept on trying to participate in the conversation between me, Leslie and Ann, but I heard breaking news next to us.

Finally realizing I was being extremely rude to my friends, I leaned over and whispered in Ann's ear, "These runners next to us are talking about canceling this year's Portland Marathon".

The marathon was a big deal in Portland, with thousands of runners, and I couldn't believe my ears! I don't remember much about what Ann, Leslie and I talked about that night over dinner…but I remember Ann giggling about my eavesdropping. She must have been thinking, "You can take a woman out of a newsroom. But you can't take the newsroom out of the woman." I was forgiven for not giving our get-together my full attention. Now that Ann's gone, I wish I had.

I broke the story the next day. Sports desks across the city had no clue the race was called off. Good scoop, but a friendship opportunity missed almost entirely.

When Ann and I couldn't find time to see each other, the phone was our refuge. It was hard to catch up when Ann was on the road, and I was a busy single mother raising my daughter with this all-encompassing broadcasting job. Unless, of course, there was an emergency like being shot at by a .22 semi-automatic pistol to light up our phone lines together again.

When Ann was working there was no time to talk, since she totally immersed herself at trials, interviewing detectives, medical examiners, victims and families. At these times, we both knew a quick check-in wouldn't suffice. We'd need more time to download, explain how life was working out. There were never quick catch up phone calls between us. We'd hunker down and gab.

When phone conversations with Ann dropped off around 2010, I figured she was consumed with researching or writing. I didn't give our hiatus much thought. Or at least I thought I didn't.

For some reason, in that period of time, Ann was constantly on my mind. My calls to her went unanswered. Then, her voicemail messages were full. I'd wake up each day pledging to call her, until the days flittered away too quickly without making contact. Days, then weeks, went by. My daughter was college-bound and life was big. Finally, I called Leslie, who relocated outside Seattle, not far from Ann. Still no word. More time passed and I figured Leslie, or Ann would get back to me when they could. But the whole situation felt very wrong.

I finally found out what was going on when Leslie, who was exhausted, found the words to call me back. Leslie let me know Ann, who was almost eighty years old, was in the hospital with a life-threatening illness. This shock came out of the blue for me. How could this vibrant, seemingly-healthy friend be on the precipice of life and death? She'd had medical issues, always controlled by medication, but this trouble was far worse. But at the time, I had no idea the fight she was up against.

Somehow this illness quickly reached a startling fever pitch. At home, Ann noticed a stiff neck but kept writing. Her book *In The Still Of The Night* was almost done. Next, she was having trouble turning her head. As the symptoms worsened, she medicated to quell the pain. But still she worked. Finally, the pain was so excruciating she was rushed to the emergency room.

At the hospital, Leslie got heartbreaking news. Doctors said her mother had a 50/50 chance of survival "but she may not make it through the week." Leslie was distraught. "My mom was out of her mind for weeks," she told me. Ann was restrained in a hospital bed, incoherent because of a mysterious infection. Imagine seeing your mother, your rock, in a hospital bed so incapacitated that the nurses used straps to hold her down and the doctors didn't have a diagnosis?

The family, sick with worry, stood vigil by her bedside, along with Ann's best friend Donna Anders.

Test after test was done. The family sweated it out a week while waiting.

Finally, an answer. Well, a partial answer. Ann had a spinal infection, most likely in her neck. Serious enough to kill her, but doctors didn't know what *kind* of an infection. Spinal Meningitis was ruled out. But the illness showed eerie similarities. But with no definitive cause, the medical staff suggested a course of action: To save her, heavy duty antibiotics or antifungal medicine would drip through Ann's veins. Pain meds would be adjusted to give Ann a break from suffering.

Spine infections are very rare, so how could Ann have contracted it? The infection usually spreads through the bloodstream from an infection elsewhere in the body. Bladder infections or wounds are common sources. But a cause was never found for Ann's. Leslie remembered Ann, always the animal lover, feeding raccoons before getting ill. But Ann never mentioned being bitten or punctured by claws. Still, a raccoon's saliva in an open paper cut is enough to trigger a devastating reaction. Again, nobody knew the cause.

Slowly, the treatments got to work. Ann's fever went down. The shivering chills lessened, as did the muscle spasms. The improvements were encouraging, but the family was warned that Ann might never be the same. Chronic inflammation from the infection might have paralyzed her. At best, Ann would need a wheelchair, at worst she'd be paraplegic. Leslie said, "We didn't know if she'd be able to walk or ever be well enough to go back to writing." Nobody knew if or how much the infection damaged her nerves or brain.

Still with more time, Ann's health steadily improved. She believed the same angels who protected her as a child were still with her. Divine intervention, medical science or both— Ann Rule made a *miraculous* recovery.

At almost eighty-years old Ann had to learn how to walk again. One step at a time. It took three months.

She steadily built her strength for daily tasks we take for granted. Ann's amazing comeback earned her the nickname "The Energizer Bunny" from a family member–the old television ads with a battery-powered bunny that slows to a stop, but drums incessantly when all juiced up again. A few months before, Rule sat at death's door, but now Ann was full speed ahead again, banging her drum.

When Ann was well enough to talk, we got back to healthy gabfests on dark evenings by phone. I apologized for not being there for her, because I then understood the gravity of what she had been through. I asked to be put on the call list if anything, anything, happens again. Ann saw it as a miracle she survived. She was hardy stock.

When Ann finally finished *In The Still Of The Night*, she

accepted my invitation for an interview at the Portland, Oregon, television station where I co-hosted an afternoon live talk show. When Ann was ushered in behind the scenes, the program had already started. I felt like tearing up, on air, at the mere sight of my friend WALKING into the studio, but our program was broadcast live and Ann was still off camera waiting in the wings.

My co-hosts, Jenny Hansson, Hayley Platt and I were yakking on air about some other topic, which was completely incongruent with crying about seeing my friend just as I remember her! But there she was: Ann Rule was back, and on top of her game. I admit to being a bit surprised by how good she looked. You'd never know this woman had almost died; she was on point and, as usual, a great interview. Her appearance bumped up our ratings that day. That old Midwest by Northwest spirit, or her personal "spirits" put the author's next four books back on top.

This woman took a hit and kept on going, and going, and going. Her schedule of trials, research, books, television movies, promotional tours and bookstore talks were racing right along.

Chapter 33
Rule's Relief

Ann didn't stop. She was now weeks from her eighty-first birthday and keeping the schedule of a much, much younger person. She was doing great. And yes, she'd written another book.

After the publication of *Practice To Deceive,* about another Washington murder case, Ann was heading to a book signing. Her best friend Donna drove her to Whidbey Island, where the crime took place, for the event. I think Ann said the signing would take place at a restaurant.

This trip would change her life.

As Donna got out of the car to lock it, she lost sight of Ann across the passenger side. Rule got out but took a bad spill. She was lying on the ground and that's why Donna couldn't see her. Rounding to the passenger side, Donna asked Ann, "Can you move, Ann?"

By this time someone, either another driver or the book signing, saw a woman down and came running out.

"Call 911!" Donna shouted.

When Donna knelt down next to her friend to give her comfort, Rule didn't cry nor moan in pain. "Ann had a very high pain threshold," Donna remembered later, and she was witnessing it again while Ann was on the ground.

By the time the ambulance arrived, Leslie was on the phone with her mother saying she'd be at the hospital when Ann got there.

This was one book signing she'll have to miss.

Ann fell hard. Her hip was broken. And it was a bad break.

In Seattle's Virginia Mason hospital, Ann's life was not at

risk, but she needed a full hip replacement.

Despite the success of the surgery, Ann couldn't go home without extra help. Both of her daughters and one son jumped in, taking turns taking care of her 24/7 for more than a month. They were there for Ann, but couldn't stay forever. Ann's relatives were very involved in her life, but she was confused, and her memory got rather fuzzy.

Leslie cobbled together a schedule for home caregivers going forward.

Later on, when I found out what happened, I called Ann at home. Listening to the sound of her voice, and knowing she's now in a wheelchair, I stifled my worries.

"Ann, I'd like to come visit," I said. "And cheer you up."

Ann's voice lifted, "Really? I'd sure like that."

I headed up to her home in Normandy Park, south of Seattle, that weekend.

Seeing her in a wheelchair broke my heart. But I never let on. After all she'd been through, here was yet another harrowing experience she was coping with the best way possible. I was there for T.L.C. and to supply laughter as the best medicine.

Ann was able to take a few steps with a walker, but it took tremendous effort. She never complained, but thankfully Ann had prescriptions for pain, an enlarged heart, high blood pressure, and I'm not sure what else. She also needed oxygen and a breathing machine at night while she was sleeping.

One afternoon when we were in her bathroom, Ann told me, "I'd really like to pay you for what you're doing for me, Anne." I told her absolutely not, this was what friends did for each other. This seemed to ring true to her and we never discussed it again. But the look on her face told me she was appreciative.

Ann was frustrated because she could no longer live alone, and she would probably need caregivers for quite some time. She cherished her independence. She wanted to live on her own and take care of herself.

My parents, nearing their nineties then, wanted the same thing. Ann's condition was different from my folks'. I'd sweated bullets and had a tremendous struggle to get them into assisted living when their cognitive abilities began to fail and their home was no longer safe. Moving them was one of the hardest decisions I've made in life.

With resources and help, Ann was cheerful in her upscale but modest ranch-style place with a nice open format kitchen/living room. As before, her habits were unchanged. In the morning, she'd read tabloids (a not-so-guilty pleasure) over a cup of coffee, usually in bed. After watching *The Price is Right* with fellow animal lover Bob Barker on television, Ann wheeled to her office to write. Always reading her last-finished chapter first, before working on the next. She put in a few hours, albeit a little less than before the accident.

Then life swooped in and took control. Ann was admitted to the hospital several times over the next year. She missed her deadline to turn in her manuscript for *Lying in Wait.* Leslie had been helping with book research and Ann's editors asked her to complete the manuscript. The last Ann Rule book was published shortly before Christmas, 2014 and quickly soared to the top of the *New York Times* bestseller list.

I visited Ann as often as possible, staying for four or more days at a time just to be with her and give caregivers a break. Each time, I'd shove down the worry knowing most people over seventy live an average of three-years after breaking a hip. Surely such generalizations were wrong in her case. Not Ann, I'd tell myself. How could medical experts possibly apply that edict universally?

Other friends and family would drop by regularly to show their love while I was there. Or perhaps, I was the visitor, and they were just doing what they always do, while I was there? Each gave kindness, encouragement, humor, support and generosity to Ann.

Together, we all witnessed Ann's lifelong resilience.

Ann and I spoke in July, 2015 about getting together again. Her hushed voice gave me the feeling she was searching for privacy. Maybe my private friend didn't want caregivers to overhear her conversations? I didn't know, or understand it. After asking if she was alright, Ann assured me she was, and would arrange my visit. I felt unsettled not knowing why her voice, just above a whisper, seemed different. Ann was eighty-three years old and life was veering out of control. There were serious family troubles during this time, but all charges against her sons were later dropped, and their names completely cleared. But that's a story I'll leave to the family to talk about someday, if they choose.

My trip was on the calendar for the coming weekend.

Next thing I knew, Ann was rushed to the emergency room again.

I left for Seattle on my birthday in mid-July of 2015 to see Ann. I planned to stay in a hotel, learning Ann was in the hospital at the Highline Medical Center. The weather was clear and bright, almost 80 degrees. Driving three hours north, I pulled into the parking lot in the early evening. It was still light and there was a nice warm swift breeze when I rolled down my window. I saw Ann's best friend Donna Anders and one of Ann's caregivers crossing the parking lot to their cars. They'd been with Ann in Room 510.

Donna said she was glad Ann would have another visitor tonight, explaining she'd made belated plans for her birthday (which happened to be the day before mine) that evening and would come back tomorrow. I knew from past experience that Ann felt safe whenever Donna was there, and I'd be her stand-in for the time being.

From Donna, I learned Ann had been rushed to the hospital when medical issues got out of hand at home and took too long to resolve. Ann liked to chew on ice in her refreshments so at first everyone thought a jagged piece of ice had cut her gums. The issue, more dire than known, caused bleeding that couldn't be stopped.

Now in ICU, it appeared the complications had caused a stroke.

Ann was resting when I arrived. When she opened her eyes and saw me, a flicker of friendship passed between us. Ann was unable to speak.

I sat. I felt the warmth of her tiny hand, tools of her trade, under mine.

Leslie spent hours with her mom each day. After I arrived, Leslie and I slept on the floor by Ann's bed. The nurses gave us blankets and pillows and somehow we managed to get some rest on the floor of Room 510. We whispered back and forth about Ann, and caught up on our lives. My old neighbor and I were together again.

Ann's family was relieved to have me there, and it gave them a chance to go home and refresh. They agreed that someone close to Ann should be at the hospital at all times.

"I know my mom will be safe with you there," Leslie told me.

The next night, one of Ann's nice nurses, Steve Ettinger, brought me a recliner to sleep on– real luxury compared to the floor. I had no idea how long I'd be there with Ann.

Knowing Ann loved animals, I read aloud a chapter of James Herriot's *All Creatures Great And Small.*

"Ann, should I keep reading?"

No, she shook her head.

Ann was clearly tired of the subject matter, having read it before.

Instead, I picked up the *Seattle Times* and started reading a front-page feature story: "Beatrix The Beaver, Caught And Waiting For Love." Beatrix, kicked out of her parents' home, a celebrity in Lake Forest Park, needed a mate to set up housekeeping once resettled on U.S. Forest Service land.

Beaming her wide smile. I could see Rule enjoyed Beatrix's hijinks. Normally, Ann would have had some choice remarks about the bold antics of this little beaver looking for a date. Watching Ann relax a bit made me happy.

Later that morning, I hoped to ask some serious personal questions.

"Ann, can I ask you something?" I was searching here, "You don't have to answer, but I see how hard you're trying..."

Ann nodded yes.

"I want to help you in any way I can," I said. "That's why I'm asking these questions, okay?"

Yes, again.

"I see how tired you are, the amount of strength and endurance this takes. You're amazing. Can you tell me, and I apologize for asking, but I'd like to know how much strength you have to continue?

YES. YES. She was confident about it.

"Okay, good Ann. Let's make some plans." I pulled out my reporter's notebook, not for a story, but to take notes on her wishes. "Let's make a list of who you want to see most."

This made her very happy.

I knew Leslie was coming back and Donna too. As I said the names of those closest to Ann, I asked for her to confirm each name written on my reporter's notepad. I then got their numbers and called or texted each of them personally, saying, "Ann really wants to see you today, can you make it this afternoon?" As they filtered in one at a time, each sat by her bedside alone. Each of them was stunned, not knowing what the future held.

Friends who heard about Ann came to the hospital too. Celebrity Seattle attorney Anne Bremner, who'd represented Ann previously, came to see Ann and to reminisce about their almost forty years of friendship. Anne held her hand and made her laugh. While interviewing Bremner in the summer of 2024, she remembered being starstruck the first time the two met, when she was a prosecutor in Seattle. Bremner read all of Ann's books and has the memory to prove it. She's still known nationwide for representing high-profile clients and as a popular television analyst.

Then, late on July 25th, the last relative arrived and I knew Ann would be in good hands. We compared notes, sharing what I'd seen so far about Ann's care and visitors–a good meeting to be sure.

Ann was asleep when I tiptoed into her blindingly bright ICU room very late that night. I wanted to see my pal one more time before I left. I would not wake her, of course. I passed my hand very lightly, almost not touching at all, over the back of hers.

I drove home from Seattle to Portland very late that Saturday night, going over the events of the last three days, mostly alone with her and not really knowing what would happen next. It was already early Sunday by the time I arrived home.

I tried to catch up on sleep most of the day Sunday, but it

was restless at best. I didn't feel like doing anything. I got a call from a relative, saying Ann was resting in a quiet hospice room away from the glaring ICU and watching her favorite television shows, like the *Price is Right.* There was nothing more that could be done for Ann but help her rest comfortably.

The day passed, the sun set. I could not settle.

I turned on most of the lights in my house, hoping to feel less alone, I guess. I'm a night owl, but even though I was still worn out, I couldn't sleep, doing absolutely nothing but watching the hour hands wind forward on my side table.

Then I heard a shrill three part howl across the street. It sounded like a wild animal. I tensed up, wondering what the heck was going on out there! Instantly, I thought that somebody had shot the wild coyote that prowled here and wounded the poor animal. My windows were wide open in the summer heat and I knew where the shots came from, right across the street from the room I was sitting in. The shots and the sounds were so clear. It was unconscionable that a neighbor, with no skill, would have done such a horrific job of it. Give it two more ticks of the clock, then, one, maybe two more shots rang out followed by two more short, neck-straining howls. It was 10:40 p.m.

That sound and the silence that followed, I will never forget.

Ann Rule had died only ten minutes before, on July 26th, 2015.

Is it naive of me, or just otherworldly, to believe Ann visited me that night? She believed angels were her guardians. Their wings lifted her up again and again through illness and injury to rise like a phoenix to continue with her unbelievable talent, foresight and gifts.

Or did my friends' soul transcend time and space to send a signal from an animal? If Ann were here, she'd unequivocally say, "Yes, this happens."

I'm not sure how to reconcile these emotions within me.

But, since the moment the coyote spoke, I've always sensed Ann was saying goodbye to me. Not in pain, but in passing.

Chapter 34
Legendary Rule

Thinking back over my thirty plus years of friendship with Ann, and after researching more about her life—her beginnings as a jailhouse kid hearing the confessions of killers, her struggles as a single parent and her meteoric success and disappointments—I know why we were friends. She genuinely wanted better lives for all of us, readers or friends.

I don't think Ann ever expected the level of meteoric worldwide success she attained, but she worked for it. Every. Single. Day. For decades. It was that touch of "pick yourself up by your bootstraps" creed that we related to so sincerely. In 2011, during a Public Broadcasting interview, she said she couldn't imagine *not* writing. "I suspect I'll go until I can't pull myself up to the computer anymore," Ann said, laughingly.

Ann always wanted to know the *why*. Curiosity made her a life-long learner, even years after her college degrees went into the file cabinet. The penchant to find out why in every case helped her find answers for readers asking the same questions.

Ann's books broke barriers by painstakingly dissecting the behaviors of murderers, their childhoods as antisocial psychopaths, and writing about it in a way we could all understand.

Ann Rule reminded us what habits made it easier to avoid being prey to killers: walk with purpose, know where you're going, be aware of your surroundings, and don't accept a stranger's advances no matter how handsome, charming or slick their stories are. If being forced into a car, or shots are fired, then scream and run like your hair's on fire. It's hard to hit a moving target.

Today the number of serial killers is dropping. Yes, monsters are still out there, but their numbers have dwindled since the advent of DNA testing, cell phones, and new investigative techniques, like forensic genealogy, as well as the exponential increase in video cameras on businesses, streets and doorsteps and ViCAP.

Ann was one of the first authors to figure out that serial killer's strike in waves. Their obsessions build and build until they kill again. As you watch news reports, you witness this bewildering cycle. When the thirst for power and domination is quenched, they go back to seemingly normal lives, blending in with the rest of us. Shockingly, we always learn these brutal murderers had jobs, wives and families which helped them blend in. The insatiable urges might lie dormant for months or years, then cycle back around again for the next hunt and kill. Over and over the restless continuum ebbs and flows.

Ann spoke all over the country to law enforcement conferences, sheriffs' associations, the FBI at Quantico, Virginia, and even the United States Senate, about the behavior and repetitive habits of murderers. Rule took the time to be certified by law enforcement associations on the West Coast, she thought like a detective, and her work informed theirs in turn. Investigators asked her to consult on their serial killer cases. Using her years of book research, she gave concrete examples to drive her points home. Before detectives shared information freely or the advent of the internet, her speeches spread the word to smaller communities nationwide. Critical information for small town investigators working in departments without resources, enabled them to expand their thinking. Rule won the Washington State Governor's Award for extraordinary leadership in law enforcement circles.

Foremost, Ann became a legend by reinventing the true crime genre for new generations.

But for me, the most lovable and admirable aspect of Ann Rule was her humanity. Humanity is a word for the collective, but a seemingly lofty word for individuals to live up to. At its essence, the word dictates an understanding and a kindness toward people, and compassion. A precept every person taken in violence, including their families, has a right to. You learn about *humanity* in Rule's books, because Ann could put herself in every mother's footsteps. No parent wants their child to be a number or a victim. There is no escaping evil, but Ann celebrated the greater good we often overlook.

Ann's writing heralded the investigative heroes who relentlessly work on all night stake outs, or studying blood spatters and bullet trajectories, examining tiny tell-tale signs left on human bodies, running test after test on the most minute specks, and so much more that goes into the work of solving crimes and prosecuting them.

Every time you turn the first page of Ann's books, or can't stop reading in the middle of the night, fighting the alarm clock for just a few more pages, you're deep in a suspense far greater than yourself, witness to the flaws and frailty of humanity, just like Ann.

I made this card for Ann's memorial service. It was passed out to every visitor. Author collection.

Afterword

Ann Rule was exceptional to me. And so is the photograph of her on the cover of this book. The cover photo is my most cherished picture of my friend Ann.

This photographic jewel is a story unto itself.

I'd seen it before I met Ann at the Downs trial. To me, this look has always been her calling card of sorts: black detective hat, dark sunglasses, trench coat, handcuffs, a provocative leg, and bright red shoes, stiletto, atop bestselling books.

There's even a toy gun in her front pocket, which you can see if you stare long enough!

Campy, sure. But this one photo encapsulates to me her humor, her willingness to set herself apart and *her story.*

I often told her how much I loved this picture and asked who took it. Ann had an original but she couldn't quite remember the name of the photographer who sent it to her. But he was a really nice young man, she recalled.

From the time Ann agreed to allow me to tell her (our) story, I looked for this unknown photographer, figuring he was lost to time. How would I ever identify him to get this great shot of Ann decades ago?

My search went on for years, and I mean *years.* Not only while I wrote this book, but long before. I liked it that much. If Ann's name ever came up, I'd often ask photographers I worked with, "Hey, there's a fantastic picture of Ann Rule dockside in Seattle with her first two hardcover books underfoot and she's wearing *red shoes.* Have you seen that photo? Do you know who took it?" A shot in the dark at the cosmos.

I know it's hard to believe that I'd find anyone that way,

but journalistic circles are pretty tight, and photographers never forget a signature shot like that once they've seen it.

As I mentioned, the photo was taken in the early 1980's and I was now still trying to trace the source by 2015! A lost cause right? But I kept searching, nonetheless.

When I left reporting and anchoring to pursue garden writing, I got a few great jobs. One, an Emmy winning gardening show on Portland's best-rated television station *and* shooting videotapes for my favorite publication in the Oregonian newspaper's *Home and Gardens of the Northwest*. A gem of a woman, Kay Balmer, ran the section, and I pitched the idea of me doing garden videos as the paper broke into the digital world. My timing was great.

The newspaper sent some fantastic photographers into my garden. We'd shoot a month's worth of video garden stories in one day, all before noon, which required well-planned scripts and even better staging to have everything ready and in place, as we moved from one two-minute story to another for the newspaper webpage.

Kay, who's gone now (and I still miss her), liked what we were doing so the assignments continued. She was quite a woman, with a sense of humor Ann Rule would have admired.

After a few years of shooting these garden videos, I met Randy Rasmussen, who enjoyed gardening and was a purist. We did lots of videos together and I was really jazzed about his work. One day, as Randy was loading up his gear, he asked me what I was doing that weekend. Now usually I'd have said, "I'm digging up this or that, and whatta think if I move this here and that there?" But on this occasion, I was thinking about my visit to Ann's that weekend. I blurted out, "I'm going to Seattle to visit my friend Ann Rule."

"Really?" Randy said. "I know Ann!"

"Hey, wait!" I said, excitedly. "Maybe you'll know the answer to a mystery I'm trying to solve! I've been looking for this one picture of Ann Rule forever, and *cannot* figure out who took it back in the '80's? She's wearing red shoes."

"I took that picture," Randy said.

"NO! Really? What?" I was gobsmacked. What were the chances?

In his long career working as a photojournalist, Randy photographed Ringo Starr, Bette Davis, Jack Nicholson (on the toilet, as requested) and other Hollywood stars. Then, with 52 years having a lens over one eye, he confirmed it: He snapped *the picture.*

My ship finally came in!

Low and behold, Randy told me the story about that day! He'd been feeling a little queasy but wrote it off. He'd be flying to Seattle to meet the famous up-and-coming author Ann Rule, and he didn't want to let her down. He was really looking forward to working with her. So off he went.

It was no easy task to get the shot. Randy and Ann had to wait on that dock until just the right light silhouetted her perfectly. I love the flash photography lighting- which balances the natural light behind Ann with the slow richness of the Kodachrome film. Photographers will wait as loooong as it takes to get just the right shot to make the 'magic' happen. And they did wait quite a while.

Temperatures on the sound can get quite chilly at sunset and Randy was feeling fluish. Unlike the other impatient stars he'd photographed, Ann was willing to wait for the perfect shot. She was shivering cold, and he was sweating it out. Their collaboration was fantastic.

Click, click, click.

The shot was in the can.

Except Randy was now feeling very ill. And Ann started taking care of him like he's one of her sons!

"We'd never met each other before," Randy said. "But she mothered me on that shoot...I was sick as a dog."

Rule ended up driving Randy back to the airport for his return flight to Portland.

Fast-forward now to the day back in my garden, when the light bulb went off over my head about this photo.

"Randy, you would not believe how long I've been looking for that ONE picture!" I told him. "That was you? It's incredible! I've been researching a book about Ann and I want it for the cover."

"Everything felt right on that shoot," Randy said. Except for his fever.

Fate? Coincidence? Angels? Or write it off to just plain good luck, the iconic photograph of Ann had been locked in Randy's safe for decades! I felt then that I was destined to write this book.

Ann Rule left her readers volumes to remember her by, but *this* picture reminds me of that small town girl who wanted to be a detective, but grew up to write arresting stories.

Acknowledgments

First and foremost, I'd like to take a moment to celebrate my enduring friendship with the extraordinary Ann Rule. Ann, you are missed and I pray I've done you justice in this living portrayal.

There are legions of people who helped in the development of this book. I am humbled by their truthfulness, willingness to offer suggestions, and hold my hand when things got rough. To Leslie Rule, Ann's daughter and bestselling author, I'm grateful for the photographs, friendship and encouragement you gave freely. Her upcoming book *Ann Rule: The Extraordinary Life of the Queen of True Crime* will detail more of her mother's life.

For Doug Welch, lead investigator in the Diane Downs murder case, my ride or die friend on our exhausting research trip into Ann's Michigan childhood. Tracy Barry, for her wise counsel, never ending support, love and laughter over 35 years of our "WE" friendship. My daughter, Haleigh, for the light and love she brings to my life. Ann's cousin's Jim and Mary Sampson, thank you for sharing your hilarious memories and a cozy fire together in your Michigan lakeside cabin. To Bette Mae Settecase, who is gone now, for providing an insider's glimpse of Ann through college and beyond.

Thank you to bestselling true crime author Kathryn Casey, Ann's friend and mentee, for sharing her insights about Rule, writing a review of the book and taking a chance on a new writer. Pulitzer Prize-winning editorial cartoonist and columnist for the San Francisco Chronicle, Jack Ohman, for years of friendship and reading the manuscript. JO, author, editor, for her expertise, advice, and nimble pen. Bob Kerns and Rebecca Force, formerly of KEZI television in Eugene for supporting our half hour documentary about killer Diane Downs. And entertainment lawyer, Kohel Havers, for giving this book his keen legal eye. Jeff Patterson, for his stunning cover graphics (www.jeffpatt.com). Thank to Julie Mallory, the National Treasure, for your help.

About the Author

Anne Jaeger spent four decades as a journalist, a career that paralleled her 30-year friendship with bestselling true crime author Ann Rule. The two shared extraordinary adventures, covering some of the same notorious killers and reflecting on chilling childhood encounters with murderers.

Their lifelong bond began at the 1984 trial of Diane Downs, an Oregon woman who shocked the nation by shooting her own children, killing one. Rule described Jaeger's groundbreaking television documentary on Downs as "the seminal personality profile" of a murderous mother.

Jaeger's immersion in the story extended to Hollywood, where she played herself as a reporter in the movie adaptation of Rule's book *Small Sacrifices*, starring Farrah Fawcett.

Over the years, Jaeger hosted an Emmy-winning garden show filmed in her own vibrant acre garden. She has also been a talk show host, a newspaper columnist for the *Portland Tribune*, created digital garden videos for *The Oregonian*, and authored and hosted a popular gardening DVD for the paper.

When she's not writing or digging in the dirt, Anne enjoys time with her daughter, who is a dedicated teacher, hummingbirds, and her charming Scottish Fold cat, Nona.

Printed in Dunstable, United Kingdom

64601919R00153